Don't Take Love Lying Down

Brad Henning

WINEPRESS WP PUBLISHING

© 2003 by Brad Henning. All rights reserved.
2nd printing in 2007.

Cover Design by Jerome F. Petteys.

Packaged by WinePress Publishing, PO Box 428, Enumclaw,
WA 98022. The views expressed or implied in this work do not
necessarily reflect those of WinePress Publishing. The author
is ultimately responsible for the design, content, and editorial
accuracy of this work.

Books are available in quantity at a discounted price. Contact
Barbara Henning at barbarahenning@yahoo.com or call 253-
848-2239 for more information.

ISBN 1-57921-494-0
Library of Congress Catalog Card Number: 2002109828

To my wife, Barbara
and my two kids, Chris and Becky

Table of Contents

Foreword 9

Acknowledgments 11

Introduction 13

What This Book Is *Really* About 15

Let's Start with a Quiz 23

SECTION ONE: DIFFERENCES

Chapter 1. "Relational" Meets "Impersonal" 29

Chapter 2. He Said . . . She Said 55

Chapter 3. *Sports Illustrated* Meets *Better Homes and Gardens* 75

SECTION TWO: LOVE

Chapter 4. Definition of Love 101

Chapter 5. Evaluating Your Relationships 133

SECTION THREE: SEX

Chapter 6. Sex 165

Chapter 7. Why Wait? You've Got to Know the Whole
Person...179

Chapter 8. Why Wait? You Have to Build Trust in the
Relationship 203

Chapter 9. Why Wait? No Comparisons Later 211

Chapter 10. Why Wait? So Best Sex Is Not Destroyed 223

Chapter 11. Why Wait? No Pregnancy or Abortions................239

Chapter 12. Why Wait? No Diseases 255

Chapter 13. Why Wait? No Hurt, Guilt, or Fear (Now or
Later) 281

Chapter 14. Why Wait? No Bad Reputation 293

Chapter 15. Why Wait? Don't Steal from Someone Else's
Marriage 305

Chapter 16. Why Wait? To Protect Society 311

SECTION FOUR: GIRLS ONLY; GUYS ONLY

Chapter 17. For Girls Only 339

Chapter 18. For Guys Only...383

Chapter 19. One Last Thing..419

Appendix...423

Foreword

Happy, loving relationships between two people can develop only with time, honesty, and hard work. The kind of love that I'm talking about here can never be blind. It sees clearly, but with compassion, kindness, humility . . . **blah, blah, blah** . . . yeah, and if you already knew that, you wouldn't be sitting here reading this book, now would you?! So, OK, let's try to figure all this out. Go get yourself a couple of cookies and a glass of milk while I reach into my **vaaaaasst** wealth of knowledge and experience, and then you and I can have at this guy-girl stuff! Seriously . . .

—BRAD HENNING

Acknowledgments

I want to thank everyone in the world for helping me write this. There's the acknowledgments. (This book is going to be a lot shorter than I thought.)

From here on out it gets a little tougher.

Introduction

Hi. I'm Brad Henning. Who are you? (Put your name here:_____.) Nice to meet you. (That pretty much covers the introduction.)

What This Book Is *Really* About

A long time ago, far, far away (sounds like the beginning of a science-fiction movie, doesn't it?), something took place in my life that changed forever the way I lived, thought, and felt. And, to be honest, it's taken the rest of my life to figure it all out. I'm still not done and never will be, which is really depressing. It all started in the seventh grade when this . . . this . . . *thing* happened to me that I never recovered from. I remember thinking at the time, no, probably wishing (I didn't do a lot of thinking in the seventh grade), that this "thing" would just go away and leave me alone. Then again, sometimes I wished it would hang around some more. I never could really understand it (it was just too complicated for me), and when I asked my guy friends about it, they just stared at me and drooled. Which led me to believe one of two things:

1. This "thing" was really dangerous
or
2. "It" sucked all your brains out when you weren't lookin'.
Or a third possible thing:
3. Maybe all my friends were idiots!

Now, after many years of studying the situation, reading about it, and watching with great interest, I have concluded, in my humble opinion . . . it's all three!!! And just what was this . . . this *thing*? GIRLS.

It's not that I didn't like girls or anything, but every time I got around them I felt stupid. Most of my guy friends felt stupid around them too. A friend of mine saw a girl coming down the hallway at his school one day, someone he really liked, and he was so shook up at the sight of her that he walked right into a concrete wall. If he didn't feel stupid before, he did then! See, girls think guys are stupid, but actually we're not. *Before* a guy sees a girl, he's minding his own business and everything's fine. He's not stupid. Then when he sees a girl, *that's* when he turns stupid. So being stupid isn't really his fault, it's hers.

Back to this "thing." This "thing" started happening to *me*. Now the seventh grade is traumatic enough: pimples, jock straps . . . you know, so adding this "thing" was overwhelming! And none of it was my fault.

Now stop right here and notice how this works. You've *got* to get this. There's this "thing" and a guy immediately knows it's his fault. What? His *fault*? *What's* his fault? Man, he doesn't even know what IT is! But sure enough, he's wrong! How could he be wrong or be at fault if he doesn't even know what *it* is? All I knew then was, *Anything bad that happens in a relationship is always the guy's fault.* (Not really, but that's the way it seemed to me. More on that later.) But hey, I was just a guy having fun, minding my own business, when, BLAM! GIRLS happened. I liked it. But it was definitely *my fault!* That's also when I started hearing the female battle cry that rings in my ears to this day. It's the cry that can be heard, everywhere you go, almost every day, in every school in America: "Guys are all JERKS!!" Now, I'll admit that stuff is our fault a lot of the time, but most of the time we're just being (how shall I say it?) guys. But girls make us out to be such morons. In fact, I started being embarrassed over just *being* a guy, 'cause as soon as I walked into a room, some girl would say, "It's your fault!" "What's my fault?" "Yoooou know!"

But I have a question. (And this is where it gets weird.) I say this with no malice at all, but if guys are such jerks, why are almost all girls' magazines dedicated to "Getting Your Own Personal Jerk"? It seems like that's all they talk about! Why would a girl want one? If guys are such losers, then why is a girl so eager to find her own personal "loser" to marry and live with for the rest of her life? Most girls dream about that Big Day: meeting that special "Jerk"—then falling in love, getting married, and raising a family. WITH A JERK!!! It dawned on me one day that maybe it's not the guys who are stupid! In fact, if guys are supposed to be the lamebrains, who *raised* them to be that way? Think about it!!! MOM did!

Well, as time passed I began to see how cool girls really were, how different they were from us guys, and because I was getting tired of having to wash guys' butt prints off my car windows, I ventured into the world of "Dating." I know a lot of people don't use that word anymore, but there doesn't seem to be another word that communicates this . . . "going out stuff." If you use "going out stuff" every time you talk about . . . this . . . "going out stuff," it's just too many words to say every time you want to talk about the . . . well, the "going out stuff." So for now we'll use the term "dating" if you don't mind.

To show you just how ignorant I was, I thought being with a girl would be a piece of cake after hanging around with guys so long. You know, having to make all those big decisions every day. Decisions like: "Should I get up today?" "Should I wear clothes?" "McDonald's or Taco Bell?" Things like that. But the Girl Thing was totally different. Now I had to ask myself: "Has this shirt been washed in the last two years?" "What do I do with the hair under my hat?" And of course the thing every guy has to deal with if he hangs around with girls very long: CHICK FLICKS! Now what's *that* all about? All girls do in those movies is giggle, fall in love, and talk to the trees for the rest of their lives. Chick flicks . . . *That's* where girls learn all that stuff about how to drive guys crazy. Those movies are ridiculous! Nobody blows up, there's no guys rippin' each other in half with laser guns, no girls in bikinis chasin' after

the good guy. . . . You know, *realistic* stuff. No, I was entering a totally different world. And it scared me to death!

Everything started to get confusing. I started questioning why we guys do the things we do. For example, when two guy friends first meet in the hall at school, what do they do when they greet each other? "Wassup?" Then they slug each other! Or they do something like one guy I saw. He was jumping up and down, stomping on his best friend's books while the guy who owned the books was beating the stew out of him. Yup. That's what best friends are for.

Or how about this one? I visited a school not long ago, went in the front door where the main office was, and I was just hanging out, practicing my "stand." (You know . . . the "stand?" You can't just stand there with two flat feet, hands at your side, staring. You have to pose like James Dean.) Anyway, while I was standing there, two guys (I found out later they were friends) came in the front door, karate-kicking each other in the crotch! Several girls waiting in the hall were watching these guys and shaking their heads, the whole time thinking . . . "Morons! They're all Morons!" Now some guys don't go in for all that violent stuff. They've graduated up to more sophisticated forms of greeting behavior, like CHEST BUTTING! But whatever their behavior, it's definitely guys' fault! And, according to girls, they're all Jerks!

But come on ladies, guys are just being guys. It's no big deal. We're just having fun. Why take it so seriously? When a guy opens a door for a girl, and then when she's halfway through, slams it in her face, he's just having fun. He doesn't mean to hurt her. It's just a guy thing.

Come to think of it, why are *girls* the way they are? Girls are way too hard to figure out. When two girl friends (who haven't seen each other for at least two minutes) meet in the hallway, do they do the "Wassup-slug" thing? Nooooo!!! What do they do? Man, they run at each other, jump into each other's arms, screech at an unbearable decibel level, then hold hands as they skip down the hall. They'll even go into First Period, sit down, and comb each other's hair, for crying out loud! Guys, of course, stare at them in total disbelief.

Then there's the age-old question: "Why do girls go to the bathroom in groups?" I actually had a guy write me a letter and ask, "Do they need help in there?" One brilliant guy wrote me an answer to that: "I think they need a spotter!" (I don't know exactly what he meant by that and, furthermore, I don't really *want* to know.) I think the real reason they go to the bathroom in groups is because they do *everything* in groups. They go in there, where it's safe, and they talk . . . about everything! Especially about guys. That, by the way, is where they decide it's the guy's fault!

Guys, on the other hand, when they go to the restroom, just go in and GO! No talking, no thinking (no washing hands), then they leave. It's a totally different scenario than for girls.

Just for discussion's sake here, let's say a men's restroom has four urinals in a row. And let's say there's a guy using Urinal Number 2:

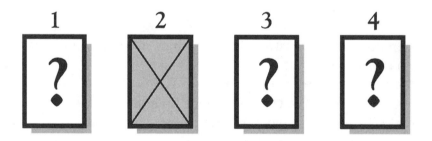

You ask any guy, "If Number 1 is open, Number 2 is being used, Number 3 is open, and so is Number 4, which one will *you* use?" Every guy will tell you, "Number 4!!!!!" No guy will ever come in and use Number 1 or Number 3, 'cause the guy at Number 2 will freak out! He's just minding his own business, not talking to anyone, and you come in and use Number 1 or Number 3, RIGHT NEXT TO HIM, and that's waaaaay too close. "Hey, man, back off! Number *Four's* open! Don't you know the rules?"

Or how about if there are six urinals and Number 1, Number 3, and Number 5 are being used, what will he want to do now?

WAIT!!! (Or use a stall.)

That's right! Guys have rules, especially about bathrooms, and all guys know them. They didn't have to read them in a book, or have anyone explain it to them. They just know.

When guys are in a restroom they don't look in the mirror and say, "I look just terrible!" secretly hoping someone will say, "Oh, Steve, you look great!" They don't ask each other how they look, they don't comb each other's hair or borrow each other's makeup, and they don't hold hands as they skip down the hall looking for the next group activity. No way! Guys just pee, peek, and leave! That's it.

So why are guys like that? Why are girls the way they are? And how on earth can the two ever communicate with each other? Why does it have to be so hard? Why is it that even though guys really try, they just don't seem to get it?

Well, that's what the first part of this book is all about—the differences between guys and girls and how they communicate with each other.

The second part of the book is all about LOVE. That's right. More songs have been written about love than about any other subject. Same with movies. But do people really know what love is? Nope. When I do an assembly I always ask the crowd, "How many of you have ever had a boyfriend or girlfriend tell you, 'I love you'?" (A whole bunch of kids will raise their hands.) Then I ask them, "How many found out they lied?" Almost all the *same* hands will go up. Amazing! When I taught a pre-marriage class I'd ask each couple, "Do you really love each other?" With sheepish, silly grins they'd say, "Oh yes! Forever!" But then I'd ask them to *define* love and they would go brain-dead. I don't know if I ever had a couple "IN LOVE" who could define it. So I will. In fact, by the end of the chapter on love you're going to know whether or not your boyfriend or girlfriend really loves you. Guaranteed! It's really very easy as long as you're honest.

The third part of the book is about SEX. Yes, sir, the chapter every guy has already turned to, to see if there are any pictures. But not so fast, guys. You can't skip the love part and jump into the sex part and expect it all to work or make sense. It won't. So be patient. If I'm gonna help you have the best "sex life" possible (and I'm going to), it all has to go together. I can promise you it will be entertaining. Lots of nude pictures, drawings, and . . . (not really, but now I have your attention!)

At the end of the book we'll get into some other stuff just for girls and some just for guys. Feel free to read the chapter about the opposite sex. In fact, I kinda hope you do; but remember that those chapters will really be aimed at specific issues that guys or girls need to hear about.

Anyway, there are lots of other things in this book to get to, so let's go. I hope it helps. If it doesn't, I've just wasted the last three years of my life on writing when I could have been out fishing.

Happy reading,

BRAD HENNING

Let's Start with a Quiz (Oh boy, can we?)

LUANN reprinted by permission of United Feature Syndicate, Inc.

How much do you really know about the opposite sex? Most of us guys are clueless. We brag about knowing everything, but we feel about as smart as a hamster. For instance, listen to this guy's letter:

Dear Brad,

I wish you would have gone further into the issue of why girls are so hard to get along with and why when you think you've finally got them figured out they totally flip and what they want isn't the same as what they used to want when you didn't know what it was they wanted.

—Jeff

Or this guy:

Dear Brad,

Thanks for coming. I felt everything you said was true! I have a good friend who lives next door and she gets mad at me sometimes and I don't know why. When I ask her why, she says, "I think you know why," when I honestly don't have a clue. Then she gets mad at me because I'm too insensitive to know why she's mad at me. It makes me so frustrated I want to cry. Could you please tell girls that us guys are stupid and really don't know why they're mad at us, and if they told us we could fix the problem.

Thanks,
Jim

Some people (except Jeff and Jim) reading this book for the first time may think they already know all there is to know about the opposite sex and really don't need to read all this stuff. I've had kids write me saying so. In fact, *I* used to think that way myself until I slugged a girl I liked (and if that's not a compliment, I don't know what is) and she never spoke to me again.

So before we go any further, here's a little quiz to help you understand whether you need to read this book or not.

Quiz: How Well Do You Know Men and Women?
(Answer True or False)

1. Men communicate what they are feeling.   T   F

2. Men apologize if you prove them wrong.   T   F

3. Women can do anything men can do. Maybe better.   T   F

4. Women have better hearing and smell than men.   T   F

5. Women have it much harder in life than men.   T   F

6. Women think about sex about as much as men do.   T   F

7. Men can be hurt emotionally as easily as women can. T F

8. You can tell a guy likes a girl when he ignores her. T F

9. Women are generally comfortable with their bodies. T F

10. Most women think men understand them, but they don't. T F

11. Men get to the point much quicker than women do. T F

12. Men are far more competitive than women are. T F

13. A man will tell another man almost anything about himself. T F

14. Women tend to marry men thinking they can change them. T F

15. Men marry women hoping they will never change, but they do. T F

16. Men have more fragile egos than women. T F

17. More women than men are dissatisfied with their bodies. T F

18. Women solve problems faster than men. T F

19. A man's self-esteem is directly connected to performance. T F

20. For women, giving advice is showing love. T F

21. Women take what others say at face value. T F

22. Men fear abandonment more than women do. T F

23. Men communicate to gather information. T F

24. Men talk about what they have been feeling. T F

25. A woman's brain compartmentalizes ideas, thoughts, and feelings. T F

26. Guys have a hidden goal of changing the women they love. T F

27. Academically, women do as well as men in all subjects. T F

28. Men talk more about "things" rather than about people. T F

29. Women move on after an argument more easily than men do.   T   F

30. Sexually, women tend to be extremely visual.   T   F

31. After a divorce, men tend to be less healthy than women.   T   F

32. Most single guys want to marry virgins.   T   F

33. For a woman, looks are a highly desired quality in a man.   T   F

34. Guys look for end results more than the challenge.   T   F

35. For men, honesty is a highly desired quality in a woman.   T   F

36. Guys tend to give sex to get love.   T   F

37. Men tend not to get hints or read minds.   T   F

38. Women are more spontaneous than men.   T   F

39. Men have larger stomachs, kidneys, livers, and appendix.   T   F

40. Men can tolerate higher temperatures than women.   T   F

41. Men outspend women on a daily basis.   T   F

(To find the answers, turn to page **666**.)

Section One
DIFFERENCES

Chapter 1. "Relational" Meets "Impersonal"

Men and Women are Different.

Pretty profound, huh? Actually, we're different in hundreds—no, probably millions—of ways, which is great. I like it. Wouldn't it be horrible if men and women were the same? After all, variety is the spice of life! Anyway, I've read lots of books and articles describing those differences, and I am always amazed at just how different we are.

LUANN reprinted by permission of United Feature Syndicate, Inc.

Being married as long as I have and having two kids of my own (a boy and a girl) has shown me just how different guys are from girls. You can't get away from it. Some of these differences are inborn and, like it or not, there isn't much you can do about it. Other differences, though, come from our society. We tend to treat little boys and little girls differently. When we give dolls to one and guns to the other, we can't help but influence the outcome to some degree. Then again, if you give a doll to a little boy, he'll more than likely use it for a gun or a hammer, and bang its head against a wall! And if you give the girl a gun, she may try to tuck it in bed at night as she sings it a lullaby.

Some people really want men and women to be the same and I can kind of understand why. I think it's because they worry that the opposite sex may gain some advantage or "have it better" if they admit there are differences. But let's not make things worse by saying there are *no* differences just because we've blown it in the past. That will really screw things up! (And by the way, if you really don't think there's a difference between guys and girls, buy a couple of playoff tickets and go see for yourself.)

A List of Differences

Let me start out by giving you a short list of differences. Very short! In the appendix at the end of the book I'll give you a bigger list, but here is a taste of what I mean.

Men snore more.
Men fight more.
Men change their minds more.
Men's blood is redder.
Their daylight vision is better.
They have thicker veins and longer vocal cords.
Guys lose weight quicker than women do (Hmmmmm!).
Guys' metabolic rates tend to be higher.
A woman's skin is 10 times more sensitive than a man's.
More guys are left-handed.

Color blindness is 16 times more common in men than in women.

Stuttering is four times more common in guys than in girls.

A guy's third finger is usually shorter than his index finger.

A woman's third finger is usually longer than her index finger. (I'll wait here until you have thoroughly examined your OWN fingers!)

More guys have ADD than do girls.

Women have better senses of hearing, taste, touch, and smell.

One Egg?!

Then there's this difference. (Now ladies, I don't mean to embarrass you, but . . . this really is funny.) Girls, every 28 days your body will produce one egg. (By the way, I didn't know this before, but the other day a doctor told me that a girl, the day she's born, has all the eggs she's ever going to have. Something like 400,000 of them!) Now when guys hear that "one egg every 28 days" thing, we just want to laugh. Why? Because every 15 minutes the average guy's body will produce up to 750,000 sperm! Every 15 minutes!! So every 28 days a guy will make over two billion sperm, compared to that ONE egg from a girl. That's two billion to one!!! Theoretically then, one guy in one day could produce enough sperm to impregnate the entire world! And I know some guys who'd like a shot at that! One guy was so impressed with that fact that he wrote me and said, "Just call me The Sperminator!"

OK, I've gone a little off the point here. (Hey, it's a "guy thing," OK?) Come back to the "guys are different from girls" thing. Is it really that big a shock to anyone that we're so different? No. Man, LOOK AROUND! You can see it everywhere!

She Totally Disagrees!!!

And speaking of the differences . . . you know the only people who get mad at me or want to argue about this stuff being true or not . . . are women? I've had girls come up to me after assemblies and get all over my case: "That's not true! That's really not true,

and furthermore. . . ." Guys on the other hand, if they disagree with something I said, will just flip me off and walk out! "That guy's so full of!@#$%&*@#$% . . . ! Who gives a @#$%@#$%!"

A mom once came with her daughter to hear my talk. They arrived early, so they introduced themselves to me. I told the mom it was nice to have her there, and that she was lucky to be early because there was only one padded chair in the auditorium and she could have it. She glared at me and said, "Do you think I need it?" Ooooooh! Scary!!!

Women Tend to Be More Relational

Dear Brad,

It's a no-win situation. If you're impersonal to a girl you end up ticking her off and if you're personal then you end up in some deep strings-attached relationship. Now if you find an impersonal girl and you're both impersonal, you usually end up ranking each other down to the point where you rarely talk anymore. Finding that delicate balance of being one of the boys and knowing when to shut your mouth takes a lot of time and for me a lot of apologies to people for being rude.

Steve

Women, by nature, tend to be relational. It's not that men can't be relational, or at least *learn* to be, it's just that women *naturally* tend to be more relational than men are. Even their bodies respond to relationships! A woman counselor once told me that if a woman started a new job in an office made up almost entirely of women, within six months or so her monthly cycle would occur at the same time as all the other women. It's a natural response to being close to each other. She doesn't choose that, it just happens. (And by the way, if a guy dares to bring that up at the office . . . he's dead meat!)

An article in *USA Today* reported a new high-tech computer strategy aimed at young teenage girls. Girls and their families evalu-

ated certain computer games for their sales appeal. One game, called "Girl Talk" (Hasbro: Windows CD, $29.95: ages eight to 12), was designed to be played by a group (up to four in number). Subjects for discussion included "Boy Buzz," "School Daze," "Chick Chat," and "Home Sweet Home." But get this! An incorrect answer resulted in a fate worse than death: the unlucky girl got one of 10 zits on her "digital persona." Most of the girl "evaluators" had a riot, and couldn't stop playing and talking about the game.

In "Starrier Soccer" (Purple Moon: Power Mac and Windows CD, $29.95: ages eight to 12) girls are supposed to help "Ginger" make decisions that will affect how she gets along with her team-mates and will prepare her for the big tryouts.[1] Can't you just see guys playing this game? "OK Ginger . . . Blammmm!! Take that!" Which illustrates that . . .

Guys Tend to Be Impersonal

Dear Brad,

My boyfriend and I went to the waterfront one night. It was a beautiful September evening and there was a gorgeous full moon that lit up the water. Well, my initial thought and comment was, how romantic the setting was, etc. But, the first thing out of his mouth was, "Yuck, it smells like dead crabs out here!"

Jennifer

Guys tend to be more impersonal than girls are. You can see it in everything they do; from the movies they see, to the computer games they play, and the way they eat. Watch a bunch of guys play basketball on an outdoor court on a hot, summer day. You know how it goes. The guys will drive up, put their shoes on, choose up teams, shoot around a bit, and then proceed to kill each other. Within five minutes one guy sets a pick; he comes around the

---

[1] By the editors of Family PC, "From Giggles to Gumshoes, Girls Get to Play Their Way," *USA Today*, April 7, 1999.

corner—slams into another guy—then both guys start yelling, "Foul!!!!!!!!!!" They're about 6 inches from each other's faces, yelling at the top of their lungs, spitting the whole time . . . "I can't believe you did that! What are you, some kind of @$#%*!#(@ idiot?" . . . **AND THEN THEY GO EAT!** Girls look at that and ask, "Hey, aren't you still mad at that guy?" The guy says, "No, man . . . We're hungry!" ("What fight?") I mean it's no big deal. Who cares?!!

What happens when two girls get in a fight? How long does it last? Yeah, you aren't kidding. Some of you girls are still mad at that girl in your seventh-grade class. You can remember everything she said to you. If you see her in the hallway at school, you'll say to your friend, "Oh my gosh, oh my gosh . . . *that's* that girl. Do you know what she said to me in the seventh grade?"

Guys don't even *remember* the seventh grade! They kinda think, "Man, you only got so much space in your brain, so why fill it up with stupid stuff?" Right?

"Relational" Meets "Impersonal"

Now, here's where it all starts to fall apart. What happens when a guy and a girl get in a fight? Who always looks like a jerk? HE DOES! Now he probably isn't a jerk, but *he looks like one.* I mean, think about your mom and dad when they get in a fight. I'm sure you've heard something like this:

MOM: Do these pants make me look fat?

DAD: Well, now that you mention it, they do look a little tight . . .

MOM: So you think I'm FAT!

DAD: Noooo . . . you asked what I thought and . . .

MOM: . . . and you think I'm FAT!!

DAD: All right, I called you fat. OK, I'm sorry. Can we just move on now?

MOM: Nooooo. You're gonna pay for that.

Poor Dad! What started out as a simple question turned into a major fight and he never saw it coming. For months he's in the doghouse, but he forgets WHY! So one night, after dinner:

DAD: Hey, aren't those pants getting a little snug?

MOM: Aaaahhhhhh! That's exactly what you said six months ago, July tenth, seven o'clock, at McDonald's!

Then she quotes everything he said.

DAD: What? I didn't say that!

MOM: Oh yeah, you did!

So, who looks like a jerk? That's right. He does.

When guys talk to each other it's totally different. Guys *love* to put each other down—they even *practice* putdowns. It's almost become an art form with some guys: "Hey, is that your head, or did your neck throw up?" Or, "Man, you're so ugly you'd make a train take a dirt road!" Did you know guys in the NBA vote on who has the biggest "trash mouth" in the league? I think it's kind of a status symbol.

At this point you guys might just as well write this on your forehead so you can see it every day in the mirror: "**I will pretty much always look like a jerk!**" Now I don't think guys *are* jerks (well, some of us are, but so are some girls) but much of the time we just *look* like jerks. I think it was Tim Allen who said, "It's not our fault we're jerks. We were born with a 'jerk gene.'"

Who Wins the Argument?

Think about this: When a guy and a girl get in an argument, who tends to get over the argument quickest? Yeah, usually the guy does! That's a good thing! But who *solves* the argument? She

does! 'Cause she won't drop it till she knows he understands just how much he screwed up, and she's sure he won't do it again. She's convinced that he just didn't understand what it was that made her feel bad, otherwise he wouldn't have said it. She figures if she tells him again he'll finally get it and won't ever do it again.

> SHE CALLS THAT COMMUNICATION.
> HE CALLS IT NAGGING!

"Goll, can't you just drop it?" "No, 'cause you just don't understand . . . blah, blah, blah!"

Guys Treat Everyone the Same

Here's another problem. Guys treat everybody the same. Now that sounds good at first, but it gets guys in trouble all the time. Remember what happens when two guys meet each other in the hallway? What do they do? They just go, "'Sup?" then smack each other in the arm, sending books flying! Then it turns into this big body-slamming thing. It's fun! They don't mean anything by it. They're just screwing around. So when a guy sees a girl he knows walking down the hallway, what does he do? "'Sup?" He smacks her in the arm, sending *her* books flying. When he did that to his best friend they both picked up their books and went away laughing. When he does it to this girl, SHE'S MAD! "Don't you know I'm a girl?" With a stupid grin on his face he says, "Yeah!!!!!!!" (He doesn't get it.) The girl goes home with a bruised arm and her mom asks, "What happened?" "He likes me."

But hey, guys treat everyone like that. Girls, you gotta know it's kind of a compliment to get slugged by a guy. He's inviting you into his world, and guys don't take that lightly. He's kinda saying, "Hey, you're one of us!" A guy doesn't slug a girl he doesn't like. Slugging is a playful thing to him, but it's a bruise to you, and now he looks like a jerk.

By the way, this is the same reason a guy will open a door for you, then slam it in your face when you're halfway through. Some

guys are being mean, but most are just having fun. (They do this kind of thing to *each other.*) He doesn't really mean to hurt you.

Guys seem to think girls are just . . . guys . . . with different bodies on . . . and they like that. A LOT! So guys *treat* girls as if they were guys. They also try to *talk* to girls the same way they talk to each other . . . and that's a guy's **FIRST BIG MISTAKE** when it comes to girls!!! Now this needs a bit of explaining.

The Guy in the Mirror

Have you girls ever seen a guy standing in front of a full-length mirror when he doesn't know you're watching? Almost all guys do the same thing. They go into this flex mode. They pose, grimace, curl their arms like a gorilla: "I'm here to PUMP YOU UP!" It's the Arnold Schwarzenegger thing. (Is that how you spell that guy's name?) Guys will even do this in *groups,* pushing each other out of the way trying to hog more of the mirror. It doesn't matter how much a guy weighs either; 300 pounds or 95 pounds. Not long ago I read that 68 percent of all guys who stand naked in front of a mirror *like their bodies.* You know, they just think it's cool the way it works and looks and everything.

The Girl in the Mirror

But given the same scenario, only 22 percent of girls like what they see in their mirrors.[2] Most girls look in the mirror and get depressed. Then they try to "fix it"! Something's always wrong and something always needs fixing. Women are much more critical about their bodies and their looks than guys are. I think that's why girls' purses are so huge. They have to bring all their "tools" with them, ready to "fix" whatever could go wrong.

So here comes some guy down the hall, not thinking about anything in particular (certainly not about what he saw in the mirror that morning). He sees a girl he knows and blurts out, "Hey, nice butt!" Now he doesn't mean anything by it at all. He's just screw-

---

[2] Daniel Evan Weiss, *The Great Divide* (New York: Poseidon Press, 1991), p. 198.

ing around. What he doesn't know is five minutes before he said that to her, she was looking at her "butt" in the mirror, *didn't like it,* and now this **MORON** brings it up!!!! Or how about this? I heard a guy say something like this to a girl: "Your hair looks really nice! . . . YOU don't, but your hair looks good!" Now he thought he was being hysterically funny! She didn't. She chased him down the hall, throwing books at him.

A teacher heard my talk one time, and came up afterward and handed me a letter. I'm guessing she was about 40 years old, but the letter told about something that happened to her in the fifth grade. (What are you then, about 10 years old?) On Valentine's Day the coolest guy in her class gave her a handmade card. She was so excited to get it that she ran home, locked herself in her room, and finally opened the card. Here's what he had written:

Roses are red
Violets are blue
You have a nose
Like a B-52.

Now, thirty-some years later, guess what's the first thing she sees in the mirror every morning? Her nose! She *still* isn't over it! After 30 years!

Then there was the guy who walked up to a girl and said, "Can I pop it?" (She had a pimple.) No comment!

Here's the all-time worst thing I've ever heard a guy say to a girl. This guy was standing in the hallway, talking to the girl. His attention seemed to be focused more on her face than on what she was saying. She kept talking, he kept staring, until finally she couldn't stand it anymore. "What?! What are you staring at?" He squinted his eyes, moved a little closer, took a deeper look at her, and said, "When you gonna shave that mustache?"

A Memory Like a Steel Trap

When a guy makes comments about a girl's body in any way, it can really hurt. I have asked hundreds of students this question: "How many of you, both guys and girls, can remember something that somebody said to you—and I don't care how long ago it happened—but it hurt so badly you'll never forget it?" In any given group about 25 percent of the girls will raise their hands. Usually only one or two guys will raise their hands. That's pretty common.

Guys, remember this. Just because it's no big deal to you doesn't mean it's no big deal to her. Girls can be deeply hurt by what is said to them, and they remember those comments, sometimes for years. Not only that, they remember WHO said it to them. That means if you've ever said something like that in the past (and probably all us guys have), that one girl you said it to can make the whole school think you're a jerk, just by repeating what you said. But hey, wait a minute, girls! Is that fair? The hardest thing you may ever have to do is forgive a guy for stuff he said to you in the past. Us guys *do* make mistakes sometimes, and sometimes do dumb things, but that's no reason to hang it over our heads *for the rest of our lives.* Yes, a guy *does* need to know that what he said hurt you. (Remember, even though you think he already knows, he may not.) So tell him, and allow him time to change. If he doesn't change, don't date him. Some guys will never get the picture, and I guess that's OK 'cause some girls won't either.

Just one more warning here. Guys, listen to this letter.

Dear Mr. Henning

In like 7th grade there was this girl on my bus that had messed up teeth and she was kinda chubby. (She was in 8th grade) She had a major crush on me and she would always sit with me and try to be really nice and well she was. One day we were all talking and someone asked me about her and she heard me say "I wouldn't touch her with a ten-foot pole." I just blew it off and forgot about it. She moved up to high school the next year and she moved and didn't ride my bus any more, so I didn't see her for about a year and a half. Well when I got to high school and I

saw her my jaw dropped to the floor. She was so hot. I expected her to talk to me because we hadn't seen each other for a long time. Well she didn't say a word and has completely ignored me ever since. At the end of my freshmen year a good friend of mine who had a class with this girl had mentioned my name for some reason and she told her everything and said she went home and cried all the time after school because of what I said to her.

Let the Competition Begin!

Who do you think is more competitive, guys or girls? Most people think it's guys. I don't. I think it's girls.

Now I'll admit that guys compete at almost everything. In fact, to most guys life is kinda like a big, fun game. For example, if one guy comes into a room and belches, what will every other guy in the room do? ***Bwwouaahhh!!!*** If one guy eats five Oreo cookies in one bite, the other guy will eat six. If all the guys in a class leave school to go to McDonald's and each guy drives by himself, what will happen between the parking lot and McDonald's? That's right . . . a race! Ever play poker with a bunch of guys? They'll kill for a quarter! You can say, "Man, listen, I'll just *give* you twenty-five cents." He'll reply, "That's not the point." See, it's the competition that's fun! Two guys will come into an empty auditorium—no one else is there—hundreds of empty seats to choose from, but they will fight for the same chair. Why? 'Cause it's FUN! Girls watch guys do stuff like that and think, "MORONS! They're aaaaalllllll MORONS!"

At a college near my town two guys were competing at jumping out of their dorm windows. Last I heard they were up to five or six stories. The only rule was they couldn't break anything. Can't you see Matt pointing his finger at Rob with a laugh, saying, "Ah ha! You broke a leg! Doesn't count!!"? "Dang!" says Rob, as he crawls up the stairs for another shot at it.

When I was in college there were even guys competing to see who could pee across the road—and one guy did it! He became a role model to all the rest of us!!!

Girls, on the other hand, compete on a very personal basis. Let me tell you a story to illustrate.

Nightmare at the Senior Prom

Let's say you're going to the senior prom with your boyfriend, and after hours of searching you find the perfect dress. You get your hair done, have a manicure, and go to the big dance. Out on the dance floor you notice a really cute girl walk in the door at the far end of the room. She's wearing YOUR dress! What would you feel? What would you do? (Guys, trust me here. I've used this story in lots of assemblies and girls answer everything from "I'd kill her!" to "I'd rip the dress off her!" At which point most of the guys in the room yell, "Hey! I'd pay five bucks to see that!")

Now most girls won't say this out loud, but here's what most (not all) girls would be thinking: "THAT GIRL looks better in MY dress (it's not *her* dress, it's *my* dress) than *I* look in my dress!" Or she might say, "I look far better in MY dress than SHE looks in MY dress." Then all night long those two will stay at opposite sides of the room, keeping track of each other, because neither one wants to be caught side by side while everyone else judges who looks better in the dress. (They just *know* everyone else is totally focused on comparing the two of *them.*)

But girls, if your boyfriend noticed that girl's dress when she came in the room, what would he do? He'd POINT IT OUT! "Hey, she's got the same dress on!" See, to him this is really funny. You know why? Think about it. What are all the guys at that dance wearing? THE SAME THING! Do guys care? Heck, no! Guys would be laughing their heads off. "Hey, Harry, dang nice cummerbund you got there!" "Well, Fred, dang nice of you to say so!" Guys don't care about stuff like that. We don't *remember* stuff like that! Girls do.

I went to a friend's party once, all by myself. I wore a blue blazer, khaki pants, brown shoes (very cool shoes), white pinstriped shirt, and a brand-new Nordstrom tie. I LOOKED GOOD! I was just hanging around trying to look cool when in the door came a guy with the exact same stuff on! I'm not kidding. Identical! So, not

knowing what else to do and not knowing the guy, I walked up to him and introduced myself. I told him I thought he had great taste in clothes. "Well, so do you!" he joked. We laughed and spent the rest of the night side by side, asking people, "How do you like my friend's clothes?" It was great fun. (Morons!)

What to Wear? What to Wear?!

So who DO women dress for? Each other! Lots of girls have told me the first thing they do when they come into a room is look around to see what all the other girls are wearing. One girl told me that in the morning when she gets dressed she is thinking, "I'm going to look better in this dress than Jennifer would. . . ." Not all girls are like that, but many are.

Guys *never* do that. They dress the way they want and don't really give a rip what anyone else thinks. They don't give it a second thought. Some guys don't give it a *first* thought! And they certainly don't walk into a room and check out what all the other guys are wearing. But girls do.

Don't think so? A high school psychology class sat studying quietly during first period when suddenly five girls, who everyone knew, walked into the room. They entered the front door, walked straight through the room, and left through the back door. As soon as the girls had gone, the teacher got up and said, "OK, I want each of you to take out a piece of paper and pencil and, by yourself, describe what each of those girls was wearing." Every guy in the class put down "T-shirt and jeans." But the girls? Well, the girls started their lists by naming each girl, then writing down her size, the brand, the color . . . everything! The guys just shook their heads.

Miss America

Think about this. Every year about 75 million people watch the Miss America pageant. Do you know who those people are? I figured it would be guys, but nope, 75 percent of the viewers are women! There are 750,000 beauty contests in America *every year!*

All for WOMEN.[3] That's unbelievable! We all know men watch women, but *women* watch women even more.

Who Do You Watch?

I was at a basketball game one night, and all through the game guys were walking by, messin' around. Some girls watched them and talked about them, some giggled. The guys in the stands couldn't have cared less. But when a gorgeous girl walked by, everybody, guys *and* girls, watched her. She almost stopped the game. If a good-looking guy walks by with a beautiful girl, everyone watches the girl; they rarely watch the guy.

OK, who do girls dress for? They dress for each other . . . and the competition is fierce. So if a guy goes around making comments about a girl's body, body parts, her clothes, or her looks, or if he makes derogatory comments about her physical appearance, *even in fun,* he's in big trouble. She'll remember what he said, sometimes for years. Not only that, she may begin to fear that the way she looks doesn't "measure up;" that "something's wrong": "I'll never look as good as the others. I *hate* my body! I want to hide. I've got to do something quick." She may even think, "I want to die!"

Ken and Barbie

From childhood to adulthood, women want to be pretty. Little girls play with dolls and start believing they will never get Ken if they don't look like Barbie. The pressure never lets up. But do you realize that if you projected Barbie's measurements into real life she would be 36-18-33? The measurements of the average contemporary fashion model are 33-23-33, and most girls know they don't measure up to models, let alone to Barbie. About 33 percent of American women wear a size 16 or larger. The average "size-6" model is 5 feet, 9 inches tall, and she weighs 110 pounds! That's

[3] Warren Farrell, *Why Men Are the Way They Are* (New York: Berkley Books, 1986), p. 70.

why 50 percent of American women are on a diet at any given time, and together they buy about $33 billion worth of diet products every year.[4] They're trying to compete.

Eating Disorders

Do you know what anorexia is? It's an eating disorder where a person refuses to eat normally and usually loses a lot of weight in the process. Bulimia is a similar eating disorder, only bulimics go on eating binges and then make themselves throw up. Both disorders are very complicated and hard to treat. Both anorexics and bulimics are obsessed with being thin. Do you know someone who is anorexic or bulimic? Do you know a *guy* who is anorexic or bulimic? Probably not. The National Association of Anorexia Nervosa and Associated Disorders says that over 8 million people in this country suffer from eating disorders. About 90 percent of them are women.[5] Why is that? I think it has a lot to do with this competition among women, their tendency to take things so very personally, and their dissatisfaction with their own bodies. An eating disorder involves all kinds of other issues, so it goes much deeper than just being female. If you're anorexic or bulimic, your whole personality is wrapped up in it. You live with it all day, every day. Very few guys understand what this feels like, so they just keep on making comments. They don't know that what they're saying could be the "last straw" that launches a girl into a destructive disorder.

Where Did It Start?

One summer I got to speak at Malibu, a Young Life camp in Canada. After I shared all this relationship stuff with about 300 high school students, a girl came up to talk to me. She introduced herself. "Hi. I'm anorexic and bulimic. Can I talk to you?" I said, "What was your name again? Anna—, what?" "No, I'm anorexic."

---

[4] *People*, July 3, 1996, p. 71
[5] National Association of Anorexia Nervosa and Associated Disorders: *www.anad.org/who.html*, February 25, 2002.

(I felt stupid!) This was years ago, and since I had never really talked to a girl with that kind of problem before, it was a chance for me to understand a little more of what anorexia was all about. So I asked her, "When did all this anorexia stuff start? I mean, did someone do or say something that set it off, or—?" She didn't even let me finish the sentence before she blurted out, "I'll tell you *exactly* when it started! I was walking through the mall, arm in arm with my boyfriend, when this really good-lookin' girl came walking by. My boyfriend saw her and turned to stare at her. I got so mad that I yanked on his arm really hard and, since his head was turned, it snapped his neck. It really hurt him 'cause he kinda bent over, holding his neck. I just turned my back on him, letting HIM feel the pain! What I didn't know was he was kinda checking *me* out from behind. When I finally turned around (he was still holding his neck), the first thing he said to me was, 'Hey, you're gettin' a little big in the rear, aren't ya?' Right then I vowed to myself that no one would *ever* say that to me again."

That poor girl went on a crash diet and almost died . . . *because of one comment from a guy!* It can happen just that fast.

"Onion Butt"

After one of my talks a girl came up to me in tears. She told me how her boyfriend would hold up pictures of *Playboy* centerfolds and compare her to the models: "He wants me to have an 'onion butt' just like all those naked girls do." Onion butt? What the heck is that? She described how an onion, sitting on a counter, has a smooth curve under each "cheek," and that's what he wanted her to look like. What a moron!

I have piles of letters from girls who know absolutely when they decided to change—to try to live their lives for someone else's dream—to be the perfect girl for some guy who didn't deserve a second thought. Some girls have even died trying to be perfect. But in spite of the risks, many girls still try to conform to a ridiculous image 'cause it hurts too much to be rejected. The comments go too deep.

When a girl hears this kind of comment, no matter who says it to her, she has two options:

1. Conform to what someone else wants you to be, or *thinks* you should be, and, in the process, lose your identity and self-image. (The cost of doing that seems unimportant *at the time.*)

OR . . .

2. Stand up for what *you* believe is right, and possibly be laughed at or be rejected by the group. ("You're not pretty enough, you're not skinny enough, you're not sexy enough, you're not having enough sex, you're clothes aren't nice enough, you're too smart, you're too dumb . . ."or, "Sorry, only onion butts here.")

It's sad, but a lot of people won't risk being laughed at (rejected), so they just go along with whatever everyone else wants or thinks. Later on they find out they don't even know who they are anymore. They've forgotten how to think for themselves.

Walkin' on Eggshells

So what's all this like from a guy's point of view? Most people never consider what all this personal/impersonal stuff might mean to a guy. I remember one time, when I was in high school, I made some lame comment to a girl and she ran away crying. Right then it hit me. "You mean I gotta watch what I say to every girl, from now on, or this could happen again?"

When an "impersonal" guy has a girlfriend, he can count on the fact that one day she will feel hurt by something he says. He didn't *mean* to hurt her, but she's hurt anyway. His guy friends aren't that sensitive, so he has to learn about the female world by *trial and error*. In the process he learns that being with girls is downright scary. "Get close to a girl and you can get in trouble. BIG trouble!" No guy *wants* to hurt the girl he cares about, but he's pretty sure

he will. What frustrates him is that he didn't see the first mistake, and therefore he has no clue how to see the next one before it hits him in the face. He starts walking on eggshells.

So girls, what's it like being a guy? Let me put it this way. How would you like to be a guy who's about to go on a date with a girl, and you know, even before the evening begins, that you might say something that could throw her into a tailspin or eventually even kill her? How would you girls like being in his place? Would you be a little nervous? Would you be walking on eggshells, too?

One more little note here. Girls have to watch what they say to *each other*. Sometimes girls say or do the cruelest things to each other—things that are never forgotten. So it's not just guys who mess up.

Guys Are on a Mission, Girls Are on a Picnic

Guys tend to be GOAL-oriented, and girls tend to be DETAIL-oriented. Men want to accomplish something. Women want an experience. If you don't believe this, watch your mom and dad when they drive to a home they've never been to. She's looking at houses, flowers, little kids playing in the sprinkler; he's running yellow lights and trying to find shortcuts. When they arrive at the house, she comments on how nice the drive was, and he brags, "Yeah, and we made it in twenty minutes flat!" Goals . . . details. Accomplishment . . . experience.

What's the Goal?

Why is it that guys can play full-court basketball, nonstop, for three hours, with no problem, but be totally exhausted after fifteen minutes of window-shopping with a girl? (I can hear all you guys cheering.) It's because with window-shopping there's NO GOAL anywhere in sight. It's BORING!!! (At least to him.) In fact, if you ask a girl what she's looking for when she's shopping, she'll say something like, "I don't know, but when I find it I'll know." The guy is ready to fall on the ground and die! Now when *he* goes to the store, he knows *exactly* what he needs, buys it, and goes home. Period. Mission accomplished. Let's get on with life. If he doesn't

need anything, why would he want to wander around in a store? There's too much else to do! For a girl, shopping is a social occasion that may or may not result in a purchase. Girls shop with their friends *just to be together.* They talk, try on outrageous clothes just for the fun of it, find little presents for each other. . . . If they really *are* looking for something, they want their friends to help them choose it. Who wants to show up at school in an outfit that no one else likes?

With that in mind, picture a girl shopping with her boyfriend. After 15 minutes he's bored out of his mind and keeps asking when she'll be done. He wonders why she doesn't get on with The Mission so they can go do something important. Like basketball. Now she's thinking something entirely different: "I asked you to come shopping so we could just *be* together. You can be with your guy friends for hours at a time and never get tired, but you're with ME for 15 minutes and you're bored. You must like THEM more than you like ME!" He thinks she's wasting time; she thinks he doesn't like being with her.

There is a way out! Ladies, tell your boyfriend that you would like to spend some time together and go to the mall. Let him know that you'd like to "just look at stuff" with him for 45 minutes, and then grab a bite to eat. Don't make him suffer! Shopping just isn't a guy thing. Guys, your girlfriend is asking you to be a part of her life—to see what kind of "stuff" she likes—to let her see what kind of "stuff" *you* like. Look at this as a cheap date! Free entertainment! A way to earn lots of bonus points!

Destination or Journey?

Guys, have you ever gone on a hike in the mountains with a girl? Help me here. What's the goal of a hike? Yeah!!! To get to the top! All guys know that. "All right, we've got an hour to get to the top . . . let's GO!" With grand visions of climbing Mt. Everest or somethin', you're off. Your girlfriend, however, has spent the whole week getting ready. She's packed a lunch, her camera, extra film, sunscreen, water bottles, insect repellent. . . . Within five minutes, what's she doing? Looking at the flowers, squirrels, chipmunks,

talking to new people, taking pictures of stuff. . . . Taking group pictures with the chipmunks. Talking to the chipmunks. Feeding the chipmunks. You're going crazy!!!

> GUY: Hey, we've only got fifty minutes left. We're never gonna get there. The goal is to get to the top!

> GIRL: Wait a minute! If you can't enjoy the trip, talk, see things, feed the squirrels, why would you want to get there?

> GUY: Because it's *there!!!*

> GIRL: That's dumb.

When Sex Is the Goal

NOW . . . think about sex. (I can hear all the guys: "*Finally* we're getting somewhere!") Hey guys, what's the goal? . . . To get to the TOP! Right? Yeah!!! But the girl says, "Not necessarily. If you can't enjoy the trip, talk, see things, and talk to the squirrels, why would you want to do that?"

> GUY: Aaaaaaaaaahhhhh . . . 'cause it's there!!!

> GIRL: That's dumb.

This next question may seem totally out of place, but follow me. . . . Girls, when it comes to sex, why is it that *some* guys (not all guys) at your school will go to bed with the "easy" girls, but those "easy" girls always get dumped? (You don't believe that? Look back just two years at all the kids you knew were having sex together—are they still with the same person? Almost never!) Now think about this a second. If sex was all the guy wanted, he would never dump her. Shoot, he could have sex any time he wanted to, 'cause she's easy. So why does he dump her? *He reached his goal*

... *NEXT!!!* So even when it comes to sex, a guy is goal-oriented. If a guy reaches his goal (sex with Girl No. 1), what will he do next? He'll move on to another goal (Girl No. 2)!! Having an "easy" target isn't any "fun." At a high school assembly in Seattle I asked the 900 students, "So if the guy can have sex any time he wants it, and she's easy, why does he dump her?" One guy way up at the top of the bleachers yelled out, "'Cause *that* was no challenge!" I thought the girls were going to kill him! But he was telling the truth.

See, a lot of guys will go after the sex stuff all right, but most guys don't want an easy girl. Ask them! It erases part of the "thrill of the hunt" that most guys feel. How many girls do you know who, after giving in sexually to a guy, got dumped the next day? I've got hundreds and hundreds of letters from girls, all telling me practically the same story: "He told me he loved me, so I let him, then he dumped me. Now everyone thinks I'm easy."

Easy Girls Get Dumped

Listen, I'll bet there isn't a guy in your school who would disagree with this next statement, 'cause believe me, I've asked:

"If a girl's easy to get in bed, she isn't worth keeping."

All guys know that!!!!

Now I'm not saying she's worth less as a person now, 'cause she isn't, but guys will tend to not want her if she's easy. Why? If a girl's "easy," that means any guy could get her. And if *any* guy could get her, that means that *he's just "any guy."* "THE HECK I AM!"

MTV's *Singled Out Guide to Dating* put it this way:

Your plumbing says, "Hook up ... with anybody," but your pride says, "Except her."[6]

---

[6] J. D. Heiman and Lynn Harris, *Singled Out Guide to Dating* (New York: MTV Books/PocketBooks/Melcher Media, 1996), p. 12.

Girls, He Wants to "Win" You!

No guy wants to think of himself as just "any guy." A guy wants to *win* the heart of a girl; he doesn't want it handed to him. The easier she makes herself, sexually or otherwise, the more he will stay away. He wants to believe he was good enough to have "won" her—that he has something no one else has. It makes a statement about who HE is. (It also makes a definite statement about who SHE is.) Lots of guys have told me that once they found the girl they really wanted, they didn't want to have sex with her and "ruin her." We'll talk more about that in the chapter just for girls.

Goal-Oriented: Good News, Bad News

So. Guys are goal-oriented. It's hard to get a lot of them to slow down long enough to see other things in life. Things like "relation-ships." Have you ever watched a guy who is really into football? The day of the Big Game he comes to school with his "game face" on. "Game face" means his whole life is wrapped around that night's game. He can't talk or think about anything else but the game. His girlfriend meets him at his locker.

GUY: I'm gonna kill those guys! YEAH!

Right then she decides it's time to have a deep, heart-to-heart talk about their relationship—where it's headed, how serious it is, do we really love each other, etc. All he can say is, "I'm gonna kill!"

GIRL: What?

GUY: I'm gonna kill those guys!

GIRL: Can't you think about anything else except football?

GUY: Nooooo.

GIRL: Don't you care about US?

GUY: I'm gonna kill!

GIRL: That's totally disgusting.

She walks off, leaving him banging his head against the locker, yelling, "I'm gonna KILL those guys!"

Here's the funny part of this whole thing. Ladies, the thing you don't like about a guy *now* is the thing you may like the most after you're married to him. What do I mean by that? Have you ever heard a girl say something like this about her boyfriend? "Is *that* all he ever thinks about?" Now *that* could be sex, sports, cars, food, money . . . he's just really focused on one thing at a time. She feels ignored.

But now, ladies, let's say you're married to a guy who leaves for work at 7 A.M., briefcase in hand, wearing his three-piece suit. Two minutes later he comes skipping back through the door, tears his tie off, and announces, "You know, I changed my mind. I just feel like staying home today and watching a little television, having a Coke or two, and, oh, I don't know, taking a nap. . . ." Would you put up with that, ladies? No way! You'd tell him, "Get your butt out there! And don't you let anything keep you from reaching your GOAL." You *want* a guy who sets goals 'cause he knows where he's headed, and he's not easily sidetracked. Nothing stops him. (That's the very thing you hate about guys in high school.) You don't want some wimp who changes his mind every five minutes or is just plain lazy.

It takes a while for most guys to find the balance, and, of course, there are some guys who never do. Some guys are all play and seem like they will *never* get their act together. Later in life those same guys will live, breath, eat, and sleep their work, and never have time for the things that count the most; things like relationships with their wife and kids. Life requires balance in all kinds of areas, and it may take a while for us guys to figure out just what that balance is. Most guys will find it. Some won't.

Don't Be a Wimp!

One more thought. Back in the '90s you started to hear a lot of women say they wanted "a sensitive, caring man." You know, the kind of guy who's not afraid to cry at a chick flick. But I've found that most girls, at least by their actions, don't really want a "sensitive, caring" guy. What???? That's right! What kind of guys do most girls date? If you look closely, you'll see it's obvious that girls don't really want the "sensitive" kind of guys. Girls *seem* to want guys who are actually . . . well . . . JERKS!

Be Confident

I'm sure you've probably noticed that a lot of great girls go out with "jerk" guys who treat them like dirt. Why? Because there's something about that kind of guy that says, "I'm confident and I don't need any girl. I don't need anybody! I know what I want and where I'm going." (Which may be in the wrong direction, but that doesn't really seem to matter.) "I got lots of other girls who would love to go with me, so make up your mind! I don't have all day here." He may be a jerk, but girls seem to want him anyway. Why? He has strength (good or bad), and therefore "potential." The wimpy guy may be nicer, but the "confident guy" usually gets the girl.

So, the way to get a girl must be to treat her bad, right? NO! (Although some guys might actually think that.) No, that's not the solution. Guys need to always treat a girl right. But remember, there is a confidence factor that has to show through. Guys, be confident in the fact that there are girls who *will* go out with you. And try not to get depressed if the first girl you ask out turns you down. I have talked to some girls who said they will turn a guy down the first time just to see how he'll react. Will he act like an idiot, start rumors, get depressed—what? If he says something like "Hey, no problem! Maybe some other time," then she might think, "Uh-oh, maybe I blew it. Did I just let a good thing go? Darn!!" But if a girl turns a guy down for a date and he falls apart or gets ticked, she knows she made the right decision.

If that guy moves on to another girl and asks her out (not in front of the first girl, by the way) it may show the first girl that he has guts. Most girls want that in a man. Desperate guys (or desperate girls, for that matter) are never attractive. Being desperate says you'll take *anybody,* and no one wants to accept a date feeling like they're the last resort.

Chapter 2. He Said . . . She Said . . .

The way guys communicate is totally different from the way girls communicate. All you guys reading this, you've got to understand this part, 'cause this is where guys mess up the most. In fact, I'll bet most of your dads *still* don't get it. I learned about this the hard way, which is where I'm usually at my best. (Not to say I've got it all figured out, even yet.)

Words, Words, Words

The average guy uses about 12,000 words a day. Did you know that? The average woman uses about 24,000 words a day . . . *twice* as many as a guy. Think about your parents. When your dad gets home from work at night, what does he do? He sits down with something to drink and watches TV. Yeah, 'cause *he's done!!!* He's used up his 12,000 words and wants to shut up. Then mom comes in:

MOM: How was your day? You know what the kids did today? The dog barfed on the carpet and . . . (I have 12,000 more words to use up!)

DAD: Mmmmm. . . . (I don't want to talk. I used up all my words. I'm done.)

MOM: . . . and then my mom called, and you wouldn't believe . . .

DAD: Uh huh. (I wish she'd leave me alone.)

MOM: . . . and my sister and her husband . . . Are you listening to me?

DAD: Huh? Yeah. Hey, I'm trying to watch this game. . . .

MOM: Well, this is important! How can you be so insensitive? You just don't care, do you?

DAD: No, I don't! I JUST WANT TO RELAX AND WATCH THE GAME!

Or, sometimes it goes like this:

MOM: We never talk!

DAD: OK, talk.

MOM: I can't.

DAD: Why?

MOM: I don't mean *I* want to talk, I want *us* to talk about what you're thinking and feeling . . .

DAD: I'm not thinking *anything!*

MOM: You just don't understand, do you?

DAD: You got that right!

They get in a big fight that can last forever. They don't realize there really *is* a difference, not only in *what* they communicate but also in the *way* they communicate.

Girls' Letters, Guys' Letters

Over the years I have received thousands of letters from students. One day I decided to compare a stack of guys' letters with a stack of girls' letters to see what the difference would be. It was pretty comical.

Girls' letters are usually one to seven pages long, neatly written (sometimes in colored ink), and very personal (usually telling about boyfriends and how things are going, or whatever disaster is in the making, or how they have been hurt). One girl wrote an 11-page letter that included everything from stuff about her boyfriend to her favorite flavor of Jell-O, which happened to be red. (I knew you'd want to know.) And I swear girls must go to a special class somewhere, where they learn how to FOLD letters into *little tiny packages* that, once you unfold them, will never go back to their original shape. Maybe these girls will work for a map company some day! You can never get maps to fold up the way they came either.

Guys' letters are totally different. They're usually two to three *sentences* long and, a lot of times, have drawings all over them. They rank on girls for being weird, and then they usually say something like "Gee, I thought you were funny . . . come back again and tell us how to get girls . . . ha ha ha." One guy signed his letter, "The Pimp."

Here are some letters from guys. I actually keep a file of pictures guys draw. And just in case you're thinking these are grade school kids, they're not. They're high school.

And here is how the typical guy letter goes:

Dear Mr. Henning,

Thank you.

Jeff

That's it. That's the whole letter.

Or here. How about this letter? I think it's the funniest letter I ever got from a guy.

Dear Mr. Henning,

I thought your speech was pretty cool but, ha ha, I wrote longer than a page, ha ha, I wrote longer

than a page, ha ha, I wrote longer than a page, ha ha, I wrote longer than a page, ha ha, I wrote longer than a page, ha ha, I wrote longer than a page.

> Sincerely,
> Josh

A guy once wrote me a letter while sitting in study hall. Everyone else in the room was supposed to be writing to me too. He wrote the typical one or two sentences, thanked me for coming, and signed it. But his P.S. said it all:

P.S. The girl next to me just wrote you three pages in the same time it took me to write this. How do they do that?

What Do You Mean, "I Love You"?

When guys talk, they tend to communicate information about things and ideas and what they are thinking about *right now.* They are far more spontaneous about what they say and do. Is there anything wrong with that? Heck no! It's fun. Can it get a guy in trouble? Ohhh yeah! Especially when he's talking to a girl. If a guy hasn't spent much time thinking or planning what he'll say to her, he's in big trouble, 'cause she's been planning for *months.*

When girls talk they tend to communicate what they have been thinking, feeling, talking, praying, sharing, thinking, talking with their friends about . . . all for the sake of being close with the person they're talking to. So here's what happens in a relationship.

Let's say a girl really likes a certain guy and has been talking to all her friends about him for months. He finally asks her out, and on the second or third date she turns to him:

SHE SAYS: I love you.

WHAT SHE MEANS: I love you, this could last a lifetime, we might be talkin' marriage here!

Clueless about what's been going on in her head for the last three months,

HE SAYS: I love you too! (He just thought of that.) (He's also wondering where he can find something to eat.)

SHE THINKS: He said "I love you" back! He must think, feel, and mean the same thing I do. (I love you, this could last a lifetime, we might be talkin' marriage here!)

But next week, the guy is telling a different girl, "I love you." (He just thought of that, too.) (He's also hungry again.) The first girl finds out about what he said to the other girl, and she's mad!

SHE SAYS: You said you loved me, and that this was going to last a lifetime. We were talking marriage!

HE SAYS: I did not. Last week I said I loved you, and I meant that. But now I love her. (He's also thinking, Gee, is there a pizza place somewhere around here?)

SHE THINKS: How could he love me last week if he loves her now? He must have lied to me! I'LL KILL HIM!

HE THINKS: Man, after three dates she's got me walking down the aisle!

Soooooo, who looks like a jerk? Yup, he does. Now girls, follow closely here. This is important.

In this story, did the guy ever lie? Now wait . . . did he? NO, but it *looks* like he did. Now do some guys lie when they say, "I love you?" Of course. Do some girls lie? Yeah. But remember, this girl had put *months* of thought into her "I love you." The guy only said what he was thinking *at that moment*. Even though he was being honest, his spontaneity got him in trouble. He told the truth both times, but now he looks like a jerk.

Reading Between the Lines

Here's the problem. Because guys *look* like they are lying, girls don't trust them. So girls start studying guys to see who's lying

and who isn't. Girls weigh every action and listen to every word a guy says. They even read *between the words*. Beware: they can find "meaning" that a guy never, ever, meant!

Guys, here comes the biggest tip I could ever give you:

It's not *what* you say to a girl that counts, It's *why* you said it that counts!

When a girl gets a letter from a guy, what's the first thing she reads? The end! She goes right to the end of the letter (which is usually only one page) to see how he signed it. "Love, Steve." (Ahhhh!) THEN she goes back and reads the rest of the letter. Not only does she read *what* he said in the letter, but now she also tries to read *what he meant* when he said it. Girls will practically X-ray a letter to find the "why" of what a guy said!

I have an article from *YM* magazine entitled, "His Love Letter Dissected." In it they showed a letter some guy sent to his girlfriend, and they sliced and diced it into "why" he used every word. He starts out, "Hey Emily." Then, with a little red arrow pointing to the side they said, "'Hey' is good. It means he feels comfortable enough with you to chuck the old-fashioned 'Dear' opener. He's also trying to be cool."[1]

I can guarantee you'll never see something like that in *Sports Illustrated*! In the same magazine was the feature, "Decoding His Postcards." (I don't know what they're talkin' about. Most guys don't even *write* postcards!)

Or how about the article that basically says reading his butt (swimming trunks) will tell you what kind of relationship he is capable of. What???!!! I'm not making this up.

Or my favorite, "Decode His Love Style." How, you may ask, does one *decode* someone's love style? By reading the guy's facial features, of course! Whoever wrote this piece thinks you can know men by *analyzing* what they *look* like.

---

[1] David Cook, "His Love Letter Dissected," *YM*, June/July 1996, p. 60

Wide forehead: Clever and spontaneous.

Straight eyebrows: Majorly committed.

Round eyes: Hard working and somewhat stubborn. (Round eyes? Of course they're round. What did they think they were, square?)

Wide nose: Edgy and wild. (Wild? Ha! The guy's been in one too many fights and got pounded!)

There's more but I'm sure you get the picture. WHAT A CROCK!!! They could make Hitler look like the Hunk of the Year according to this "analysis"!

Trapped!

See, girls are so intent on "knowing you" that they sometimes get carried away, reading into everything you say and do. They can trap you into saying things you don't mean! How?

A guy from my hometown told me that one night, right in the middle of a date, his girlfriend looked at him and asked, "Do you think I'm skinny?" Now come on . . . what's he supposed to say to that? He started to freak out because he knew anything he said was gonna be wrong. Finally, with sweat running down his face, he came up with what he thought was the right answer. "I think you're just right!" (He's thinking, *All right! Got out of that one.*") Was she satisfied with that? Noooo. She replied, "Nahhhhhh, come on, really, do you think I'm skinny?" "No, really, I think you're just right!" But she kept pushing: "Oh come on, be honest and tell me the truth. Do you think I'm skinny?" By that time he saw where this whole thing was going, knew he couldn't back out, and blurted, "Well, OK, you're skinny." "YOU ARE *SUCH* A LIAR! Come on, tell me the truth! Do you *really* think I'm skinny?" Now he's getting ticked. "I already told you the truth . . . TWICE! You didn't like either answer I gave you!" Not to have her question so easily tossed aside, she put it to him one more time: "No, really, be seri-

ous, tell me the truth." Desperate to end the inquisition, he played his final card. "Well, I don't know. . . . Man . . . well, OK, maybe . . . you're a *little* overweight." "OH! YOU THINK I'M FAT????!!!!! I can't believe you *said* that! You're such a jerk! And by the way, have you looked in the mirror lately? You're no Chippendale Dancer yourself, you @#$%^&*!"

At that point he thought, "Man, screw this! I can hang out with the guys all day long and not get into trouble like this. If I tell her the truth, I'm a jerk. If I lie, I'm a jerk. No matter *what* I do I'm a jerk!!"

I can go up to any guy and say, "I think you're fat!" and most guys will come back with something like, "Well, you're bald!" (Because I sorta am.) Who cares?!! No big deal. Guys don't care about stuff like that. But guys, you don't do that with a girl. You may never hear the end of it. (Especially if she's bald.)

What You Do, or What You Mean?

Men live in a world of action. To them, action means getting the job done in the most efficient way possible. Women live in a world of words and meaning. In their world, both words *and* actions have a "deeper meaning." Guys, can you see trouble coming?

Let's say the CEO of a big corporation suddenly remembers today is his wife's birthday, and it's already two in the afternoon. Panic! He's got a 2:30 meeting with a big client, and it won't be over until 5:30. But he has a secretary! He tells her to make dinner reservations and sends her out with $200 to buy his wife a dress. "She likes blue, she's a size 8, shops at Ann Taylor. . . . Oh! And make sure it's gift-wrapped! Get a card and sign my name for me and put everything in my car before I leave for home." (He's just being efficient.) When he gets home he hands the gift to his wife and sings "Happy Birthday" to her with a smile on his face. What he doesn't know is that his wife was at Ann Taylor that afternoon *and saw his secretary buy the dress for her.* So before she even opens the gift, she says, "Thanks for the BLUE dress." (Ooooops!) Does she want the blue dress? Not now! But the dress isn't the issue. If

her husband had been the one to go to the shop and buy the dress for her, she would have been thrilled. But because the *secretary* ran the errand, the gift didn't count. He thought the *gift* was what she wanted. She thinks *taking the time* to plan and shop is more important. Now if she had had *her* secretary go out to buy him a basketball for his birthday, would he have cared? No way! He's got a new basketball, and what's wrong with that? But she's thinking, "It's not w*hat* he gave me, it's the effort that he put into the gift that counts."

It gets worse.

Women Test Their Men!

Any girl who has dated a guy for any length of time at all has probably "tested" him to see *why* he does *what* he does. (When I bring this up in an assembly it's fun to watch girls, because they all look up with a funny grin, which turns to a smirk, and then it's the "Who, me?" expression.) Did you know some girls have actually broken up with their boyfriend *just to see what his response will be?* (And girls think GUYS are jerks?) Here's another way girls test us guys.

If I Have to *Tell* You, It Doesn't Count!

If you ask a girl what she wants for her birthday and then run right out and buy it for her, IT WON'T COUNT! She won't want it. It's not special. She may keep it, but she is disappointed. Why? Because if she had to *tell* you what she wanted, that means you weren't paying attention. (She has been hinting for months.) And if you weren't paying attention, it's obvious you don't really care. And if you don't really care, then the only reason you bought it in the first place is because *you* want something. Therefore it doesn't count!!! Get it?

Once my wife asked me what I wanted for Christmas. (This was in September.) Well, how should I know? I hadn't really thought about it. So I took 30 seconds and said, "I want a basketball and a cordless Makita drill." You know what she got me? A shirt. Hand-

made. It had one of those little tags on the back of the collar that said, "Handmade by Barbara." It was the ugliest shirt I have ever seen! I never wore it. What's funny is years later I was sitting at our cabin in the mountains, reading a book, when I looked up and saw my shirt in a *quilt* on the wall! "Hey, that's my ugly shirt!" My wife didn't think that was funny.

Back to Christmas . . . I politely thanked her for the shirt and asked where my basketball and cordless Makita drill were. She said, "Well, I knew you would really want something I made myself more than those things." Nooooooo . . . I don't think so!!! See, to her, what was important wasn't *what* she gave me, as much as *the effort that went into the gift.* The WHY of it. She put *herself* into that gift.

That was *her* gift to me. Now let me tell you what I gave her. It all started two days before Christmas (the two-day thing is key here, guys). I asked her what she wanted, and she said, "Ah . . . is this the first time you've thought about this?" "Yeah." "Well, in that case, I want a baseball bat." At that point I was totally lost. I had no idea why she wanted a baseball bat so I just figured that's what I'd give her.

Another Christmas, after we'd been married a couple years, I wrapped my wife's presents all together in one great big package. See, to guys, bigger is always better. I got her a mop, a fern, a stepladder (so she could get to the dishes without having to ask me to help), and a laundry basket. What a guy! She burst into tears and ran upstairs, and all I could think was, "I done good!" Yup, I thought she loved it. Later she came downstairs, took me by the shoulders, sat me down, and told me for the first time what I've been trying to tell you these last few pages. Where do you think I learned all this stuff? Not from my guy friends. (I just found out that, years ago, one of my guy friends gave his new wife a fan belt and a "Fix-a-Flat" for Christmas. Just makes ya feel warm all over doesn't it?) (Way to go, Ron!)

Not *What,* But *Why*

So guys, remember these two things. It's not *what* you say that counts so much, it's *why* you said it. And it's not *what* you give to

a girl, it's *why* you gave it that's important. It's what's underneath. This will probably drive you crazy, but get used to it! Girls read between the lines their whole lives.

Now with this next example I'm going to save you guys *thousands* of dollars! Trust me.

Hey girls, pretend you have a boyfriend. He's really good looking, he's fun, and he's FILTHY RICH! I mean this guy has bucks! He can buy *anything* he wants, so girls, don't think about cost here. OK, let's say you can choose to receive one of these three things from your boyfriend. You can have:

1. A dozen long-stemmed red roses, OR . . .

2. Two red roses and one white one (still long-stemmed), OR . . .

3. One red rose.

Twelve, three, or one. Which of these three choices do you think most girls want? I've asked this question hundreds and hundreds of times over the last 10 years, and I'd say about 75–85 percent of all women, regardless of age, will say they want *one red rose!* By the way, I've had guys literally yell out, "They're lying!" Now some guys already know *how* most girls will answer, but what they don't understand is *why*. Why one instead of 12? Here are the five most typical responses I get everywhere I go.

One rose is:

1. Thoughtful

2. Meaningful

3. Special/sweet/personal

4. Romantic

5. Symbolic

In case you don't know what "symbolic" means, it's like this. A guy buys a girl One Red Rose. When he gives it to her, she sees that he understands that when a guy and a girl love each other, two individual people who are now together, it's almost like they are one. The flower is red, and red means love. (One guy said it meant blood!) She thinks he spent the last few days wandering through a field of roses trying to find the ONE perfect bloom that means "US." (Actually, he went to Safeway to buy it and can't figure out what the heck she's talking about.) Symbolic.

Now here's the tricky part. YOU GUYS THOUGHT YOU GAVE HER A FLOWER!!! Ha! Ha! Silly you! No, in fact, you gave her all five of those things above. For some reason, *one* flower means all of that, but *twelve* doesn't. Ladies, the guys are reading this, and because they don't think this way, they say to themselves, "Well, hey, if . . .

ONE FLOWER = thoughtfulness, meaningfulness, romance, etc., etc.

then

Twelve times one = **ANYTHING I WANT!!!!!!! Yeeeaaaahhhhhh!!!**

Weeds Will Do . . . (!)

For those of you who can't afford even two bucks for a rose from the grocery store, here's an alternative. I heard of a 15-year-old guy who really liked this girl and had been taking her out for several months. He didn't have his driver's license, so he had to walk to her house. It was summertime, and as he walked he started picking weeds. By the time he got to her door he had this big bouquet of weeds! He knocked. She opened the door and said, "Hi, come on . . . ARE THOSE FOR ME?" Embarrassed, he looked down and said, "Yeah, but . . . they're just weeds." She was so excited she lunged out of the door, tackled him to the ground

(smashing the weeds between them), and gave him a big kiss. He was so confused that later, when he wrote me a letter, he said, "You know what? I'm just going to give her *stupid stuff* from now on!" He won her heart but had no clue why.

After a parent meeting, a woman told me this story. Her husband came home one night, opened the trunk of his car, and it was full of beautiful flowers. It took four or five armloads to get them all in the house! The next night he came home with a trunkload of long-stemmed roses. Now guys, do you have any idea how much that could have cost him? Hundreds of dollars! This routine went on for almost two weeks . . . until she found out where he was getting all those flowers: the MORTUARY!!!!!! NOW did she want those flowers? NO! Why not? Were the flowers thoughtful, meaningful, romantic, special, or symbolic? Not to her! All she could think was, "They're for dead people!"

No Formulas, Thank You

Guys, now that you know about the one-rose thing, you might make the mistake of thinking you've got it made. I mean, you're not stupid! One rose ($1.98) versus a dozen ($25). Looks pretty obvious to me! BUT . . . Let me add one more thing to the rose illustration. Women don't want to feel like you're using a "formula" on them. If, from now on, every girl in school starts getting one red rose from her boyfriend, the whole thing isn't special anymore. Is this "formula" thoughtful or meaningful? Special, sweet, or personal? Romantic? Symbolic? NO! Not if every girl in school is getting the same treatment! If this happens at your school, all the girls will change their minds and want, oh, two pink carnations. Or whatever. Then you guys will all think, "That guy who told us all this 'rose stuff' was wrong." Hold on, though. Has your girlfriend really changed? No. Remember, it's not *what* you give her, but *why* you give it that counts. She wants to know that she's unique, that you love *her,* and that you're listening to *her.* Have you learned a *system,* or is this the real thing? (Guess who is still being tested here?) (To solve that problem, one guy I know grows all his own flowers for his girlfriend and brings her a new flower every day.)

Worst Date

Let me add another dimension to this. Let me describe for you the worst date a girl can go on.

(Guy comes to the door, knocks, she opens it.)
GIRL: Hi! What are we going to do tonight?

GUY: I dunno. Whadda *you* wanna do?

Now why do most girls hate that? Well, let me ask you this, Is this date going to be:

Thoughtful? No.

Meaningful? No.

Special, sweet or personal? No.

Romantic? No.

Symbolic? Well . . . sort of . . . (but for all the wrong reasons).

Does it look like the guy has put any effort into this date at all? No! It feels to her like he doesn't give a rip about her.

Best Date

Ah, but what about THIS date?

(Guy comes to the door and knocks.)
GIRL: Hi. What are we going to do tonight?

GUY: Ah . . . well, I can't tell you (smile). But you need to wear something warm (smile), we'll be back about 11:30, and if your dad or mom is home (smile), I need to talk to them before we go. But we've got to hurry! (More smiles)

OK, girls . . . WOULD YOU GO? *You're darn right you would!* Why? Here's why. Is this date:

Thoughtful? Yes!

Meaningful? Yes!

Special/sweet/personal? Yes!

Romantic? Yes!

Symbolic? Yes!

When I've used this illustration in assemblies, I've had girls jump out of their chairs saying, "YES, YES!!! I'd go on a date like that *anytime!*" Then I ask them, **"Why? He's GOING FISHING!!!"** Now I know you guys won't believe this, but most girls will shout, **"So what? I'd even go fishing with a guy . . . *IF HE'D THOUGHT ABOUT IT FIRST!"***

So guys, see what's happening here? A girl would even go *fishing* with you (or whatever), something *you* really like to do, but she needs to know you planned it—that you were thinking about *her* the whole time.

Just for You, Girls (Guys . . . You'll Love This)

Girls, let's say you do go fishing with that guy, and while you're sitting in the rowboat you see an extra fishing pole. You ask, "Hey, wait a minute . . . this is my fishing pole, that one's yours over there, but whose is that one at the front of the boat?" What if the guy says, "Well, gee, I don't know. Let's take a look." He grabs the pole and reels in a bottle of sparkling cider and two wine glasses! Will you ever forget that date? No way! How much did that date cost him?

$1.98!

(That's what sparkling cider costs.)

Come Monday morning, will you tell every girl in school about that date? Oh, yeah.

But now, watch how quickly that same date can change because "it's not *what* he gives you, but *why*."

You're sitting in that same boat, and you've just asked the question, "This is my fishing pole, that one's yours, but whose is that one at the front of the boat?" Now, instead of sparkling cider, up comes a six-pack of Bud Lite. What are you thinking now? "Hmm-mmmm . . . Is it *me* he loves, or is it *something he thinks he can get from me (when he gets me drunk) that he loves?*" See? It's not *what* he gave you, it's *why* he gave it! (By the way, in about 80 percent of high school pregnancies drinking is involved. Does that make you wonder a little?)

A guy wrote to me about that very thing.

Dear Brad,

I'll tell you honestly that I am a virgin, but I also love women with a passion and probably would not mind losing it. Anyway the last couple weeks I have gone out and gotten drunk with this girl I really like. By the end of the night we are all over each other. Anyway, I feel horrible because I think she feels like I'm taking advantage of her, but I'm not. I like her a lot. I feel like I've ruined any possibilities of a relationship because of this. What should I do? I like taking her out sober but I don't know if she will respond the way I want, and I'm too chicken to ask . . .

Jason

Jason's girlfriend should start asking herself some questions.

Best Date I Ever Heard Of

One warm summer evening a guy asked this girl if she wanted to go for a rowboat ride on the lake. She said, "Sure!" So out they went, rowing on the lake. Suddenly, up out of the water came a scuba diver! He swam right up to the boat and presented a bottle of sparking cider on a fancy tray. Then he disappeared into the water. The guy pulled out two wine glasses from under his seat, set them down next to him, and just kept rowing, like, "You know, this happens all the time."

What do you think the girl was doing? TOTALLY FREAKING OUT! Do you think she will ever forget that date? No chance! She loved it! Will she tell every girl in school what he did? Oh, yeah!! How much did the date cost? $1.98! Now when I tell *this* story in schools, there's always some guy who's thinkin', "Yeah, but what about the scuba guy?" Man, that scuba guy would do the same thing for anyone who'd ask him, but NOBODY EVER ASKS!

Be Original

A little warning, though, guys. Never try to totally duplicate someone else's dating idea. That would tell a girl that you were too lazy (or dumb) to think of it yourself.

One year a ninth-grade guy came to an assembly where I told the story about the rowboat and the scuba guy. The following year I came back to that same school to talk to the *new* ninth graders, and this guy sneaked in to hear my talk all over again. When I started to tell that story, he started to freak out, making panicky motions to get me to stop telling the story. Well, I didn't understand what he was trying to tell me, so I finished the story, and as I did he just gave a big sigh and dropped his head into his lap.

Sitting in the same row, about 10 or 15 seats to the left of this guy, was a ninth-grade girl. She had been listening intently until I came to the scuba story. Then she slowly started to sit up, and her eyes got wide. She turned toward the tenth-grade guy and, with an angry, tight-lipped expression on her face, she gave him a look that could kill. He had *duplicated* the date!

So What Do You Want?

Any guy who's creative with the things he does on a date, as long as he's doing them for the right reason, can win the heart of almost any girl. Guys, the real question here is this: Do you really care about the girl you are dating, or are you just looking for a system that will get you what you want? Let me tell you, every girl wonders about that and is asking that question of every guy she goes out with.

Girls, I know I've been talking mostly to the guys here, but you need to understand something. Guys don't read minds, and they don't get hints. They never will. You can hint to your boyfriend all day long and he'll never get it. You have to tell him what you're feeling, thinking, wanting, or needing. When he asks you what you want for your birthday, expect to get what you tell him, but also let him know that you like surprises, or that you would love something that would remind you of your relationship together. Something a little more personal than your very own baseball bat.

Chapter 3. *Sports Illustrated* Meets *Better Homes and Gardens*

Guys tend to value freedom. Girls tend to value security. If you take the time to watch, you can see it everywhere.

For instance, you ever watch what happens when a couple is about to get married? Go to the guy's bachelor party and you'll see it. Now wait, I mean the normal kind of bachelor party, not the Jerry Springer kind, with the naked-lady-jumping-out-of-the-cake deal, OK? For those of you who are new to the strange phenomenon of bachelor parties (both the good ones and the bad ones), there's a joke that goes on the whole night. All the single guys are (jokingly) trying to talk the poor sap out of getting married. "Hey, man, she's never gonna let you play sports, ya know. No more poker parties, no more huntin' trips . . . BALL AND CHAIN." By the way, what is the ball and chain? The new wife, of course, and doesn't she just *love* to be thought of as a dead weight around her new husband's neck?!!

Now have you ever been to a girl's wedding shower? Totally different. What are *they* doing? The bride-to-be is holding up all the see-through stuff and giggling, and all the girls are saying, "Oh I wish it was *me* getting married!" They even keep track of who gave what, so they can send little thank-you cards later. Do guys do that? "Dear Fred, Thanks for the hot dogs! Love, Steve."

So picture this. At the wedding, her life is about to BEGIN (security), his life is about to END (no more freedom), and somehow these two are going to live happily ever after! Yeah . . . RIGHT!

So Many Women . . .

LUANN reprinted by permission of United Features Syndicate, Inc.

Us guys are afraid we're going to miss out on something better if we "settle down" too soon, so settling down isn't all that attractive to most of us. One page in MTV's *The Singled Out Guide to Dating* was dedicated to the different terms men use to describe relationships: couple, dating, girlfriend/boyfriend, going out, just friends, relationship, seeing each other, together. At the bottom of the list was this comment: "Number of *handcuff symbols* indicates estimated relative degree of freedom surrendered. The greater the number of symbols (handcuffs), the greater the threat to your *stud status*." The term "seeing each other," for instance, had only one set of handcuffs, while "going out" had the most: four.[1]

Cosmopolitan once tried to explain why guys don't seem to want to settle down with one particular girl. In the article entitled "Why Do Men Want to See Other Women?" the author said it like this:

---

[1] J. D. Heiman and Lynn Harris, *Singled Out Guide to Dating* (New York: MTV Books/PocketBooks/Melcher Media, 1996), p. 12.

"I am encouraged to look elsewhere exactly because I am in a relationship and she thinks I'm kind of sexy. I figure I'm on a roll: "That's one down; bring on the other 2,822,063,999!"[2]

Freedom! Us guys enjoy life *now*. Why screw it up? Why limit yourself to one relationship when you can have the whole thing? It's kinda like, "So many women, so little time."

Even though not all guys are like the guy in *Cosmopolitan,* you girls probably *think* we are, and therefore we seem sort of disgusting. But the reality is that we are just different (*and* disgusting). However, if you think it's only guys who are weird . . .

Catch the Bouquet . . . Catch the Man!

"America's Funniest Home Videos" can be very educational when it comes to stuff like this. One clip I saw opened with a bride about to toss her bouquet after her wedding. Now, help me out here, what happens if you *catch* the bouquet? **NOTHING!!!!** Nothing happens at all. But single women go through this ritual at every wedding, thinking, "If I'm the one to catch the thing, I'll be the next one to get married!" Ridiculous. But it's the same thing at every wedding: the bride turns around to the mob of women behind her and says, "Are you ready?" They all start elbowing for position, getting ready for the throw. But at this particular wedding, after a bunch of predictable fake starts and way too much giggling on the part of the bride, she finally chucked the bouquet . . . but *a little too far.* It flew over the heads of the women and landed *under the wedding cake table* . . . then, believe it or not, two women dove for it! I'm not making this up. Those two women were actually duking it out under the table! Finally one of them captured the bouquet, but only after her dress was practically torn off her. Now come on, all those women had to know they weren't really going to be the next one married just because they caught some bouquet, right? I mean, these are *grown women* we're talkin' about here! I must be missing somethin'.

---

[2] David Jacobson, "Why Do Men Want to See Other Women?" *Cosmopolitan,* October 1997, p. 58.

Catch the Garter . . . and Die!

Now think about guys at a wedding. Think back to the last wedding you went to. When the guy goes to throw the garter, what happens? It's unbelievable. This same scenario plays out at almost every wedding. The groom peels the garter off his bride's leg (while the guys are all doing catcalls) and gets ready to toss it, but when he turns around to say, "Ready?" no one's there! Not one guy is within a hundred yards of that thing. What *are* they doing? Eating! (Or putting condoms on the car.) (Which, guys, is really tacky!) But that doesn't stop the desperate women of the church! They round up all the single guys and herd them back into place behind the groom. With their hands stubbornly planted in their pockets (they're not *about* to catch the dang thing) all the guys watch as the groom finally zings the garter. Then all heck breaks loose! Guys start running for the exit doors, chairs are knocked over, and, as expected, the garter plops to the floor, unclaimed.

Just about then, the curious little 3-year-old ringbearer-kid toddles over and picks the thing up. The whole crowd applauds and cheers. The poor little guy has no idea he's getting married next month to the lady with the torn dress. She's 40. The guys all go back to what they were doing before they were interrupted, which was eating and blowing up condoms. Yea!! Sound stupid? Well, we keep right on doing the same dumb thing at every wedding! It's Freedom's last stand against Security.

The "C" Word

Retail America will tell you the truth about guys wanting freedom and girls wanting security. Go to any store that sells magazines, and I'll guarantee there will be at least one magazine for women featuring an article on "How to Get a Guy to Commit." Do freedom and commitment go together? Not in a guy's mind, they don't! Nooooo!! I assure you, you'll never see an article like "How to Get a Girl to Commit" in *Sports Illustrated.*

You think it's different in college? Think again. Waiting to meet a friend of mine at a local college, I stood in the lobby of the

student union building. There happened to be a magazine rack beside me and, being kinda bored, I started looking at "women's" magazines and compared them to "men's" magazines. It turned out there were three guy-type magazines—all sports. No big deal. The front covers had pictures of stuff like some boxer beating the snot out of some other guy, demolition derby crashes, kamikaze snowboarders, things like that. But here's a short list of some of the magazines for women: *Bride, Bridal Fair, Bride Book, Brides, Modern Bride, Seattle Bride, Bride Guide, Weddings, Wedding Planner, Bride Dresses.* Some of those magazines were over an inch thick! By the way, do you know what the world's largest magazine was? *Brides* magazine. The record issue weighed 4.8 pounds and had 1,270 pages of at least a gazillion different wedding dresses. As far as I was concerned, they all looked the same![3]

Now here's a question for you. Name one "groom book" for guys. Go ahead. Ahaaaaah, can't do it, can you? NO WAY! Why? There aren't any. (Unless you count *Playboy* and *Penthouse*.)

Women's Magazines

Anyway, bride books, *Seventeen, Cosmopolitan* . . . What's in those suckers, anyway? For a long time I was too chicken to look, and I wasn't going to ask. All I knew was I didn't get a manual *that* thick when I bought my pickup! I suppose all guys, at one time or another, have taken a peek in one or two girls' magazines. We might feel stupid doing it, but it's pretty enlightening! When I finally did look, I found that the more you read those magazines, the more you realize that the articles are aimed at us guys:

How to Get a Guy to Notice You

How to Lose That Extra 50 Pounds So Guys Will Notice You

Major Makeup Tips So Guys Will Notice You

---

[3] *Brides* magazine, February/March 2000

How to Know If He's Lying

Will Your Man Cheat?

Does He Really Love You? (10 ways to know for sure)

How to Kiss (I actually saw this one! You think a guy needs to be taught that?)

What Guys Hate in Bed (Always *wanted* to read that one)

Can This Marriage Be Saved?

Can you imagine an article in *Sports Illustrated* like, "Can This Marriage Be Saved?" No way! Maybe, "Can This BASEBALL MERGER Be Saved?" Now THAT I could imagine!

One magazine had an article entitled, "Butt Blasters!" Hellooooo! I still have no idea.

Check out the ads. Makeup! Tons of it!! Should have bought stock in that industry years ago! Did you guys know there's make-up *underneath* makeup? Makeup to take off makeup. Makeup to keep your skin fresh and alive so you can kill it tomorrow with even more makeup. There's makeup that wouldn't come off in a hailstorm! You've got eye liners, eye shadow, eyebrow pencils, blushes, foundations, hair softeners, hair conditioners, volumizing stylers (?), and tints. Lipstick ("kiss-proof," of course), lip gloss, hair sprays, deodorants, and wax. (I'm not even gonna ask.) Stuff for pimples, fingernail polishes, and polish removers. Everything to "fake a perfect face." Did you guys know they even have soap with oatmeal in it???? Wheaties . . . now I could understand that, but oatmeal?

I remember going one day to pick up something at a friend's house. A woman I didn't even know answered the door and acted like we were long-lost friends. Turned out I'd known her for years, but I'd never seen her without makeup. Didn't even recognize her. Scaaarry!

Men's Magazines

Men's magazines are a totally different story. We're talkin' paintball wars, slam-dunk contests, batting averages, and just about anything that has an engine mounted on it. (Guys will go into Home Depot and drool over a riding lawn mower, the whole time wonderin' "just how fast that little hummer'll go.") (Did you know there's a national lawn mower racing association?) If it's fast, loud, or smells like a locker room, guys will love it. Instead of the little fold-out smelly strips for perfume that you find in women's magazines, guys' magazines would have strips that smell like gun oil or basketball leather. Instead of ads for cover cream, they'd show pictures of all the stitches the goalie on some hockey team has accumulated in his career (I actually saw that in a magazine once). He doesn't want to cover all that up, he's displaying scars proudly, like each one's a medal.

Do Women *Really* Want Freedom from men?

Publishers print magazines to make a profit. They print what people will buy. They sell advertising space based on the hottest sales. *By what they buy,* are women and girls saying that they really want to be free and independent of men? Do these magazines *encourage* girls to be independent of men? No! Do they seem to say that a woman's security (at least financial) is to be found in a man? Yes! Are men's magazines training men for relationships? Obviously not!

A Guy's Ultimate Dream

Now I've been around guys a long time, and I've been observing girls all my life, and I've come to the conclusion that there is one huge difference between the sexes that is basic to all the others. I'll warn you guys that this is going to make us look pathetic for a minute, but hang in there. Remember, I'm a guy, so trust me here. I'm not trying to bash guys, but I think it's time for a little honesty.

If you asked a guy, "What is your ultimate dream?" (we're talkin' ULTIMATE here—if it wasn't wrong, and nobody would get mad at him) I think most guys, if they were honest, would answer something like this: **"I want access to as many beautiful women as I want, without being rejected by any of them."**[4]

Many girls

One Guy

(By the way, when I bring this up in school assemblies, the guys at this point do one of two things. They either start catcalling, whistling, and whooping it up, or they get reeeal quiet.) Now I'm not sayin' that every guy just wants to take every girl he sees and slam her into bed (well, some guys do, but most don't go to that extreme), it's just that he wants *access* to all those girls. But the rejection part scares him to death! He wants *them* to want *him*.

In *YM* magazine there was a perfect illustration of a guy not wanting to be rejected. It was in the *You've Got Mail* part.

> I'd been thinking about breaking up with my boyfriend, but I hadn't made up my mind. He heard a rumor that I was planning to dump him, so he sent me an e-mail saying that if I was going to end things, he was doing it first. Then it said that if the rumor wasn't true I should forget the whole thing and we'd still be together! —Samantha[5]

---

[4] Actual quote, "Access to as many beautiful women as desired without risk of rejection.", Dr. Warren Farrell, *Why Men Are the Way They Are* (New York: Berkley Books, 1986), p. 18.

[5] *YM*, February, 2002

Absolutely the scariest thing for any guy is to *take the chance of being rejected by a girl HE thinks is beautiful.* The more gorgeous she is in his mind (the more chance he has of lookin' stupid), the less he will want to risk asking her out.

Guys' Biggest Fear? Rejection

Why do guys enjoy magazines like *Playboy* so much? (Even though it's not good for them.) Because all those gorgeous women are available to him, and NOT ONE WILL REJECT HIM! They won't yell at him, "Hey, quit staring, you jerk!" Pornographic pictures don't talk back, they don't get mad, and they don't say "No!" to you. They are always ready and available, and never keep you waiting. They don't care if you miss their birthdays, and you don't have to spend a lot of money on them before they will like you and give you what you want. Pictures don't even care if you look at other pictures, and you can change pictures whenever you want. You don't have to risk talking to them and saying something stupid, and you don't have to call and talk for hours on the phone the next day, increasing your chance of saying something *else* that's stupid. All of that adds up to a rejection-free "relationship."

This is why almost 100 percent of all porn is aimed at guys. If you don't believe that, try to name just one pornographic magazine for women. Did you say *Playgirl?* Yup, 'cause it's the only magazine people ever seem to come up with. But *Playgirl's* circulation is extremely small, and a huge chunk of the subscribers are *men.* Most women don't really like or want pictures of naked men. *Pornography for women is almost nonexistent.* A few years back a women's magazine conducted a survey, asking women if seeing pictures of nude men was a turn-on to them. Four out of five women emphatically replied, "No!" It's not that women don't like sex. They do. But the display of nude male bodies isn't really what attracts most women. *Playgirl,* for instance, isn't among the top 100 magazines in the United States, but *Playboy* is the 14th best-selling magazine in the nation. It beats out *Newsweek, Redbook, Cosmopolitan, Seventeen,*

Martha Stewart Living, National Enquirer, U.S. News & World Report, Woman's World, Mademoiselle, and *New Woman.*[6]

Good Looks? Even Guys Don't Agree

At this point a lot of you girls figure that all men are looking for The Perfect Babe, and that *Ordinary Old You* doesn't stand a chance. But you're wrong. You have to understand something here. Each guy has a different idea of what "good-looking" is. I know that's hard to believe, but take any five guys from your school and stand them in a row. Then have every girl in school march past those five guys. Will the guys agree on who's good-lookin' and who isn't? Absolutely not! One guy will say, "Goll . . . she's gorgeous!" but the guy right next to him will say, "What? Are you blind? You need glasses!" If you still don't believe that, sit on a bench at the mall and watch married couples go by. I can tell you right now, when you see some couples you'll say to yourself, "Why on earth did he pick *her*? Man, I *never* would have picked that girl!" But *he* did. Why? 'Cause the guy thought she was the most beautiful thing he'd ever seen. That's why some of your dads have said to you girls, "Oh honey, you'll get a guy someday." (Don't you hate it when they say that?) Yeah, well, you may hate it and not believe it ('cause you think that's what *all* dads are supposed to say), but he's telling the truth. So ladies, don't be too hard on yourselves. Someday there will be a guy who thinks you're the best-lookin' girl he's ever seen. If you don't believe me, go back to the mall.

If I'm So Pretty . . .

Every guy wants a gorgeous girl (or at least one HE thinks is gorgeous), *but he is scared to death of being rejected by her.* So OK, every guy has his own idea of what's good-looking. Fine. But as everyone knows, there's always one or two girls in every school

---

[6] *The World Almanac and Book of Facts 2000* (Mahwah: World Almanac Books, 1999), p. 182.

who everybody knows are pathetically beautiful, and all the guys turn to mush whenever they walk by. To the rest of the girls it just doesn't seem fair. Most girls would give anything to look like them, but if you think about it, having good looks like that might not be all it's cracked up to be. Here's why. Those girls may be the most gorgeous ones in the whole school, but in any school *the most beautiful girls usually get the fewest dates with the kind of guys they really want to date.* I know you don't believe that either, so let me share some letters from a couple of Those Girls. I have lots more where these came from.

Dear Brad,

I have a question that you don't necessarily have to answer. I am a freshman at _____High School. I have a lot of friends, both guys and girls, and the majority say that I am pretty. All I ever hear from family, friends and even people I don't know is how pretty I am. I am smart, I dress nice, and a lot of people think I am funny, but I don't have a boyfriend. I went out with one guy in the 7th grade for a week, but that is about it. Some of my friends who are not necessarily prettier than me, always have boyfriends. What I want to know is, if I'm so great how come guys, even if they do like me, they don't say anything or ask me out? Is there something wrong with me?

Thank you

Dear Brad,

I was talking to one of my guy friends and I was telling him how no one would ever ask me to go on a date. I asked for his opinion and he told me truthfully, "Don't get upset for me telling you this, but almost all the guys I know do like you but they are afraid that you will turn them down."

Shannon

What is happening to these girls? Is there something wrong with them? No! Think about it. Girls, what's the Number-One biggest fear for a guy? The fear of being rejected by a girl he thinks is beautiful. The more beautiful she is to him, the more he fears being rejected by her. So the real problem is that the "good" guys (the ones a girl would actually like to marry someday) are all standing around looking at the gorgeous girl and saying to each other, "You ask her out." "No, I ain't gonna ask her out. You ask her." "Nooooo. . . ." The closer they get to her, the greater the chance of rejection, and that scares each of them to death.

So the girl will go home, look in the mirror, and think, "Everyone *says* I'm pretty, but nobody's askin' me out." So she puts on tighter, wilder clothes and goes back to school thinkin', "*That* ought to get them to notice me." And boy, do they notice! Now they're blown away more than ever. "Ooooohhh my gosh . . . you ask her out." "No way man, you ask her." "I'm not gonna ask her. . . ."

Now she's *really* frustrated . . . and confused. Everybody's lookin' but nobody's buyin', and she can't figure it out. Home she goes, back to the mirror. This time she's made up her mind. She thinks, "I'll do *anything* I have to (even SEX), to get a boyfriend! And I don't care *who* he is. The next guy who asks me out, I'm sayin' yes!" So she puts on a skimpy top (maybe a low-cut crop-top with spaghetti straps) that shows off her belly button, and a really short skirt. (By the way, there isn't a guy alive who, when he sees a girl wearing one of those crop-tops, doesn't hope she'll bend over. Come on, girls, what do you want us guys to look at . . . YOUR EYES?) Or she might wear those low-cut jeans that reveal her thong panties when she bends over. Determined to be noticed, she goes back to school, and, by golly, it works! They notice her all right, but now, besides being afraid of rejection, the good guys are a little afraid of being accepted! As beautiful as she is, she's beginning to look a little dangerous. So the very guys she wanted to attract begin to move on to the more approachable, less intimidating girls.

But waiting in the wings is a guy who wants only one thing (sex), and since she now looks like a willing partner, (I mean hey, look at what she's wearin'.) he asks her out. He's been watching

her all year. He recognizes the signs, and he's ready to make his move. She knows his reputation, but she is desperate now. She says yes, halfway believing she can *change* him even though no one else has been able to. He takes advantage of her sexually and dumps her the next day. But because she's always received attention for being pretty—for being the girl every guy wants to date—she is absolutely shocked to find herself dumped. "How could this be happening to me? I'm not a one-night stand! I'm not that kind of girl!" And she isn't.

What Happened?

What was it about that gorgeous girl that made that kind of guy want to date her? Was it her personality? Her mind? "Boy, can she cook and sew!" Yeah . . . right! It was her sex appeal. "She's HOT, man!" The only reason any guy would want to date her is because of her body and her looks. He can't possibly know anything else about her because her appearance blinds him to everything else!

What the gorgeous girl failed to understand is that even a "user" guy fears rejection. Yeah, he wants her for sex—he even knows that she'll keep giving him what he wants because she's desperate for attention—but he dumps her anyway. Why? 'Cause he's not stupid. He knows that eventually, when she figures out he was just using her and that he's not the kind of guy she wants to spend the rest of her life with, *she'll dump him!* And who is it that dumped him? Only THE MOST GORGEOUS GIRL IN SCHOOL, THAT'S WHO! Can he allow that to happen? Noooooo!!! So what does he have to do? HE HAS TO DUMP HER *FIRST!* "Hey man, I had to dump her 'cause (OK, come up with something quick here . . . gosh, what . . . oh, oh . . . yeah), she wasn't any good!" (Ever heard *that* said about a girl?) He got his ultimate dream, didn't get rejected, and he feels like he had some fun in the process. NEXT! On to the next girl in his Ultimate Dream. . . . Now are all guys like that? Absolutely not. The problem is most girls don't know how to tell the good guys from the bad guys.

A Girl's Ultimate Dream

Now let me tell you what I think a girl's ultimate dream is. If girls were asked about their ultimate dream, I think most girls would say, "I want to find me one guy—just one—who understands me, will treat me right, and take care of me for life . . . but they're all a bunch of jerks!"

One girl

One guy

A girl doesn't want a "bunch" of guys drooling over her, or even access to as many guys as she wants. She just wants ONE, but he has to be a very *special* one. He can't be some idiot who doesn't communicate with her, or who doesn't care about how she feels about things, and just lives his life between his legs. He has to be the kind of guy who listens to her, has a good sense of humor, is fun, and has a very special potential that will make her feel . . . secure. What's amazing is most girls say the guy doesn't even have to be all that good-looking. Good looks are a plus, of course, but it's a guy's *potential* for success and financial security, plus the way he treats a woman, that keeps her attention. At the 1997 annual meeting of The American Psychological Association, researchers reported that "women rank a man's salary and earning potential above attractiveness, education or occupation as a key criterion for selecting a mate."[7] The more attractive a woman thought *she* was,

---

[7] Mark Bowden, "Of Nice and Men: Study reveals women prefer not so macho." *Tacoma News Tribune,* Friday, April 14, 1995.

the more she could demand top income potential from a man. So she'd use sexual attraction as bait to get the kind of guy who would translate her ultimate dream into reality. And that ultimate reality is all about SECURITY. (More about that in chapter 17.)

Go back to the magazine rack, and you'll see what women *really* want. They might *say* they want careers and power, but look at what they actually spend their money on. Of the top 100 best-selling magazines in the United States, these are the most popular women's magazines. Look at their annual number of readers. (And remember, these figures don't include women who *borrow* magazines from each other!)

Better Homes and Gardens	7,613,249
Family Circle	5,004,902
Good Housekeeping	4,584,879
Ladies' Home Journal	4,575,996
Woman's Day	4,242,097
McCall's	4,202,809[8]

Better Homes and Gardens almost outsells *Cosmopolitan, Glamour, Vogue, Mademoiselle,* and *New Woman* combined.[9] What does that say about what women *really* want? They want security! Lots of it. And where do you suppose these women will find that security? In their better homes and gardens, and in their family circle. And who will pay for those better homes and beautiful gardens? Hmmmmmm???

The Manhunt Begins

A girl's search for her Ultimate Dream begins somewhere between the seventh and eighth grades, when she begins to turn from a little girl into an adult. Her body begins to change dramatically; she gets taller, "fills out," and begins to look like a real woman. She

---

[8] *The World Almanac and Book of Facts 2000* (Mahwah: World Almanac Books, 1999), p. 182.
[9] *Ibid.,* p. 182.

becomes very aware of guys, and guys obviously become very aware of her. Problem is, most of the same-aged guys haven't begun to change physically yet. Think back to seventh grade . . . remember how much taller most of the girls were than the guys? At that age most guys are about one-and-a-half to two years behind the girls in physical maturity. That's the reason junior high girls, if they're dating, usually date guys three to five years older than they are. It's because of the differences in their maturity levels. Guys catch up eventually, but it takes a while.

So the junior high girl comes to school looking and feeling totally different than she did in sixth grade. She's turning into a real woman, and it feels good. (Scary, but good.) But when she looks around she sees all the guys her age standing in a corner spitting loogies and farting. Suddenly reality sets in, and she gets depressed. "I'm never gonna find a guy. Look . . . they're all morons!" So she thinks, "OK, if I'm never going to find a guy *exactly* like what I want (I mean look at 'em!), I'll find a guy that's *closest* to my dream, I'll do anything I have to, to get him (SEX), and once I get him, I'LL FIX HIM!" This brings us to "The War Between the Ultimate Dreams."

The War Between the Ultimate Dreams

If a guy is the sort of guy who only wants sex when he wants it and where he wants it, can he just go up to a girl, tell her what he wants, and expect some action? No! He'd probably get slugged! He has to be smarter than that. To get the girl he has to convince her she is going to get her dream: one guy who will treat her right and take care of her for life—the Knight on the White Horse. He has to tempt her with *just enough* of her dream (knight, white horse, castle) to convince her to give him what *he* wants (One Sexy Damsel).

If a girl wants a particular guy can she just waltz up and tell him she is looking for a Knight on a White Horse who will settle down with her for life and raise a family? No! He'd take off like he was shot from a cannon! To get that guy she has to convince him he's gonna get *his* dream: One Sexy Damsel who won't reject him.

They both disguise the truth to get what they want. When they finally do come together (and have sex) they are doing it for totally different reasons. She uses sex to get him. Yeah, she might enjoy the sex, but she does it mainly out of the pressure to keep him. She isn't *driven* to sex like he is. He's having sex 'cause he thinks it would drive him crazy not to! He tells her he loves her, but he's thinking, "Man, I'm on a roll! Wait till the guys hear about this!"

Once they've had sex she thinks she's got her dream, and starts Making Plans, but the next thing she knows, he's dumped her for some better-lookin' damsel down the road! After all, he's just being consistent with his dream . . . many girls, rejected by none. He dumps her first (so she *can't* reject him), and then he moves on—NEXT!

She is in total disbelief that her plan didn't work. ("How could he do that to me?") She thinks she loves him! She always wanted to marry the first man she made love to, and she thought he was THE GUY! She tells herself, "I'm not the kind of person who jumps into bed with just *anyone*. . . ." ('Cause that would make her a "slut.") She wonders why she couldn't keep him. "Maybe I'm not pretty enough—I know guys want gorgeous women. . . ." So now she starts working really hard on her looks and body. She uses every trick she can to attract the guys. But now she finds herself even more rejected by the very guys she would like to date. They're afraid to be rejected by the most beautiful girl in school, and the more beautiful she becomes, the more *unlikely* the good guys are to ask her out!

Dear Brad,

I'm a sophomore right now, and I've had about three boyfriends in my entire life. Pretty sad, huh? Even after your speech I still don't really understand why. Everyone tells me how beautiful I am, and how I can get any guy I want. Yeah right. In my dreams maybe. And when I finally do get a boyfriend, it lasts for a few weeks at the most, (and let me say that I am still a virgin, and I never get far enough in a relationship to even get into all that stuff) but then he'll call, and tell me things are moving too fast, or it's just

not working out, or some other lame thing. Everything you say though, is so true. I get so fed up with guys not asking me out I just come to school trying to dress a little sexier everyday, and everyday I try to act a little more flirtier, and everyday it doesn't work. So, what am I supposed to do?????? Even though I say to myself that there is nothing wrong with me, deep down inside I try to think of ways that I can change myself to make the guys want me, and ask me out, but nothing ever works. But you really got me thinking that if I go to school dressing all sexy and stuff, that sex is all that they will expect from me and once they get it, they'll dump me. So how am I supposed to get a boyfriend? Answer me that please!! I'm just so sick of being alone.

Sophomore Girl

But I'm Not Like That!

Then a new guy asks her out and she thinks, "OK, that last guy didn't work out, but I know *this* one will." Sure enough, the same thing happens, and she gets dumped. Again.

She tries over and over, moving from guy to guy, being sexual with each one, all the time thinking, "I'm not that kind of girl." And really, she isn't. But other things begin to happen. Trying to win each new guy, she spends more time on WHAT she is (a beautiful object) and less time on WHO she is. What she doesn't realize is that she is slowly becoming a "thing" to be possessed: beautiful, but shallow. She isn't *trying* to become "sluttish," but her reputation is being destroyed. People won't say it to her face, but that's what they're thinking. In her mind, all she's trying to do is use her body to win a man's heart. It's her way of expressing commitment. Never mind that in the process she has gone against all her morals and beliefs. . . . She has unconsciously taken on the role of the "slut," while he basks in the glory of being the "stud." (Pimp, or whatever.)

What's Going On Here?

But that's only what is happening on the surface. Now let's look at what's happening *below* the surface.

THE GIRL: She is setting up an extremely destructive pattern for herself. "I'll give sex to get love. I'll find a guy closest to my dream, I'll do anything I have to in order to get him (sex), and once I get him, I'll fix him!" When she gets dumped or taken advantage of, she feels that she *got faked out by love and sex.* She begins to wonder if all guys are the same, and after several more guys she's convinced they are. She starts holding back her heart and her feelings, and it becomes more difficult for her to share anything with *any* man. In her mind, sex becomes connected with hurt, pain, and bitterness. Sex becomes less attractive—something to emotionally run from. She blames it all on the guys, not seeing her own responsibility for her actions. "They're all idiots!" she will say. "You can't trust any of them!" What has happened to her Ultimate Dream of one man for life? Gone. She's been reduced to a "thing," and "things" don't have dreams.

THE GUY: A girl who "gives in" sexually before marriage is helping to set a pattern for each guy she dates. He is learning, "I'll give love to get sex." What's weird is that every time she gives in to him he realizes *his system works.* When she falls for it, he thinks, "Whatever works, man!" He learns to be clever and deceptive. But as she becomes hurt, bitter, and resentful (for being used), she feels less like fulfilling his needs. She questions whether they really love each other. So he takes the attitude, "Well, heck with you, then!" and he becomes more self-centered, egotistical, non-relational, and irresponsible. He dumps her. He simply moves on to the next available female. His excuse? "Boys will be boys! If you can't handle it, get out!" She becomes damaged goods. All the guys want to look, but the good guys don't have the guts to ask her out, and the guys who DO ask her out seem like perverts. Gorgeous as she is, the more sexually active she becomes the less attractive she will be to the right kind of guy.

Hollywood . . . Dreams Come True?

Hollywood is full of women who are caught in this trap. They can't seem to find true love. Their men dump them, or treat them

so badly that these women decide they have to move on. Like "studs" on a farm, these guys mate with each female and move on to the next. So who's to blame for the mess? Out-of-control guys or desperate women? Heads up, folks! It's both.

The Manhunt Olympics

Single women on the hunt for Mr. Right are always in competition with each other. "After all," they think, "there's only so many good guys out there, and honey, you aren't going to stand in my way!" As the contests begin, girls feel constant pressure to be gorgeous and sexy, and they feel they have to stay that way forever. But there's a fine line here. If a girl becomes *too* sexy-looking, her reputation goes down the toilet. But she also thinks if she isn't sexy *enough,* everyone will think she's a loser. And, of course, girls think that being sexy and beautiful is the *only way* you can catch a guy, 'cause that's what they hear loud and clear from every corner of their lives.

All too often reality for a high school girl is this: the more beautiful she becomes, the less secure she is. She also knows she can't keep up that image forever, 'cause if the leading ladies in the movies can't find guys and keep them, how can she? If you don't believe that, find the August 27, 2001 issue of *People* magazine. The headline reads, "Everything But Love. Sure, they're rich and gorgeous. But that doesn't make it any easier to find a love that lasts."[10] Whose pictures are on the cover? Meg Ryan, Julia Roberts, and Nicole Kidman. Or look at *Us* magazine (March 18, 2002). "Smart Women, Dumb Choices. Why Successful Women Keep Picking The Wrong Men."[11] Who's on that cover? Liz Hurley. How successful have any of these women been in using looks and sex to get and keep their men? Not very. If a woman believes that's the only way to get a guy, what really happens is that she allows herself to become a "thing" to be viewed or played with. In the

---

[10] *People* magazine, August 27, 2001
[11] *Us,* March 18, 2002, cover

process *she wins the guy's attention, but not his heart.* He's attracted to her body but doesn't know the woman inside. For fear of being found out, or out of sheer boredom, he moves on.

Sassy magazine ran this article: "She's So Pretty It Makes Me Sick!" In the article, Dr. Debbie Then said, "Many beautiful women never get a chance to test themselves beyond their looks, and they live in fear of losing their looks. Plus, being beautiful can be lonely. Beautiful women find it difficult to have female friends due to the jealousy factor. And a lot of men don't approach them because they're afraid of rejection. They feel safer approaching more average-looking women." One girl confessed to being bulimic, and admitted, "I feel a constant pressure to be thin, to always look perfect. It's like I have this impossibly high standard I have to maintain at all times."[12]

Is physical perfection any guarantee that a relationship will last? Apparently not. Once again, the magazine rack tells the story. The "Commitment" articles are common in women's magazines. What's also common is they, each in their own way, try to teach women how to get that commitment by using sex and looks.

Here's a typical title from *Cosmopolitan:* "Make Him Commit 100 Percent."[13] It doesn't say, "Gosh, I Hope He Commits," or "Wouldn't It Be Neat If He Did," it says, "MAKE HIM commit 100 percent!" (Underneath the headline it says, "25 Ways to Get a Man into a *Rock-Solid* Relationship.") But if you simply look at the cover of this magazine, you'll see how they're trying to get guys to commit. How? By wearing a low-cut, let-it-all-hang-out kind of outfit! You know, the kind that yells, "I'll do anything I have to, to get him, but once I get him . . . I'll force him into a 100 percent commitment!" Now *you* tell *me* . . . will that work? NO. Proof?

The woman pictured on that *Cosmopolitan* cover is a gorgeous actress and model who lived with her actor/lover for 13 years. Near the end of that time he was arrested for being with a prostitute! Now guys, if your girlfriend was as beautiful (and as sexy) as a famous

---

12 Alison, ("She's So Pretty It Makes Me Sick!,") *Sassy,* p. 60.
13 *Cosmopolitan,* October 1997, cover

actress, WOULD YOU DUMP HER FOR A PROSTITUTE??? Yeah, you would . . . IF the only thing you wanted was sex . . . and IF the only thing your girlfriend had to offer was her looks. Beauty and sex aren't enough to keep a relationship going!

By the way, here's a list of the other article titles that were displayed on the cover of that same magazine:

1. Your Healthy Breasts
2. Are Sex Hang-Ups Sabotaging Your Love Life?
3. I Was 2 Lbs. Away from Dying
4. Oops! You Blew Him Off; Now You Want Him Back. Is There Hope?
5. Tap Into the Eerie Secret Power of Female Intuition
6. Sexy? Classy? Stuck Up? Is Your Hairstyle Sending the Right Message?

So let's recap what this magazine says is the way to get the guy to commit. You're gonna need big boobs (Look at the cover and you'll see just how "healthy" those breasts really are!), no hang-ups about having sex with him before he is committed, a sexy, thin body, and sexy hair. Of course your intuition would naturally confirm all this and send the "right message" to him through your hair!

Two Different Worlds

Men and women live in two different worlds. He lives in a world filled with options—millions of options. The world looks to him like it could give him just about anything imaginable, so why would he want to narrow down his options (by marrying and having a family, a dog, a cat, and a mortgage) and potentially lose out on whatever opportunities might be just around the corner?

A woman lives in a world of relational commitments and, therefore, a world with fewer options. But by focusing on those options she becomes much more secure in herself. Her choices

may limit her career options, but she has deeper, longer-lasting friendships, and her ties to family tend to be stronger. Because he focuses on his career and social options, his friendships are fewer and shallower.

I'm Keeping My Options Open

Because a man knows that women have the relational edge, he begins to feel inferior. Since he has few, if any, deep relationships, he can't communicate very well on an emotional level and tends to be less moral. He is more sexual in nature and feels guilty for it. He fears he will fail at commitment and deeply hurt the woman he loves. He doesn't *want* to hurt her, and he doesn't want to be "the jerk," but he's afraid he will be. His fear of failure has trained him to run from relationships. He knows that if he gets too close to a girl she might find out he's nothing but a shallow fake, so he tells himself the smart thing to do is maintain a distance and "keep his cool;" take a position of "FREEDOM FROM" everything. "At least I'm not tied down. I've got my freedom. Nobody's tellin' *me* what to do!" In the process he becomes physically and mentally unhealthy. Bachelors are 22 times more likely than married men to be committed for mental disease (and, incidentally, 10 times more likely to be put in hospitals for chronic diseases).[14]

Having come to the conclusion that he'd rather be free, his only real course of action is to "admire his options" from afar. "Look at all those girls, man!" His biology drives him to women, but he can't get too close for fear of rejection or failure. As a result he never feels the deep satisfaction in life that can come only from a committed relationship. He can fantasize over pornography or go to nude clubs, but it's all so non-relational. He can even go to bed with the real thing, but he's left feeling unfulfilled and unsatisfied because he's chosen to maintain a distance from the very thing that will bring him ultimate fulfillment: a deep, lifelong commitment to one woman.

---

[14] George Gilder, *Men and Marriage* (Gretna, Louisiana: Pelican Publishing Co, Inc., 1993), p. 64.

Great Expectations

Men and women may go into marriage with two entirely different expectations, and if they're not careful both may be doomed to disappointment! Many men marry believing their wives will never change. Many times a woman marries believing he will change into what she *really* wants. Family counselors will tell you that married women often say, "He hasn't changed *one bit* since the day I met him!" But do you see what's she been trying to do since the day she met him? *Change him!* At the same time her husband is thinking, "*That's* not the woman I married!" Why isn't she? Because she started changing the minute they got married, and it really scares him. Her desires changed, her body changed, her looks changed. She got pregnant. When the baby was born and she quit her job to be a full-time mom, he felt like he got gypped. Since he's now the only wage earner, he feels like he isn't needed for anything except his wallet. Her attention is always on the new baby, and he feels left out.

He can't help but think about how he gave up all those other women—all those "options"—to settle down with one woman who promised she would never change and would always be there, just for him. After a few years he realizes that he hardly recognizes her. His bachelor buddies seem to be having way more fun than he is. (Even though they're not.) He begins to long for the open road—the freedom he once had—but it has long since passed him by.

Summary

Let's summarize these last three chapters. Guys tend to be impersonal, while girls tend to be very personal. He tends to communicate what he's thinking right now, while she communicates what she has been thinking, feeling, talking, sharing, and praying about for the last few weeks. And while he panics at the thought of being "tied down" and losing his freedom, she seeks the security of a deep relationship. No wonder it's so hard to understand and love a person of the opposite sex!

Section Two
LOVE

Chapter 4. Definition of Love

The mess probably started when we were little kids. People would tell us stuff about love, and then our pea-brain intellects would kick in and mess it up even more, adding and subtracting what we thought was necessary, twisting it into some half-baked definition. What's funny is most adults never think to go back and challenge what they grew up believing about love. So the older we get the more we sound like little kids again.

> "No one is sure why it happens (falling in love), but I heard it has something to do with how you smell . . . That's why perfume and deodorant are so popular."
>
> Mae, age 9

> "I think you're supposed to get shot with an arrow or something, but the rest of it isn't supposed to be so painful."
>
> Manuel, age 8,[1]

> "Love is not a decision your brain makes. It's a feeling you know somewhere else, and your brain catches up."
>
> Meg [2]

---

[1] WWW.danielsen.com/jokes/KidLove.txt
[2] TIME Domestic, May 22, 1995 Volume 145, No. 21

That last quote was Meg Ryan, talking about her marriage to Dennis Quaid. Meg and Dennis got caught in a childish definition of love and it wasn't enough to keep their marriage together.

Think how weird it would be if you really *believed* all of that stuff you've been told. Poor little Manuel (who thinks you'll get shot with arrows) would be petrified if some girl on the playground told him she loved him. **Phhffft!** *"Run!!! Incoming arrows!!! Aaaaahhhhhhh!"* A high school guy named Ryan wrote this poem, and he's no better. See what you think.

LOVE

Love is very mysterious, no one
Knows when they'll find it.
Some people never find it,
Sometimes because they don't
Want to. Some do find it, and in
Many different ways. To some
It is love at first sight. Some
People say it and don't mean it,
They use it as a game. People
Think they love each other, but
They don't, which is a shame.
To some love just wasn't meant
To be, but when it is they'll
Know it. Love can be a
Wonderful thing and it can ruin
People. One can love another
And the other doesn't have to
Love the one. It can be very
Confusing but very enjoyable.
Love can take forever to find,
So if you think you have it, go
After it, cause if you don't you
Could have blown your chance
Forever.

So let's sum up here what Ryan thinks love might be:

1. It's mysterious.
2. It's a game.
3. It can be enjoyable, but confusing.
4. You may think you have it, but you could be fooled.
5. There are lots of different ways to find it.
6. Finding it can take forever.
7. If you see it, you've found it.
8. If you think you've found it, you still don't have it, so you must not see it.
9. You don't know if you'll ever find it.
10. You may have to go after it to find it, but you could miss it.
11. You will know it if you were meant to find it.
12. Some can't have it.
13. Some don't want it.
14. You may have it, but your girlfriend/boyfriend might not have it.

Weird . . . really weird!

I Love Ice Cream . . . I Love You . . . (?)

More songs, books, and movie scripts have been written about love than any other single topic, yet when you listen to the words, read the stories, or watch the screen, you realize the writers sometimes haven't got a clue either! Some artists write songs like "Love Me with All Your Heart!" and others write "Love Stinks" or "Love Is Chemical." So what's the deal?

People say they love their husband or wife, kids, dog, car, country, chocolate ice cream, or their new DVD player, and then say they love me, too. I'm confused! Do they love me like they love their dog or car, or do they love me at all? Maybe I fit in somewhere between chocolate ice cream and the DVD player. Or maybe saying, "I love you," is just a way to get me to do something.

MTV's *Singled Out Guide to Dating* injects this heartfelt sentiment about love:

> Love stinks. Sometimes it sucks. But you can't let that stop you. Despite all those misses, there are some real hits out there just waiting for you to step up with just the right look and just the right line at just the right time.[3]

Yeah, I really can see why some people think love stinks! But is what they smell really love?

If everyone has a definition of love—your parents, brothers, sisters, church, boyfriend or girlfriend, movie stars—who's right?

I AM!

Right here, in this very chapter, I'm going to give you a definition of love that will change your life forever. I'll warn you up front, though, it's gonna be different from all the other definitions you've ever heard. But when I'm done you'll know when someone really loves you, and when you love them. Everyone else will be able to tell, too. The best part is that *it's very simple* . . . IF YOU'RE HONEST!

First, though, in order to get you to understand my definition, I have to deal with some misconceptions about love, because if I don't, those ideas will be the very things that keep you from having the real thing. And if you're like that guy Ryan, the one who wrote the poem, you might never get through the confusion. So let me start by telling you what love is NOT before I tell you what it is.

Love Is Not a Feeling or an Emotion

---

[3] J. D. Heiman and Lynn Harris, *Singled Out Guide to Dating* (New York: MTV Books/PocketBooks/Melcher Media, 1996), p. 6.

A lot of people think it is a feeling; especially girls.

Dear Brad

I can't agree with you on everything you discussed, 'cause I do think love is a feeling. If love wasn't a feeling or emotion, what would you feel? How would I know if I was in love or not, if I couldn't feel it? Because, I have a boyfriend (We've been going out two months today) and I love him, so if your saying love is not a feeling, what am I feeling?

Thank you,
Katie

If love isn't a feeling, then what *IS* she feeling? She's feeling feelings! But love and feelings are not the same. Katie thinks they are, and I can understand why she feels that way, but love still is not a feeling. Here's why. Let's say that last night I went to bed with my wife. She looked great, smelled great, and, ah . . . well . . . you know, I mean . . . ah . . . all the feelings were there. Trust me!!!!!! But this morning I woke up, rolled over, and there she was—hair all screwed up, pillow wrinkles on her cheek, no makeup, been droolin' all night. She opened her eyes and, with absolutely *gross* breath, said, "Hhhhiiii!"

Bleaaaaaaah!!!!

So think about it. If love is a feeling, then last night I was in love, but this morning . . . THAT'S DISGUSTING!!! Well, dang! (By the way, she could say the same thing about me, too.) I guess I just fell out of love. So I kicked her out, and started lookin' for a new wife! After all, if love is a feeling and I don't have any feelings for this "thing" in my bed, I must not love her any more. Right? Wrong!

Are You in Control?

Now that sort of reasoning would make perfect sense IF love was a feeling, but it isn't. Here's the problem. How many people are in control of their feelings? Answer? No one is. Proof? Have you ever gotten up on "the wrong side of the bed"? You know what I mean—for no good reason you're mad at everything. You're yelling at people about the toothpaste, or your lost sweatshirt; about breakfast. Then your mom comes in (it's almost always your mom) and says, "Hey, snap out of it!" Now I ask you, does that help? Can you just "snap out of it"? No. Man, it may take all day to get back to feeling good, 'cause you can't "just quit" feeling crummy. OK then, are you in control of your feelings? No. Still not convinced? If I told you right this minute, "Be sad!" could you do it? How about, "Be angry, or happy"? No! You could *act* like you were sad, angry, or happy, but *would you be*? No.

Ladies, are you always in control of *your* feelings—*all month long?* Hey, don't get ticked at me, man. And don't try to throw it back at me, either. I've been married too long to know that sometimes a woman's period can throw her whole *week* off. (Guys, if I were you I wouldn't bring this up, 'cause you'll get it slammed back in your face. Which would obviously prove my point.)

Good and Bad Feelings

If love is a feeling (and some of you still think it is), then do you mean ALL feelings or just the GOOD feelings? How did you come to believe that? Most people have never thought about it, but they would say the *good* feelings prove you're in love. I mean, nobody in his right mind would say, "You make me sick—so I guess I must love you!" In fact, most people would say that bad feelings are proof of *not* being in love.

A girl once wrote me and said that when she heard my talk she was totally convinced her boyfriend loved her. But the minute the assembly was over she found out her boyfriend had been cheating on her the whole time they had been together. The feelings of love that she *felt* for him during the assembly immediately turned

to feelings of hate, all within seconds. She came to the conclusion that she hadn't *ever* really loved him if her feelings could turn around that fast. I disagreed. She *might* have loved him. Anger at being betrayed doesn't mean love wasn't there. But her bad feelings—her hate—came because he had lied to her, and because she had been fooled into thinking she was his only girl. Her "love" (feeling) was based on what she thought was true. I knew he *didn't* love her because of the way he treated her. Was she fooled by her feelings? Yes!

Love can make you feel good, but selfishness can bring good feelings too—temporarily. (As long as your partner gives you what you want.) So, do good feelings mean you're in love? What if you have a "bad" feeling toward a person that you thought you loved? Would it mean you no longer loved them? Could you love someone and have both good and bad feelings at the same time? Of course! Ever had an argument with someone you loved? Did you have "good" feelings during the argument? No way! Did you still love them? Yes. So love *can't* be a feeling!

Can I Be Honest with You?

If love is only a *good* feeling, that would mean that a bad feeling would be the enemy of every relationship—something to be avoided at all costs. It would also mean that real communication—sharing deeply and honestly about life—could never happen because of all the potentially bad feelings. You would be so afraid of having "bad" feelings, you could never get honest with the person you say you love. But loving communication is based on honesty, truthfulness, and vulnerability. "Am I safe telling you what I am thinking and feeling? Will you still love me? Even if it hurts you? I don't *want* to hurt you, but what if I do?" Genuine love makes it safe to bare your soul, right or wrong, good feelings or bad. If love was only a good feeling, then at the first sign of conflict or disagreement the relationship would be over. Love has to come first; then comes the freedom to share feelings. Love and feelings are very different, but both are important.

What You See Isn't Necessarily What You Get

Dear Brad,

I have recently discovered that guys usually make decisions by sight. I was involved with a guy who supposedly liked me and I asked him why he liked me out of all the other girls that were throwing themselves at him. Anyways, he said he liked me because I was beautiful and gorgeous and said nothing about my personality or the way I act. Sometimes it makes me mad when a guy only looks on the outside instead of looking at a girl's inner beauty.

> Sincerely,
> Naomi

Can you deny that the guy in Naomi's letter has real feelings for her? Of course not! He thinks she's beautiful, and that's great. That makes him feel all kinds of things, but does it mean he loves her? No. If being moved by beauty equals love, then this guy could just as easily be "in love" with the naked girls on the Internet. Does Naomi have feelings for her boyfriend? Probably, or she wouldn't still be with him. So they both have "feelings" for each other, but for very different reasons. Do they love each other? Some people would say yes, but I would say . . . not yet. Are their feelings wrong? No, not at all. Feelings are very important, and I would be very surprised to see a really successful relationship that lacked genuine, deep feeling. But feelings and love are not the same.

Love Is Not a Ditch

OK, so love is not a feeling, but it's also not a ditch. A what? You heard me! It's not a ditch.

Have you ever seen a person walking down the hall at school and suddenly . . . "Ahhhhhhhhhhhhhhhhh!" Thud. "What happened?" you yell out to them. From deep inside a hole in the middle of the hallway you barely hear them cry,

> "I fell in love! Look, right down here . . . I'm in the hole . . . in the middle of the hall. I just fell right in here. I couldn't help it."

Sounds stupid, right? Yeah, 'cause it IS stupid! Love isn't a hole. You can't fall *in* it and you can't fall *out* of it either!

I Think I Fell in Love . . . Again

I remember a guy in high school that would sit in the cafeteria every day, see a girl across the room, and, with a ridiculous grin on his face, say, "I just fell in love." Two minutes later, a *different* girl would walk by, and he'd say, "Man, I just fell in love (again)!" Somewhere down the table someone would always yell, "Hey, what happened to the first girl?" He'd reply, "Well, I. . . ." (As *another* girl walked in. . . .) "Whoooooaaaa, I just fell in love!" Three times in six minutes! He must have broken some kind of record. Where's *The Guinness Book of World Records* when you need it?

The point is that you can't fall in love 'cause there's no such thing. No such thing as falling in love? Nope, not really. You can feel physical attraction for someone—be "turned on" by just looking at a person—but it ain't love. Now this probably comes as quite a shock to you, but hang on a minute. Think about it. If you could fall in love, then you could "fall in friendship"! Yes? No? Imagine running home from school, slamming the door, dropping your stuff on the floor as you go stumbling into the kitchen, and gasping to your mom, "Mom! I just fell in *friendship!*" She'd think you were nuts! Everyone would! But if you can fall in love, why *can't* you fall in friendship?

Have you ever "fallen in love" with someone only to find out five minutes later what a bonehead they were? You're just standing there, minding your own business, and wham! You see this guy or girl walk into your next class, and you instantly "fall in love." A

couple of minutes later they push past you, ignoring the fact that they just knocked your books to the floor, and then they make some comment about how clumsy the people in this school can be. . . . So what happened to the "I fell in love" thing? Gone.

I once heard about a guy who transferred from one school to another in the middle of his ninth-grade year. He was a tall, good-looking basketball player. I mean, his first day at the new school every girl "fell in love" with him. But after two weeks every one of those girls hated him 'cause he was such a jerk. Every girl had "fallen in" and "fallen out" of love with the same guy, all in two weeks' time.

Obviously if you can "fall IN love" then you can "fall OUT of love." Do you believe that? Can you imagine marrying a person and two weeks after the wedding they decide they have "fallen out" of love (they just couldn't help it) and they're leaving you? How would you argue with that? It would make perfect sense IF you could fall in (or out) of love . . . but there is no such thing.

Remember what Meg Ryan said about love? "Love is not a decision your brain makes. It's a feeling you know somewhere else, and your brain catches up." That feeling is what most people call "falling in love." It might be the *beginning* of the real thing, but your brain had better catch up, or you're in for trouble.

Love Is Not Sex

A glance at the magazine stand would make you think love and sex are the same thing, but they're not.

Love and Sex: The Myth

Love and sex. Love and sex. They're always together. *Playboy* magazine has built a multimillion-dollar business preaching that love and sex are almost synonymous. One issue (*Playboy*, February, 1989) quotes dictionary definitions of love right on the front. (How

many guys do you think will actually stop to look at the *cover?*)
One of the definitions on the cover is: "A feeling of warm personal
attachment or deep affection, as for a parent, child or friend." Really? Have you ever had a "feeling of warm personal attachment"
to somebody and hated their guts two minutes later because you
had an argument or you found out they had cheated on you? Gee,
is it still love, then? Do you still feel the "warm fuzzies" for them?
I don't think so!

Do sex and love go together? Not necessarily. Ah—wait—that
needs explaining. What I mean is, just because you love someone
doesn't mean you have to have sex with them. That would be ridiculous. Loving your parents doesn't mean anything sexual. . . .
Loving your best friend, loving your dog, loving your brother or
sister—none of those involve sex. (I hope!)

Having sex with someone doesn't mean you love them, either.
Prostitutes have sex with people all the time. They don't love them;
they *hate* them! So sex doesn't equal love, and love doesn't equal
sex.

All the media put love and sex together. In fact, next time you
go to the movies take a stopwatch with you, and as soon as someone in the movie says, "I love you," to the other person, start your
watch and see how long it takes before they're in bed. Sometimes
it's the same sentence. That's crazy!

YM magazine interviewed a bunch of guys once and asked them
a lot of questions about love, sex, and girls. Question Number 6
asked, "Do you have to be in love with a girl before you start fooling
around with her?" They all said, "No." In the same questionnaire
86 percent of the guys SAID they thought love was more important
than sex, but they had just admitted that you didn't have to love
the girl in order to have sex with her. In fact, one guy said, "No. I
think part of falling in love with someone is finding out if you're
physically compatible." Another guy said, "No. You can't possibly
know what love is until you experience it, and fooling around is
part of the process."[4] Oooooookayyy!!!

---

[4] *YM* magazine, February 1996, p. 54.

What Kept Them Together?

Sex is an incredibly important part of marriage, but let me ask you something. Is it sex that's keeping your grandparents together? No? OK then, what is? Feelings? Sorry! It's commitment and discipline that keeps couples together "in sickness and in health. . . ." Are you going to make the same kind of commitment that has kept Grandma and Grandpa together all these years, or are you saying sex is what's gonna decide it for you?

Love Is . . .

So if love isn't a feeling, and you can't fall in it, and it's not sex, then what is it? Let me give you the best definition I ever heard.

LOVE IS
CHOOSING THE HIGHEST GOOD
FOR THE OTHER PERSON[5]

Now I know what you must be thinking. "Well, gee whiz! THAT doesn't sound very romantic!" But let me explain.

First off, you're probably wondering, "How am I s'posed to know what the 'highest good' is for someone else? I don't even know what it is for me! (And I sure as heck don't want to let someone *else* decide that for me!)" What IS the highest good for *anyone*? Can you know it? HOW?

Be All That You Can Be

Each of us comes to life with a certain purpose and potential—certain God-given character, abilities, talents, and gifts—and

---

[5] Actual quote is, "Unselfishly willing the highest good of God and His Universe", Winkie Pratney, *Youth Aflame* (Minneapolis, Minnesota: Bethany House Publishers, 1983), p. 235

the "highest good" is to be what we were created to be. To be the best we can be. Love is choosing to do everything you can to help another person become who they were meant to be. Choosing anything less is cheating them. In order to know what a person is uniquely meant to be, you have to really know them and commit yourself to them over a long period of time. The better you know them the more effective your love will be for them. Let me warn you though. Love can be experienced in some pretty strange ways. Let me give you an example.

Pretend you have a 5-year-old son who one day stomps to the dinner table and announces, "I ain't gonna eat any of this broccoli junk any more! I want *candy* for every meal and nothin' else!!" Now, as the parent of this kid, what would you do? If you don't give him what he wants (candy), he may get mad and never talk to you again. But if you give him *only* candy you know he won't be healthy (being the best he can be), and it'll be just a matter of time before his teeth rot out and he dies of malnutrition. So what will you do? Will you give him what's best for him (the "highest good") or give him what he wants? Parents who spoil a child by giving him whatever he wants may have "feelings" and "natural affection" for him, but they are not loving him; they haven't chosen the "highest good" for him. See why it's not about feelings? It's about choice.

Have you ever asked your parents for something, knowing there's no chance they'll let you have it? Why did you do that? 'Cause all kids want to know if their parents really love them. They know that if their parents let them have what isn't good for them, then the parents don't *really* love them, and most kids are *desperate* to know that they are loved. So we test our parents to see if their love (choice for our good) is stronger than just feelings.

To Have and to Hold . . . 86 Percent of the Time?

Make believe it's your wedding day. (Scary thought, isn't it?) You're the bride, all dressed up in your wedding gown. And let's say, 10 minutes before the wedding is to start (music is playing, people are being seated), your groom sneaks up behind you, leads you

away from all your bridesmaids, and whispers in your ear, "I just want to tell you one more time how much I love you. In fact, just to prove it, for the rest of my life I'm going to commit *SIX nights of every week just to you!*" OK, what would you want to know at this point? Darn right! "Hey, buddy! Wha'd'ya think you're planning on doing on the *SEVENTH* night of the week?" Now let's say his response goes something like this: "Oh . . . well, there are some *other* girls I really like, and . . . well, I want to spend *ONE* night a week, overnight, alone with them. But listen, THEY DON'T MEAN NEAR AS MUCH TO ME AS YOU DO!"

OK. Question: Would you marry the guy? Not a chance!!!!! Why? "'Cause he doesn't really love me." But wait, six nights out of seven ain't bad! I mean, hey—it's close!! It's 86 percent of his time!!! So would you marry him, or not? Of course you wouldn't! Guys, reverse the roles. Would you marry a girl who said that to you? No! And why? Because you want . . . no, you would DEMAND the very best (HIGHEST GOOD) from the person you intend to marry! You would *never* put up with second best, a "sorta" effort on their part. Only a fool would marry under those circumstances. So why are most high school students putting up with that kind of stuff in their relationships and still calling it LOVE? If you allow someone you're dating to treat you that way *now,* what makes you think anything will change when you get married?

Since all this dating stuff is really about your future marriage you better take some time to really think what "highest good" means in marriage. It means giving absolutely 100 percent of yourself to someone and accepting nothing less than 100 percent from them. Yes, they will fail at times and so will you, but if you give just a half-hearted effort you don't really love that person. And if you accept that sort of thing from them you aren't helping them to be the best they can be, either. Love is choosing the *highest* good.

Love Is a *Choice*

Love is always a choice. It's not an impulse, and it's not blackmail. When you choose to love someone, you have actually made a decision to work for his or her good. You're not just reacting to a

great body or a pretty face. Remember my high school friend who could "fall in love" with three different girls in one lunch period? That was reacting, not choosing. When you choose to love someone back, it can't be because they are forcing or threatening you. Love must be *freely* given.

Blackmail

If someone uses a line like, "If you *really* loved me you'd prove it right in the back seat of this car," thank them—a lot—for clearing up a very important thing. What is that? The fact that they don't really love you. What you do in the back seat of the car may be fun, but it's not love. What that person is really saying to you is this, "If you won't do what I want you to do, when and where I want you to do it, then I won't love you." THAT'S BLACKMAIL! Here's another way this blackmail thing works. A lot of guys have dated girls who, at the threat of a breakup, say something like "I'll slit my wrists if you leave me." That's blackmail! She's trying to blackmail him into staying! That's not love! Any time you begin to feel controlled or threatened by another person, you can be pretty darn sure it's not love. And if they say they *can't* live without you, then you better learn to live without them. They're just using you.

I've heard a lot of stories about guys (some girls, too) who have actually committed suicide as a kind of emotional blackmail. If we somehow could have talked to them before they killed themselves, and had asked them if they really loved their girlfriends, you know they'd have said, "Yes!" But did they "choose the highest good" for the girl? Not even close. They wanted their girlfriends to PAY for breaking up with them. And pay they will. They will never fully get over blaming themselves for what happened, but life will go on for the survivors. It won't for the blackmailers. The amazing thing is they call it love.

An Impulse—a Feeling

You've seen couples at school. You know the kind, the ones groping each other in plain view of everyone in the hall. They think

they're "In Love." That night they break up, and the next morning at school they start spreading rumors about each other. "Boy, I showed that @#%&*$% a thing or two! Boy, what a @#$%&* she was!" And she's doing the same thing to him. Yesterday it was love; today they can't stand each other. All they're trying to do is save their egos by saying, "The other person didn't dump me, I dumped them. I'm not a loser." What they thought was love was just an impulse—a feeling. Was it ever love? No. Love is a choice for the good of the *other* person. It's not just a thing to make *you* look or feel good.

Making Him Happy or Making Him Good?

Lots of girls will say something like "I know I love my boyfriend 'cause I would do anything in the world for him. In fact, all I do is try to make him happy." (Hmmmm . . . I hope her kids don't ask for candy instead of broccoli!) Does loving someone mean you should be willing to make them happy by giving them whatever they want? No. For instance, a girl might think having sex with her boyfriend is the loving thing to do because he wants it. But just because he wants it, does that mean it's the best thing for him? Will giving in to him teach him to be disciplined and patient, to be unselfish? Will he learn to love her and meet her needs? Will his character be better or worse? How will he treat her if he doesn't get his way? Those are things that need to be asked. Remember that the goal of love is to help the other person be their best. It's about helping them grow and develop good character.

Love Will Cost You

Loving someone is very costly. Love doesn't always bring "happy thoughts" and warm feelings. I found that out the hard way when I was in college.

Early one fall I met this unbelievable girl: smart, good-looking, liked a lot of the same things I did. We started dating. After we had dated quite a while, we were in the library studying together one night during finals week, when all heck broke loose. Now in

college, finals week can be a really tense time because so much is riding on the results. It was late and we were both studying our brains out when, out of the blue, she turned and said something to me that about ripped me apart. Since I wasn't expecting it at all it totally caught me off guard, and it really hurt. I couldn't figure out what she meant by it. (To this day I can't remember exactly what it was she said. I think I blanked it all out.) I thought, "Well, OK. Big deal. It happens sometimes." But about five minutes later she did it again! What's really weird is both times she didn't realize that what she said had hurt me.

Now you know how when you're dating someone you try to always have your good side showing? You don't want that person to know what you're *really* like, 'cause if they did they might not like you anymore? Well, when you're in college and you've been dating for six or seven months, you can't play that game 'cause you're closer to the real thing . . . marriage. By this time I was starting to see this girl, *really* see her, for the first time. Anyway, I didn't say anything, but I watched her all through finals week and I began to realize she treated a lot of people like she had treated me—only she didn't realize she was doing it. The question I faced was this: "Should I say something and risk the chance of losing her, or should I just forget it?" I mean, I really wanted to help her understand what it was she was doing. People were starting to dislike her because she treated them so badly, so in the end it was hurting her, too. Man, I was sweating BBs over it.

It finally dawned on me that if I didn't love her enough to talk to her about stuff like that, then I didn't love her enough to date her, and certainly not enough to marry her. So, with knees knocking, I called her up, met her in the library, and in fear and trembling told her what I was thinking. Well . . . she got so mad she stood up, slammed her books shut, put on her coat, and left with one final shot: "I don't know who you think you are, but I don't need this kinda crap from you!" That's a quote! That was also the end. I couldn't believe it. I had tried to do what was right, to love her the best way I knew how, and the whole thing blew up in my face. I lost!!!

Not a Fairy Tale

But, you guys . . . THAT'S LOVE! When it's real love . . . you can lose. There are no guarantees, and I lost. The movies and fairy tales never seem to end *that* way, but real life sure can! By the way, let me tell you something about fairy tales. You'll know it's just a fairy tale relationship when you hear the line, "And they lived happily ever after." No they didn't! Nobody does!!! Reality is more like "And they lived happily . . . oh . . . for a couple of months there . . . and then all heck broke loose." Now THAT'S reality! Or at least it's much closer to the truth, 'cause that's just the way real life is.

Back to my college story. Some time later I got a letter from her in my mailbox. She said she wanted to talk to me again about all the stuff I had said, and she asked if I would meet her. Now I'm no brain surgeon, but I knew I didn't want to go through *that* again. Besides, she might bring a *gun* this time! I didn't know. But I guess I was curious, so I agreed to meet her in the library. (To this day I still don't like libraries very much.) When I got there I looked around but couldn't find her, so I sat down to wait. Suddenly she appeared in front of me . . . with a gun! (No, just kidding.) She stood pointing her finger in my face (it *felt* like a gun), and with tears in her eyes she said, "You know, I've thought a long time about what you told me, and something dawned on me. I've never had anyone care about me the way you did. No one else has ever cared enough to talk to me about the things you did, and it scared me. I didn't know how to handle it or what to say. But now I know you really love me." Then she burst into tears. Me, I just sat there looking stupid. She was crying . . . people started coming around thinking I was beating her up or something. I didn't know what to do, so finally I grabbed her and held her on my lap while she cried. And, you know what? I've held her for over 32 years. Yup, THAT'S MY WIFE! When I asked her to marry me, you know why she said yes? Because *she knew I would choose the highest good for her, even at the risk of losing her.* That's real love! (And, just for the record, she has done the same for me since then, many, many times.)

Saying the Hard Things

See, love *dictates* that you and your partner say the hard things to each other, and that you stick around afterwards. If you don't challenge each other to be better than you already are, then you don't really love each other. It may not always feel good at the time, but, just like broccoli, it's good for you!

He *Says* He Loves Me, But . . .

After one of my assemblies a girl came up to me in tears. Man, she was a mess: mascara running down her face, it was terrible. I asked, "What's wrong?" She said, "My boyfriend *says* he loves me, but he treats me like dirt. How do I know if he really loves me?" Now I'm listening to this and I almost burst out laughing. (Nice, compassionate guy that I am.) I said, "Would you mind repeating that again?" She did. "My boyfriend treats me like dirt and—" "Stop!" I said. "He treats you like dirt?" "Yeah, but he says he loves—" "Wait, wait, wait! He treats you like *dirt,* and you are wondering if he really loves you?" "Yeah." "Look," I said, "Let me ask you a question. If you really loved someone would you ever want to treat them badly?" "Well, no," she answered. "OK. So if someone tells you one thing and then does the exact *opposite* of what they said, what would you call that? It's called lying, isn't it? Can you trust a liar?" "Well, no" she said. I went on. "Does he really care about you and have your best in mind? Would you want to marry someone like that?" "No!" "So, just 'cause this guy *says* he loves you, that doesn't mean he does." She looked a little fuzzy, so I asked her, "By his actions, *and only his actions,* can you say he truly chooses the highest good for you, no matter how it affects him?" At this point she just sorta laughed, "Well, no." "Then it's quite obvious he doesn't really love you! When he said he loved you he lied, because his actions prove he cares only about himself. You can't build a relationship on that. I don't care *what* he says!" We talked some more, but she kept coming back to the same thing over and over again. "But he says he loves me." She couldn't grasp the concept that love is not a word, it's an action.

Motives

When a guy says, "I love you," what's the next thing every girl wants to know? That's right. "Why? Is it *me* you love, or is it something you think you're going to *get* from me that you love?" When a girl says, "I love you," sex may be the first thing that comes into a guy's mind, but the next thing is, "Yeah, well, is it *me* you love, or do you just want transportation?" Or, "Do you really love me, or do you just want me to pay your way to the movie?" So the love question seems to come down to this: Do you love me because of something you think you're going to get in return, or do you just love me for myself?

If I could magically take the word *love* out of our vocabulary, so your boyfriend or girlfriend could never say, "I love you," ever again, how would you know if they really *did* love you? They couldn't say it, so how would you know?

BY THEIR ACTIONS!

I read an article once that said that a guy went to prison after he shot his girlfriend in the head. This man and woman were dating steadily, but one night she said she wanted to date some other guys. He was the only guy she had ever dated and she still liked him, but she really wanted to meet some other guys. He was so mad he got his gun, loaded it, and went to her apartment. Putting the gun to her head, he said something like, "If you won't love *just* me, I'll kill you!" She said she still loved him but she wasn't ready to settle down. He shot her at point-blank range and killed her.

Now suppose we could get an interview with this guy in prison (I hope he's still there), and we asked him, "Did you really love that girl?" What do you think he'd say? I'll bet he would answer, with tears in his eyes, something like, "Oh yes, but I just couldn't imagine her being in anybody else's arms but mine!" (Boohoo, boohoo . . .) "SO I SHOT HER IN THE HEAD!" Hmmmmm. Let's think about this.

> Question: Did he have feelings for her?
> Answer: Yes! Deep feelings! (tears, crying, etc.)

> Question: Did he choose the highest good for her?
> Answer: No way!

> Question: Who *did* he choose the best for?
> Answer: Himself! (Even then he messed up—he ended up in jail!)

> Question: Whose definition of love do you want to live by, his or mine?

If you choose his, you could end up dead! He defined love as a feeling he had for this woman, and his definition is the one most people believe is true. But when the "feeling of love" turned into a "feeling of jealousy," it was a short trip to "feeling like killing." Feelings and words have absolutely nothing to do with real love. Like the girl with the boyfriend who treats her like dirt, too many people have fallen in love with the *words,* "I love you." For her, the words had no relation to real life at all, but she seemed willing to blindly follow those words over the nearest cliff.

Remember the great football player, O. J. Simpson, the guy who was accused of killing his wife, Nicole? Now we may never know for sure if O. J. really did it or not, but we do know he beat her up on a number of occasions, and she had to have the cops come to stop it. I have an article that quoted O. J. Simpson as saying that if he had killed Nicole, his wife, he would have done it 'cause he loved her. Evidently someone went back and asked him if he meant

that, and he said yes. So my question here is, did O. J. really love Nicole? He said he did, but did he *choose the highest good for her?* No way! Whose definition do you want to live by, O. J.'s or mine? If you say his, you may die. By the way, ladies, he's still single, and he still has a couple of million dollars . . . anyone want to date him? You'd have to be crazy!

Just My Opinion

At this point some people might say to me, "Well, this is just your opinion about love. You can't push your definition on anyone else. It's everyone's own choice." OK, but would you say that to O. J.'s wife or to the murdered girlfriend? They're both dead because of their husband's or boyfriend's definition of love. Words mean things, and we really do live or die by our definitions.

I once had a girl come up to me after an assembly and verbally tear me apart. "That's just your opinion about love. Don't push that stuff on me!" Now I don't mind at all when people disagree with me, but I always try to watch the *way* they go about disagreeing. It shows a lot about who they are and about their philosophy of life. Notice what she was doing? She didn't want *me* telling *her* what to do or what to believe, but she expected *me* to give *her* exactly what *she* wanted. She couldn't have cared less about the way she was treating me. Her actions shouted, "You treat me the way *I* want to be treated (love ME), but don't expect me to treat you the way *you* want to be treated. Give me what I want! Cross me, and I'll rip your head off!" ME, ME, ME! Sounds like a lot of two-year-olds I know.

Back to Motives

So love is choosing the highest good and acting on that choice. Actions are *objective* (visible) proof of genuine love. But there's also a subjective (not visible, but still knowable) proof. It's not something you can see as much as you can discern or "sense," and it's extremely important.

Let me give you an example. Gary is a very good-looking guy who lives in my hometown. He has his own business and does quite

well at it. He's young and single, and loves to go out every weekend, but he never dates the same girl more than once. (You'll see why in a minute.) Anyway, he's an amazing guy to watch. Every Friday afternoon he goes to a local flower shop, buys one red rose, adds a little baby's breath and greenery, ties it all together with a little pink ribbon, and then adds a little card that says something like:

> Looking forward to being with you.
> I've been thinking about you all day.
> Just wanted to give you something
> to make your day a little brighter.
> See you tonight.

He signs the card, takes it to where his date-of-the-week works, and tapes it lightly to the hood of her car. What will she think at the end of her day when she climbs into her car and sees the flowers and the note? "Man, this guy is unbelievable! He really knows what a woman likes! Where has he been all my life?" But do you know *why* he goes to all that trouble? (He actually admitted this to a friend of mine.) "The reason I do it is 'cause I know I can get any girl I want to go to bed with me. It works every time."

He does a genuinely loving thing, right? Yeah, *but for all the wrong reasons!* He's a guy who's showing the *outward* signs of genuine love, but his motive stinks! Right actions, wrong motive. Does he love her? NO! He isn't choosing the best for her, even though *at first it looks like he is.* The flowers may fool her, but she'll learn by his *actions* what his intentions are.

Only Time Will Tell

So not only do you have to see genuine acts of love, but you also have to recognize the motive *behind the actions.* How? By watching the person over time. Only time can tell you if the actions are for real. And I'm not talkin' two weeks here; I'm talkin' months—sometimes years. Anyone can fake it for a while, and some do. Remember, all this dating stuff is eventually going to determine who you marry, so it's worth taking your time and get-

ting it right! When I meet kids who are dating and they tell me they are "in love" after being together for two weeks, I just want to gag. Their desire to be "in love" could cost them big time. See, I know guys like Gary, and, yes, I've met some girls like him, too. They can be very patient, sometimes for months, just waiting for the right time. Then, like a cat ready to spring, they jump into bed, take what they want, and are gone the next day.

But let's give most people the benefit of the doubt. There were times I wasn't real sure I loved the girl I was dating. I really didn't know if MY motives were all that pure. It took me a while to know myself. Was I being loving? Was I doing the "nice stuff" just to show off to my friends? Was it her I cared about, or my reputation? Would I do nice things for her even if she didn't know it was me who did them? Would I keep on doing those things even after we broke up? That would sure prove whether my motive was sincere or not!

One Final Test

If you really want to know if your boyfriend or girlfriend loves you, here's a pretty good way to find out.

All you girls have to do is find five girls you can really trust. Now they can't be just any old girls, they have to be girls who you know will *tell you the truth*. And this is what you tell them:

> "Let's say that love is choosing the highest good for the other person. OK. Now I don't care what you've ever heard my boyfriend say to me or about me, but by the way he treats me, and ONLY by the way he treats me, do you girls think he really loves me, by that definition?"

In the snap of a finger you'll have a pretty good idea if he does or not. Those five girls aren't emotionally wrapped up in the relationship like you are. They don't have to apologize for his poor behavior the way you do. No, they're lookin' right at his actions and judging them for what they are. If you're smart, you'll listen to them.

Guys, you may have to find *five girls* that you trust, instead of five guys, 'cause the guys may be thinkin', "Yeah, she treats you like dirt, but she's so good-lookin'! What's a little dirt gonna hurt?" Listen, I don't care *how* good-lookin' she is! I want to know how she *treats* you! Some of you guys are dating girls who treat you like trash, and you put up with it because *she's so good-looking.* What a crazy reason to stay with a girl!

The Ultimate Experiment

Think about this. What would happen if, for just one month, everyone in your school decided to genuinely love each other by my definition? That would mean treating everyone equally well by choosing the best for them, and they would do the same for you. It wouldn't matter who the other person was—guy or girl, teacher or administrator, smart or not-so-smart, pretty or average, popular or not. Everyone would treat everyone else exactly the way they themselves wanted to be treated. People would care about your life and what you were going through, and they would also be willing to talk serious stuff with you, if you needed it. If someone forgot to bring money for lunch that day, you'd give them yours. If some girl was crying in the hallway, people would be standing in line waiting to help or listen. No one would "keep score" of the things someone did to them in the past, so there'd be no paybacks. Everything would be done simply for love of the other person. Period! How different would your school be after just one month?

Of all the people at your school who say they love their boyfriend or girlfriend, how many of them love *everyone* the way I'm describing to you? Do they love just the people they have feelings for—the ones who bring them the most pleasure—or do they show a loving character to everyone equally?

One more question. How much would have to change in order for our experiment to happen *permanently* in *your* life? Do you want the real thing, or do you just want to look good? Do you love only certain people, the ones who will bring you the "good feelings," or do you love everyone? If I asked the people who know you at school, what would their answer be? Think about it.

Magic Words

"I love you." What magic words these are! We all want to hear someone say that to us . . . and really mean it. We want to know someone is thinking about us—that we're at the center of their heart and mind. You can love someone (by choosing the best for them) in a very short period of time, but *telling* them you "love" them will immediately change the dynamics of the relationship. They may be thinking something totally opposite from you and may immediately read all kinds of things into your statement, like marriage or sex, when you're not ready for either!

Love Doesn't Mean Marriage

Always separate love from marriage. You could love someone deeply but never marry them. You wouldn't dare marry someone you met two weeks ago just because they say they are in love with you. You'd need to know what they believe about love, marriage, commitment, friendship, God, etc., before you'd ever commit to that kind of relationship. You'd have to know who they *really* are. Lots of kids put love and marriage together as an excuse to have sex with each other. "After all, we're gonna get married eventually anyway, so why wait?" But that's crazy! I got a letter from a seventh-grade girl who had been dating a guy for two weeks, and now they're engaged! Wanna bet me they're no longer together? Wanna bet me they were having sex? Easy money!

Are high school students really ready for marriage? No. But *can* two high school students genuinely love each other, for the real thing? Absolutely! I've seen it. Love, yes. Marriage—not yet!

When to Say "I Love You"

So when it comes time to say those magic words to someone, here are a few things to keep in mind.

1. **THEY'RE NOT MAGIC WORDS!** When you say, "I love you," it may change nothing, or it may bring an illusion ("magic") of feelings, but love must go far deeper than mere words.

2. Your boyfriend or girlfriend may not define love the way you do. How will he or she interpret your words? If your boyfriend tends to struggle with the sex thing, the words "I love you" may carry very different expectations for him than they do for you. If you're saying it to your girlfriend, she may think you're ready to marry her.

3. Remember: you may love many people in your lifetime, but you will marry only one. You may think, "This is *the One!*" But you may feel that for *every* guy or girl you date. Saying "I love you" is not a commitment to a relationship, marriage, or sex, but as soon as the words are out, the dynamics of the relationship will change.

4. When you are finally ready to say it, mean it. Don't just say it because the other person did. Think very carefully about it first.

5. Tell them only when you have their full attention and can talk, not in "the heat of the moment."

6. Tell them only when you require nothing in return.

7. Tell them only when your actions have already proved what your words will declare.

When *Not* to Say It

1. When you just want to get it over with.

2. When you're desperate to be loved.

3. When you're in "the heat of the moment."

4. When you feel pressured, 'cause they said it first.

5. When your actions have not proved it to be true.

6. When you don't honestly love yourself.

7. When you're not sure.

8. When you have spent less than four to six months in the same town with them.

9. When you want something back.

How to Say It

It's not just *WHEN* you say "I love you," it's also *HOW* you say it. A subtle "Love ya!" is different from a low, hot-breath "I LOVE YOU . . ." in the back seat of a car. They have totally different meanings.

When I was in high school I made up my mind that I would never tell a girl "I love you," until I was willing to ask her to marry me, hand her a ring, and set the date. And I knew that would be after dating her for at least six months, or more. A lot of guys I knew would tell their girlfriends whatever they wanted to hear so they could get whatever they wanted. Some girls do the same thing to their boyfriends. I thought that sort of thing was disgusting, so I was very careful about what I said when it came to the "love thang." I'm not saying that's what *you* should do, but it really helped *me* to think straight. (By the way, I blew it only one time. I told a girl, "I love you," and as soon as I said it, I knew I lied. We broke up a few weeks later. The next girl I said it to, I married.)

One More Thing about Feelings

Now that I've explained that love isn't a feeling, you may wonder just what to do with the feelings you do have. Just because feelings aren't love doesn't mean we shouldn't want them, or that we don't have to deal with them every day. So here are a few thoughts that might be helpful.

Our minds, bodies, actions, and motives are very closely connected. You might think that what goes on in your body has noth-

ing to do with what goes on in your mind, but that just isn't true. For instance, if you tell a lie your body feels it and responds in a physical way. Your mind unconsciously communicates with your body that you are not telling the truth, and your body responds with sweaty hands and an increased heart rate. That's how polygraph machines (lie detectors) work. Our bodies are designed to help us "read" right and wrong. If someone did something really nice for you and later you found out they were just trying to rip you off, *all of you* would react. You wouldn't just get "ticked off," your whole being would respond to it. Your muscles would tighten up and ache, or your stomach would start to churn. Your reactions are deeper than just "feelings." They are physical, too.

Nobody wants physical pain, but without it, life would be terrifying. Pain is important. Why? Pain tells you when something is wrong, and that you need to "stop, look, and listen" to what that pain is trying to tell you. Without pain you could do all kinds of damage to yourself without knowing it. If you accidentally touch a hot stove, the pain you feel immediately tells you, "This is NOT GOOD. Aaaaaahhhh!" You instinctively pull your hand away so you don't get burned. You don't have to ask pain to come; it just shows up. Pain is out of your reach. You can't stop it or control it. Most of us at one time or another have wished we could turn off the pain and continue with whatever we were doing, but it doesn't work that way. If it did, we would just turn off the "pain button" until we were finished with what we wanted to do. Then we'd turn it back on after the damage had been done. If pain was never a threat, we'd never bother asking ourselves if something was good for us or not. But since it is such a threat, we have to listen to it. Kinda like "Don't tell me what to do. I'll do whatever the . . . Ooooowwwwww . . . OK, OK, I'll stop! That hurts!"

Emotional pain (bad feelings), just like physical pain, instantly gets our attention and drives us away from whatever caused it. It's as natural a response as yanking your hand off the hot stove, and it's designed to keep you from losing out on the best in life. For instance, a girl who gets taken advantage of by a guy will immediately pull away from him, at least for a while, because he caused

her to have deep, painful feelings. The pain and bad feelings made her stop and evaluate what went wrong. She learned, "Get hurt too many times by this guy and the pain might become permanent." To get rid of the pain, most people just get rid of the person who caused it. But that doesn't necessarily deal with the *source* of the pain. The pain is not the problem. The *person* may not even be the problem. What's wrong in a relationship *is* the problem, and pain gets our attention.

Pain is built into the fabric of life. Pain and bad feelings can become your best friends if you let them talk to you. Emotional pain, relational pain, and physical pain all register the same way: "This hurts, and I know I have to change whatever I'm doing . . . FAST!" Take pain out of life, and you no longer have that "early warning system" that protects you from danger that can cause permanent damage.

If you experience emotional or relational pain you can try to ignore it, but usually it hurts too much and you have to work awfully hard at not thinking about it. Remember, pain is trying to get your attention—to tell you something—to make you think. That's its job. You may tell yourself, "Thinking about it hurts too much, so I just won't think about it." But that's like the guy who read the newspaper headline, "Smoking Causes Cancer." He was a smoker, so what did he do? He stopped reading the newspaper! (????)

Instead of dealing with the real problem some people get into drugs, drinking, or sex, because it makes the feelings change or go away for a while. "I don't wanna *think* about anything. I just want somethin' to drink and to see somethin' naked. Any girl will do! At least that'll make me feel good." The sex and alcohol may feel good, but people still haven't "taken their hand off the stove." They haven't fixed the *real* problem, so the same pain will keep hounding them. Pretty soon their thinking becomes so blurred and confused that they finally conclude, "Love stinks!" and they "quit reading the newspaper."

Feelings are just tools to help you find genuine love. Feelings are byproducts of your behavior and reactions to what people do to you. If you make bad choices pain is usually the result. Good

feelings are usually the result of wise choices, but remember, feelings can still fool you.

Pain isn't the enemy, but actions can be. Good and bad feelings come and go. You can't control them, but you *can* control your actions:

- ACTIONS LEAD TO FEELINGS

- FEELINGS LEAD TO NEW ACTIONS

- NEW ACTIONS LEAD TO NEW FEELINGS

Chapter 5. Evaluating Your Relationships

Most people evaluate their relationship on the basis of one thing: is it fun or isn't it? Well . . . OK, but believe it or not, there is a higher purpose for dating than just having fun . . . and that's kissing! (Kidding . . . juuuussssst kidding.) Not that fun (and kissing) are bad, but just the same, I can have fun with (and kiss) my dog, but I certainly don't want to date or marry my dog. (She's got great eyes, but she's also got hairy feet!) Yes, dating and relationships are for having fun, but they are also preparing you for bigger and better things to come. So it's worth doing right.

When I started thinking about writing this book, one of the things I wanted to do was to come up with some way for people to evaluate their relationships—kind of a "How Am I Doing?" sort of chapter. I mean, shoot, you get grades in school, so why can't you do the same thing when it comes to relationships? Obviously passing or failing a test or a class is different than passing or failing in a relationship, but still, there's got to be a way to evaluate so you pretty much know whether it's going to turn out right or not. That's what we're gonna try to do right now.

Am I Stuck with Fate?

First of all, a lot of people think there's only ONE person out there for them and if they should somehow miss THE ONE . . . they're done for. Or they've got the idea that somehow God picks the person for them, and if they screw it up they'll get stuck with "Plan B" (the wrong person). So there you go! Eat too much pizza one night, get a bad stomach ache, make a stupid decision, and BAM! Life stinks, 'cause you chose the wrong person! Most of the people who believe that can't really explain how they came up with the idea, but they'll spend their whole life believing it. Other people think things like, "I'm too ugly or dumb . . . no one would ever want me," or, "All the good ones are gone." They are totally convinced they'll never find someone. Personally, I don't think any of that is true. It's not just fate, and there are still lots of "good ones" available. It's just that the good ones are the most picky about who they will go out with. They're also the ones you have to GO FIND. They aren't just standing around waiting to be "discovered."

So here's the deal. No one can find or choose "THE ONE" for you. Only you can do that. Yes, you can get help, but essentially you're the one who has to figure it out. Can it be done? I think it can.

A Piece of Cake

At church one Sunday our minister used this illustration to make one of his points. He took all the ingredients needed to bake a cake and placed them on a table. On another table he had a finished cake. It was a beautiful *chocolate* cake, so right off he had my attention. He asked for volunteers to come up and sample the cake, and not being a shy person, of course I raised my hand.

Well, he picked a couple of kids from the front row instead of me. (I decided never to go to that church again!) But before he let them taste the *finished* cake he said, "Let's have you sample some of the *ingredients* that went into that cake to make it taste good." First he handed each kid a spoonful of chocolate chips. (Oh man, I love chocolate chips! Dang!) The kids were *lovin'* this! Then he

reached for the eggs. Have you ever eaten a raw egg . . . all by itself? Suddenly I felt better about him choosing those kids instead of me. They choked down the eggs while all the people in the church were gaggin' and laughing. When they finally got the eggs down, he reached for the salt. After the salt it was the flour . . . then the butter . . . sugar wasn't so bad . . . then *baking powder* . . . Bleeeaaahhh! When he was finally done, the kids had turned green and were ready to die. But in the end they *finally* got a piece of the finished cake, made up of all the ingredients they had eaten separately, and they ate it with a smile. (Let me say right here that smiling after eating a piece of chocolate cake is never a good idea!)

So what's the point? The point is that you may not like eating all the particular ingredients individually, but without any one of them, the finished product won't taste good. It's the same thing with relationships and even marriage. You need *all* the ingredients to make it work. You ever eat a cake without baking powder or salt in it? Gross! Have you ever seen a successful marriage without the ingredients "honesty" or "sense of humor"? Gross! So ingredients become very important when evaluating relationships.

By the way, you ever wonder who came up with just the right list of ingredients for cakes? I mean, *someone* had to figure out what works and what doesn't, right? So who did? MEN DID! That's right. Some woman kept tryin' new recipes, and when her poor husband came home from a hard day workin' in the fields, he'd dig into the *new* cake and . . . *puke it up!* "Woman, what did ya use *this* time, cow chips?" (By the way, I think that's how cookies originally got started.) But she kept right on adding and subtracting stuff, and he had to keep right on eating away, until one day she came up with the recipe your grandma uses to this very day. That's also the reason men die before most women do!

Always Start with the End in Mind

When you're thinking about what you want in life, you have to look way ahead to the end—to see what it is you want THERE— before you make any moves HERE, in the present. Then you can evaluate and decide how to get there from here. If you don't have

a clear goal, how'll you know what to shoot at? It's like when you play darts. First you locate the target, THEN you throw the dart. Believe it or not, most people live their lives as if they can throw the dart in any old direction, then run and MOVE THE TARGET. What can I say? It just doesn't work well.

Think about many of the adults you know. (Now don't get too judgmental here.) Do you think when they were your age they could hardly wait to become what they are today; that they actually *wanted* and *planned* to be this way? Probably not. If they could do it all over again would they plan more carefully? Oh yeah! On the other hand, look at the adults you admire. Did their lives "just happen," or was there some pretty determined planning involved?

A Scary Thought

I once heard a medical doctor talk about how his life had turned out. "Once, a very long time ago," he said, "a nineteen-year-old kid decided that I would become a doctor. As a fifty-two-year-old adult, how could I have ever let some kid decide *anything* about my future?! What could that kid possibly know about who I am? But thirty-three years ago I did just that . . . I decided what I wanted to be. It just doesn't seem fair!"

That's exactly what's happening right this minute! Right now, a *kid* is deciding what will happen concerning love, marriage, and family in YOUR future. That kid is you! And sometime in the future you may be looking back wondering, "What the heck was I thinking?" So be careful. When you do your planning always start with the end in mind. And what better ending could there be than finding the right person . . .

The Right Person for What?

When someone asks the question, "How do I find the right person?" the next logical question is, "The right person for what?" The answer is obvious . . . marriage! When it comes to evaluating your present relationship with the opposite sex, you will always be evaluating that relationship according to its potential for a permanent relationship in marriage. And since marriage is the

ultimate goal of all dating relationships, it would probably help, at this point, if we define what marriage is. It may seem stupid to suggest that you might not know, but let's do it anyway. Humor me. (By the way, this "marriage potential" stuff . . . this is scaring the heck out of the guys reading this.)

Definition of Marriage

Some people think marriage is "just a piece of paper," so they choose not to do the usual church wedding with vows, rings, and "a piece of paper." They just live together. But that argument always seemed dumb to me. If marriage was only a "piece of paper," then what's the big deal? . . . SIGN THE DANG THING! If that's ALL someone thinks a marriage is (a piece of paper), then I totally understand why they think it's stupid. But that's not what marriage is. It's far more than that!

The best definition I ever heard came from a guy named Dr. Norm Wright. He said:

$$\text{MARRIAGE} = \begin{array}{l}\text{The total commitment}\\ \text{Of the total person}\\ \text{For total life}^1\end{array}$$

Marriage is the decision to share yourself physically (sexually), mentally, socially, emotionally, and spiritually with only one person for the rest of your life. Legally, both people give to each other all their assets, liabilities, and potential. The license says, in effect, "I give you my life and all it holds . . . forever. I'm holding nothing back for myself, and I'm asking the rest of the world to hold me to my promise." Author Walter Wangerin wrapped it all up this way:

A promise made, a promise witnessed, a promise heard, remembered, and trusted—this is the groundwork of marriage. Not emotions. No, not even love. Not physical desires or personal needs or sexuality. Not the practical fact of living together. Not

---

[1] H. Norman Wright, *The Living Marriage* (Old Tappan, NJ: Flemming H. Revell Company, 1975), p. 17

even the piercing foresight or some peculiar miracle of All-seeing God. Rather, a promise, a vow, makes the marriage. "I promise you my faithfulness, until death parts us."[2]

Take Your Time

Marriage, almost by definition, is two imperfect people, willing to live forever together in tight quarters, who will, in time, hurt each other. They can't help it. So they each need to know *in advance* how the other will behave when the going gets tough. How will they respond when they get hurt? (Because they *will* get hurt.) The more honest and open they are with each other beforehand, the less chance they will have of failing at their marriage. Before you promise to stay with someone forever, you'd better make sure they can stand up to the challenge. Take your time.

Ingredients for Marriage

So if someone came up with the ingredients for cakes, then who came up with the ingredients for marriage? The answer is millions and millions of couples all over the world. That's who. People kept trying this and trying that, until it became very obvious what worked and what didn't. (Seems like it would have been easier if they had consulted the One who created them in the first place, don't you think?) And you know what it is that works best at keeping marriages going? Chocolate cake! (No, just kidding again.) That's what this next part is all about.

But first let me ask you a question. What in life do you know *for sure*? Answer . . . very little. So how can you know *for sure* whether you have the right person with the right "ingredients" for marriage? You can't know . . . *for sure*. So what do you do? You have to *eliminate as many unknowns as possible before you make a commitment to someone*. The only way I know to eliminate the unknowns in a relationship is to observe that person over a great deal of time, in as many different situations as possible. You need

---

[2] Walter Wangerin, *As for Me and My House* (Kansas City: Thomas Nelson Publishers, 1987), p. 18.

to watch them in social settings (family and friends), see them at work and at play, and observe them when they think they are alone. Watch them in stressful times and when they're laid back. In other words, simply gather as much information as you can about the whole person, so you can make the most intelligent decision possible. Take as much of the guesswork as you can out of the equation.

Is Love Enough?

Is love enough to cover all life's difficulties? Depends on what you mean by "love." Many people think, "As long as we love each other, that's all we need." The problem with that statement is most people still think love is that gooey feeling—that look in the eye. But those feelings will come and go. Have your first argument or disagreement as a couple, and see just how long those feelings last. The good news is that during (and after) that argument you'll find out if all the *other* necessary ingredients are there. The argument may become your best friend. It will tell you the most about the other person. Yes, love is extremely important, all right, but there are a lot of other ingredients that are just as important. Do you like doing the same things? Can your life goals work together? Do you even have goals? What if you love the noise and pace of the city and he craves the quiet of the country? What if she wants kids and you don't? Sometimes choosing the highest good is recognizing that even though the "feelings" are there, the relationship could never make a successful marriage. True love would mean letting go.

Back to that question about why your grandparents have stayed together all these years. Is it sexual curiosity, peer pressure, and excitement? Of course not. An exciting day for them may consist of nothing more than taking a walk in the park, hand in hand. So what *has* kept them together? *Character and commitment.* And character and commitment are the only things that will keep *your* marriage together.

Reality Check

Now it's time for a reality check. It's time to take a really, *really* good look at the person you are dating or want to date. Of course no one is ever perfect, including you, but that's no excuse for not looking. Love is never blind. Quite the opposite. Love takes a good look with eyes wide open, sees all the potential for good and bad, and then makes a calculated decision. "Can I live with that person happily and *intelligently* for the rest of my life?" Brutally honest evaluation *now* will save you from disaster *later.*

Absolutely Essential Ingredients for Any Successful Relationship

So here is a list of "absolute musts" that are essential to long-lasting, successful relationships. (Especially marriage) Check the ones you know are present *right now* in the person you're dating, and make a note of the ones that seem to be in question. Don't cheat, either! If you can't be honest now, how can you be honest after you get married?

❑ **Are they honest?**
   Is the person you're seeing honest? There are a couple of kinds of honesty to think about here. First, truthfulness. Does this person tell the truth? Always? Do they withhold facts in order to bend the truth? Have they been willing to hide your relationship from your parents? Has either of you lied about your relationship to others? Do you trust the person? Would they ever cheat on you? (Not just sexually, but in other ways as well?) What's their reputation like? Do other people see them as a reliable person who will stick it out in tough times, or are they just a "fair-weather friend?" Are they committed to working out problems regardless of how they will personally be affected?
   The second kind of honesty is openness. Can this person let you see inside their heart and mind, or are they always hiding behind a mysterious, masked personality? Do they

want to be known, to grow? Do they have the ability to be open? What do you read in their eyes?

❑ **Can they admit when they are wrong?**

When was the last time you heard them humbly admit they were wrong and mean it—not because they got caught, but just because they were wrong? Do they constantly excuse their behavior by blaming something or someone else? Do they always have to be right?

❑ **Are they forgiving?**

Does the person you are seeing have the ability to forgive? Do they keep track of wrongs done to them so they can use them to get back at you later? Can they leave the past behind once it's been dealt with? A professional counselor told a story about a married couple who came to him for help with their marriage. "What seems to be the problem?" he asked. The woman said, "I'll tell you *exactly* what the problem is!" Out of her purse she pulled a one-inch-thick, typewritten manuscript, and slammed it down on the desk. The counselor, amazed at the size of the thing, asked, "What is *this*?" "It's everything *he's* done wrong for the last five years of our marriage." The counselor sat in disbelief, but finally said, "Well, now I think I know what the *real* problem is." That woman had no ability to forgive and move on.

❑ **Can they change for the better?**

Does the person you are seeing have the willingness to change? Are they stubborn? Have they ever conquered a bad habit? Do they *have* bad habits? Are they willing to talk about them and work on them? Can you live with that? Do you find yourself having to make excuses for their behavior? Can they learn from someone "less important" than themselves? Can they learn from you? Are they growing as a person? Do they love to learn new things? How well do they take criticism? Do they read? Does the relationship feel like it's tearing you down or building you up?

❑ **Do they have a sense of humor?**

Humor can get people through almost anything. It's an absolute MUST in marriage. Can they take a joke? (Can you?) Are they "touchy"? Are they fun to be around? When you close your eyes and visualize their face, do you see a smile, or do they have "an attitude"? Are they cheerful, or always down, somehow living in a "dark" kind of world? Do most people find them happy and fun to be around? Can they be serious?

❑ **Is there sexual attraction?**

Sexual attraction is normal, important, and healthy. If it's not there, something's missing. So, are you physically attracted to them? Are they attracted to you? Are they in control of that attraction, or do they seem out of control? Are they trying to control you? Do they seem to be pushing you sexually? Are you proud to be seen with them? Do they take care of themselves physically?

❑ **Do you share common beliefs?**

What would they say is the most important value in their life? Do you agree with those values? If you asked them what they believe about God, family, politics, or money, would you already know the answer, and would you agree? Do they know what your beliefs are? Do they help you toward your goals in those areas, or do they take you farther away from them? Are they living what they say they believe? Do they love your family and want to be a part of their lives, or are they taking you away from them?

❑ **Do you share common goals and life direction?**

How do they define success? What "drives" them on in life? How committed are they to what is valuable to you? What goals are they pursuing right now, and are those goals realistic? Do they ever *reach* their goals? Do you believe in what they want to do with their life, and do they strongly encourage you in decisions concerning your future? Are they energetic, or do they tend to be lazy? Do they work hard? Do they work too hard, and never have time for you?

❏ **Do you share common interests?**
Sports, hobbies, church, education, family, music, your home—how important are these things to them? Are they supportive in the areas that interest you? Are they creative or boring? What kind of hobbies do they have?

❏ **Are they disciplined?**
Can they save money, or do they spend it unwisely? Do they have to have what they want RIGHT NOW? Are they in debt? Do they finish what they start? Can they do what's right even when they don't *feel* like it?

❏ **Are they kind?**
Are they gentle to people different than themselves—people of all ages, beliefs, races? How do they talk about and treat your parents? Do they always have to be "one up" on the other person? Are they hot-tempered? How do they treat those closest to them, especially parents? Do they excuse their own behavior by saying, "I have a bad temper 'cause I'm Italian" (or whatever)?

❏ **Are they faithful and dependable?**
Are they faithful in little things? Do they do what they say they will do? Have you ever suspected them of cheating on you? Do you worry when you're separated from them? What have their past relationships been like? Do you feel secure in their love? Have they proved they can be trusted? Do they respect your sexual boundaries? Have they been committed to you for at least a year or more? Do they keep their word?

❏ **Are they patient?**
How do they react when you do something wrong? Do you feel jumped on? When you disagree with each other, do they listen to your side of the argument before explaining theirs? Do you feel free to agree to disagree?

❏ **Are they thoughtful?**
Do they remember important events and dates? Do they do little things for you "just cuz," with no ulterior motives? How clean is their bedroom? Their car? Do they pick up after themselves, or leave the mess for someone else to clean?

❏ **Are they emotionally healthy?**
Does this person desperately "need" you, seem almost driven to be with you, or are they healthy without you? Do they fall apart if they're not in a relationship? Are they an "oak tree" or a "clinging vine"? Do they need "fixing"?

❏ **Are they good at listening?**
Can they listen without arguing back? Do they love to just talk with you, or does it always seem strained? Is it important to them to remember what you say? Do they feel the need to "fix" you?

Now that you've looked closely at the person you're dating, I'll ask the question again. Does this person have those character traits or not? Can you live with that person happily and *intelligently* for the rest of your life? How would your parents and close friends evaluate him or her? Don't let anyone tell you that the opinions of others don't matter, 'cause they do.

Most, But Not All?

Could you have a successful marriage with a person who has *most* of the items on that list, but not all? Well, let's find out. Pick any one of the items listed above. It doesn't matter which one. Now, try to envision a long-lasting, healthy, successful relationship *without the one trait that you picked*. Would it work? Not a chance!! Could you have a successful marriage with someone who is kind, loving, committed, a good communicator, forgiving, etc., but feels called to be a missionary in Africa when you want to work on Wall Street? No, because you don't have the same common goals and life direction. Or maybe they have everything but the ability to admit when they are wrong. Can it work? The answer is still no.

Stages of a Relationship

How can you know in advance if a person has the qualities on the list? Or *can* you know? The answer is yes, but knowing is a process that requires three things: time, honesty, and eyes to see. Let me explain.

Almost all relationships go through stages, and the process of going through those stages is really important. It's the only way you can see if each of you has the kind of character I just described. I first heard about this years ago when two marriage counselors gave a class on relationships. It helped me so much that I never forgot it, so I'm passing it on to you.

I know you're probably thinking, "Oh great, he's gonna tell me I'm in some *stage* now!" I used to hate it when my parents would say that. "Thanks mom, I feel soooo much better! Now I know it's a *stage* that's making me feel like my parents are stupid, my brother is a jerk, school stinks, my car won't start, and the teacher doesn't understand me. Everyone will be so pleased to hear that I'm not an idiot after all—I'm just in a STAGE!" No, it probably doesn't help knowing you're in a stage, unless, of course, you could be shown when it started, why it started, where you are now, and when it's gonna be over! So bear with me.

Every stage your relationship goes through reveals something important about you or the person you're seeing. What's really sad is most relationships don't make it out of the first couple of stages and into the good stuff, 'cause they can't figure out what's happening to them. They just hit a wall, blow up, and quit. (Remember the thing about pain? Here it is again.) I think a lot of the bad stuff that happens between couples could be avoided if they knew in advance a little of what was probably going to happen. So here's an outline of what usually does happen in most relationships, and why.

Stage 1. The Honeymoon

Honeymoon

Boy meets girl. Boy and girl "fall in love." Passion builds and they just know they will be together forever. Love is such sweet bliss. They would *never* think of arguing because, "We're in LOVE!" It's exciting and fun. They begin to think, "Heck, this relationship stuff is easy." Why? 'Cause nothing ever seems to really go wrong during this time. It feels like "heaven." You might see them stand staring into each other's eyes for hours in the school hallway. They can kiss till their lips bleed. They just *know* "it was meant to be." It's forever. (Actually, it's kinda embarrassing to watch, but you know you've probably looked the same way yourself a time or two. You can't really blame them. After all, "they're in love.")

But here's what's really happening. When two people start dating they tend to put on their best "front" for the other person to see. After all, neither person wants the other to *really* know what they're like, because if they *really* knew, they might not like it. For instance, here's a scary thought. What would it be like if, even before they went on their first date, each of them knew as much about the other person as their parents knew about them? Do you think they would still be interested in dating? Hmmmmmmm? So most of us hide in one way or another. That's probably OK . . . at first, 'cause it's important for the other person to see the good things about us; that we can be nice, look good, and act right. Good for us! But at some point reality sets in. The real "US" emerges with all the flaws and problems, and for the first time the other person is confronted with the truth. And again, that's OK! That's normal. But the more desperately we try to hide our flaws, the more difficult the next step is going to be. It's one thing to have flaws; we all do. It's quite another thing to try to hide them forever. Eventually the mask starts to crack.

It happens like this. Let's say our "honeymoon" couple is at his house watching a baseball game, and she gets up to go to the bathroom. As she's walking down the hall the guy yells at her, "Hey, as long as you're up, get me a Pepsi." She stops, turns around, puts her hands on her hips, and spits back, "What do you think I am, your servant? Get the dang Pepsi yourself!" Suddenly they both realize, "THE HONEYMOON'S OVER!"

Or let's say the guy, at a real romantic moment, leans over and
. . . belches in her ear! Or during dinner at a really great restaurant
she does a "fluffy." (When guys do it, it's a fart. When girls do it,
it's a fluffy. Go figure!) At this point both are feeling like this isn't
quite what they had in mind at the beginning of their relationship.
It's not supposed to be like this! It used to be perfect. What happened? I'll tell you what happened! They just moved into the next
stage of their relationship.

Stage 2. Disillusionment (or Reality)

Disillusionment

Honeymoon

Dis-illusionment. The word "illusion" means something that
deceives you by holding up a false impression. The Honeymoon
stage is an illusion because you keep part of yourself from the other
person. *Disillusionment* is what happens when the other person
recognizes the incomplete picture and starts to see the real you.
And that can be very scary. We all want to hide the bad side of
ourselves—that's understandable. But if a relationship is going to
last, it has to be based on what's true, not a propped-up image.

So at this point you've discovered that the relationship isn't
perfect; it's not what you thought it was. You feel let down and
betrayed, somehow. The magic (the illusion of that person being
perfect) has been taken away and has been replaced by a bunch of
huge questions that have no easy answers. You start wondering if
what you see is all there is to this person. You catch yourself saying things like, "Is *that* all he thinks about?" or "Is she *always* that
scatterbrained?" Everybody else's relationships seem to be going
better than yours, and though you still have feelings for the person,
those feelings aren't quite what they used to be. This is also the

time when you start apologizing for the other person's behavior. "Oh, don't worry. He's not always like that. He just lost his game yesterday, and. . . ." Or, "She's a little grouchy today. She's on her period, and. . . ." (Guys . . . don't even go there!)

Neither of you understands what's going on. You're not sure you can keep this up much longer. You start making demands on the other person, assuming *they* are the problem, not you. Each believes the only way things will get back to normal is if the other person quits being such a weenie. After all, it certainly couldn't be *your* fault, now could it? Then, believe it or not, it gets worse. You move into the next stage . . . the Misery stage.

Stage 3. Misery

Misery

Disillusionment

Honeymoon

Don't ya just love it? It actually gets worse! Some of you have watched your parents go through this stage, and when you go through it, it's hard! Really hard! And very painful. The Misery stage is a selfish stage. You tend to be unhappy and lonely, and you feel totally deprived. You feel unheard, uncared for, and completely misunderstood. Sometimes you feel like screaming, "Somebody owes me! Somebody's gonna pay! I'm right, you're wrong! YOU need to change, not me." Again, it seems like everybody else's relationship is fine, but yours isn't. "How come everyone else is happy? No one else treats their girlfriend like you treat me! *Don't you understand your job is to make me happy?*" It feels like this stage will never end; that your life is ruined. . . . So what's the use? You think it's over.

But here's where a very interesting thing begins to happen. Since each person has no hope that the other person will ever change, they tend to take one of two roads:

1. They fall in a pile and give up on life. Their only hope is that someone will rescue them, or that the person they have been with will one day come to their senses, realize what a terrible mistake they have made, and come running back all repentant and humble.

OR . . .

2. They give up on the hope of being rescued or that the other person will ever change. They realize that if they are ever going to be happy again, it will be because *they* have taken responsibility for changing *themselves* and not their partner. They are through waiting. They are through being rescued!

If they choose the first (waiting to be rescued), they stop growing and will live in misery for the duration of the relationship (and sometimes for life). But if they choose the second alternative, they will find themselves flung into the fourth stage.

Stage 4. Awakening

Awakening
Misery
Disillusionment
Honeymoon

It's almost like the person has been in a deep sleep, and is suddenly awake for the first time, realizing all the possibilities that await them. They understand there are things in their life that need to change, and that no one else is responsible for making those changes but themselves. Being rescued wouldn't change anything. They see that no one else is responsible for making them happy. Only they can do that. They know they aren't perfect and

neither is the other person, and that's OK! They start to examine their own motives and actions, and start to accept and love themselves for who they *actually* are, not what people *think* they are, or what people *want* them to be. They begin to make actual changes in their life and begin to feel alive, as if for the first time. Life takes on direction, meaning, and freshness. Loving feelings begin to surface again. The need for fighting becomes less intense; they become more accepting and less selfish. They find that real needs, not just surface needs, are being met, and that they aren't dependent on the other person's good mood for their own happiness. All of which produces the fifth and final stage, which I call Being One, or True Love.

Stage 5. True Love (or Being One)

True Love

Awakening

Misery

Disillusionment

Honeymoon

When both people decide to move on, going from the selfish stages to a real awakening, it brings tremendous change. For the first time they begin to comprehend what real love is: a daily choice for the good of the other person and for themselves. This goes way past feelings. Being One is when two people think, act, and live their lives together. I don't mean *literally* living together, 'cause you can be dating and still experience Being One (not in a sexual way). But their lives are lived out together. They are not perfect and they know it. In fact they may even *enjoy* the fact that they aren't perfect. They are just two people who live sacrificially for one another, and their relationship is actually becoming more important than each of the two separate individuals in the relationship.

Yes, feelings have begun to come back again, too, but the two of them now know that feelings change from day to day. Feelings of love are to be deeply enjoyed but they can't be captured, and lack of feelings is no longer something to be feared. Lack of feelings may mean nothing at all. The two of them are now more committed to life than to feelings, and it's that commitment—that unconditional commitment—which brings them back to the place they originally started—the original stage they enjoyed so much—THE HONEYMOON! Is love blind? No it's not! Love is not blind. It's wide awake: looking, observing, improving, caring, growing.

We've Arrived! (or Not)

At this point some people make the mistake of thinking they have somehow ARRIVED!!! "At last we are THERE! Life is great; we are HOME once again!" Wellll . . . not quite. Because what happens next should come as no surprise. That's right. Don't you remember what comes after the honeymoon? Disillusionment . . . then misery, then. . . . But what makes it easier this time is the fact that now you can see it coming. It's like "Waaaaiiit a minute!!! I've been here before. I know where this is going. . . ." And now instead of impatience, there's patience. Instead of accusation, there's communication. Instead of pain, there is love and forgiveness. If you choose rightly, the relationship will only get better and better. If you choose selfishly, you'll get pain, hurt, and ultimately the death of the relationship.

A long time ago I was involved in the interview process for couples who were planning to marry soon. They would come in for their first session all starry-eyed and I would ask them right off, "Do you really love each other?" "Oh yes!" they'd say. "Well, that's great. That's great. Ah . . . just a question here . . . when you had your last argument, how did that go?" And almost every time the couple would say, "Oh we never argue . . . we're in love!" (Honeymoon!) Amazing! So you know what I would try to do? For the next several sessions I would do everything I could to get them to fight! I wanted to see how they would act in an argument. Would they be HONEST? Would they ADMIT WRONG when

they knew they were? Could they FORGIVE and move on in their relationship? Would they be WILLING TO CHANGE? Were they still in the Honeymoon stage, or was there a maturity in their relationship? It wasn't for *my* sake we were meeting, it was for theirs. *They* were the ones who needed to realize where they were and what was coming.

Remember when I said ALL relationships go through those stages? Let me give you a couple of examples.

Puppy Love

I have a dog. She's very cool. When my wife first found her and brought her home, we all went crazy. She was so cute. You could hold her cupped in both your hands. Such cool little ears. . . . (HONEYMOON.) Then one day, to my utter amazement (and after all I had done for this dog), she peed on my carpet. I yelled, "Hey, wait a minute! You're cute, but what's this peeing stuff??!!" (DISILLUSIONMENT.) Well, next thing I knew, that @#$%^&* dog POOPED on my carpet. And she chewed up a good pair of shoes. (MISERY.) I was ready to kill that animal. I wanted to pluck those cute little eyes right out of her cute little head!!!!! (They say only a guy thinks punting a small dog is funny.) But then it dawned on me. She didn't know the difference between the back yard and my living room rug. It wasn't really her fault. I was demanding something she really didn't understand. So off to obedience school, where *the human learns far more than the dog*. At obedience school they tell you it's not really the *dog's* fault 'cause the dog doesn't really know what's wrong. So who do they train? They train YOU—the master. (AWAKENING.) Now the dog loves me and I, as much as I might not want to admit it, love her. (GENUINE LOVE.) In fact, I loved her so much WE GOT A SECOND DOG! (HONEYMOON . . . *again!*)

My Dad's Better . . .

Or how about this example? Remember when you were a little kid and you talked about your dad? "My dad can beat up your

dad!" (Honeymoon.) Then when you got into junior high it was "My dad's a little strange." (Disillusionment.) In high school, "My dad's an idiot!" (Misery.) You're gonna have to trust me when I say that later on, after college is over and you are on your own, you'll say, "Ya know, my dad's a lot smarter than I thought!" (Awakening.) You can't see it now, but someday you will.

High School Relationships

Let's get personal for a second. How long would you say the average high school relationship lasts? One week? A month? Six months? When I ask most kids, they'll usually tell me about a month and a half. At first I didn't believe them, but that really is what most kids will say. OK, so at what *stage* would you say the average relationship in high school ends? Would you say most relationships end in the Honeymoon stage? Heck no! *They're in love!* No, most high school relationships break up during the Disillusionment or Misery stage.

But if a high school couple decides they are going to have sex, at what stage do you think they will probably start? In the Misery stage? I DON'T THINK SO! I can just hear it, "What a jerk! You miserable @#$%^&*! Hey, wanna have sex?" People don't do that! If they're going to start having sex it'll be during the Honeymoon stage because of all the feelings and excitement. "After all," they will say, "We're in love!" But that's where two people know the least about each other. That's when they are most fooled into believing they have the perfect relationship. But it's also the stage where the other person tends to hide their true self. Can you spell DISASTER?

Sex has become one of the main ways people hide from each other. We think it's the opposite. In the Honeymoon stage we think that sex brings us closer together, but it doesn't. It makes you *feel* close and "in love," but it is actually keeping you apart. Real communication takes place less and less because most of your time is spent thinking about sex (when and where) and not about the relationship. How many times have I heard kids say, "All we did is have sex. We may not have had time to communicate, but boy, we

always had time for sex." And just how long did the relationship last after that? You guessed it. One and a half months . . . or less.

Go the Distance

But there's one more question . . . at what stage will a high school couple find out if the person they are dating has the character qualities of being honest, admitting wrong, forgiving, and being able to change? Will they find out if the other person can admit they are wrong during the Honeymoon stage? NO, 'cause there isn't anything wrong in that stage. They're "in love!" Will they find out if the other person can change during the Misery stage? No, because in the Misery stage it's always the *other* person's fault. They figure, "Why change if it's not my fault?" A couple will find out if those qualities are present only when they have gone through *all* the stages together. And not just once, but over and over again. And it won't work if just one of the two goes through the stages. It's got to be both of them together.

If the average high school relationship lasts only one and a half months, and most end in the Disillusionment or Misery stage (where it's most difficult to understand yourself , let alone the other person), then most couples won't reach the last stages of development. *But that's where they would really find out the truth about their character.* If they don't go through all the stages they will never grow up in their relationship. So they start having sex during the Honeymoon stage, they end their relationship during the Disillusionment stage, but they never really get to know who the other person is, or see their real potential and true character until it's too late.

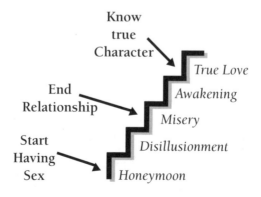

If You Don't Know 'Em, Don't Date 'Em!

Most of us date people we have known for a while, mostly because it's safer that way. But once in a while we find ourselves in a situation where we throw all our inhibitions out the window, throw caution to the wind, and go out with someone we know almost nothing about. And, just like in the movies, sometimes it works. Most of time it doesn't. But when you're in high school it's always smartest to date people you know something about. If you know a guy wants to take you out, try to find out what his reputation is. Find out how he treated the last girl that he dated. I mean, hey, if she got pregnant and then he dumped her, you've got a pretty good idea this is not going to be what you'd call a "casual dating opportunity!" Or if all of a girl's past boyfriends seem to be ticked at her, you can pretty much count on her not being all that kind and gentle a person. So don't go out with them, and don't be fooled. If they treated a person badly before, they can (and probably will) do it again.

Giving Your Heart Away . . .

What do people mean when they say they gave their heart to someone? They obviously aren't talking about the bloody, pulsing thing in their chest. So what *do* they mean?

Most people might not say it this way, but I think what they really mean is they gave the "real them" to the other person, and they were holding nothing back. Your "heart" is the REAL YOU. It's what's at the center, the core, the naked truth about you. It's the part most people never really see or know. It's you when you are most vulnerable.

Even though we mostly think of sex as something bodies do, sex is actually a part of what we call "the HEART." It reveals the deepest part of who we are. That's why we feel totally betrayed if our partner has an affair, or takes our virginity only to tromp on it as they walk out the door. A woman, for instance, doesn't feel that it's her *body* as much as it's HER that's been betrayed. The REAL HER! That's what I call the HEART.

Yes, you can lose your heart (or at least have it damaged) by way of your body (through sex), but you can also have your heart damaged by way of your mind. We all know people who have been devastated just because of the things that were said to them by their families. "You fat pig!" "You're an idiot!" "You'll never amount to anything!" Those things can go so deep, and cause so much damage, that a person's "heart" may never recover. We are all so desperately in need of being loved unconditionally by another human being that sometimes we will give our hearts to total strangers, hoping they can be trusted . . . only to find out they can't.

. . . Too Soon

Opening your heart too soon, and having it stomped on, makes you react as if you burned your hand on a hot stove. Every new relationship finds you overly sensitive and suspicious, afraid of making the same mistake again, withdrawing until finally you can't trust anyone, ever again. Now it's the FEAR of being hurt that keeps you from trying again. It's not the pain itself, it's the FEAR of the pain.

Learning to Trust

So how can you learn to trust a person? Answer . . . one small step at a time! First, get to know them and learn to trust them by telling them things about your life in the present. Things that most people know. Safe things. Little things. As time goes on let them see the way you think and what you believe in. Let them see what you feel about love, life, family, and the future. But when you begin to share your pain, hurt, feelings, and struggles, that's when things go to the heart, and that's when you become vulnerable. That's the kind of information someone could use against you by telling the wrong people. Which means you must open yourself up slowly. Very slowly! Take your time. DON'T GIVE YOUR HEART AWAY TOO SOON or things will backfire. You'll yank your heart back in pain and become overly sensitive and suspicious in all your relationships.

Ending Relationships

There are times in almost everyone's life when you've been in a close relationship, but you know you can't go any further. You care a lot about the person you're dating, but you know they aren't the one to go through life with. You may have found that your heart just doesn't "sing" anymore, even though you've tried. Maybe you aren't compatible in some area or you're simply headed in two different directions in life. You've discovered the person doesn't have the same values you do, and they don't seem able to encourage you to grow as a person anymore; somehow your relationship has become stagnant.

Because you've never made the commitment, "Till death do us part," you may be coming to the conclusion that it's time to end the relationship, and that's OK. Don't feel like you have to apologize for feeling the way you do. It's not wrong . . . on anyone's part. It's important to find out those things now and not later. By definition, dating is the evaluation process for making a bigger, lifelong commitment. It doesn't require the same commitment as marriage, but you still have to be responsible, respectful, honest, and kind toward the other person.

Terms: Dumping/Breaking up

Before I talk about ending a relationship, first let me say a bit about terminology. Sometimes the words you use can say far more than what you mean. For instance, think about the words people use to describe ending a relationship: *dumping, breaking up*. Now think about what those words *really* mean, especially to the other person.

1. Dumping: To toss out or throw away. The act of getting rid of something worthless, something you don't want anymore.
2. Breaking up: To tear apart, smash or bash into itty-bitty little pieces.

Neither one of those terms has much to do with being respectful, honest, or kind. So for crying out loud, don't use them! If you know

you need to end the relationship, then do THAT . . . end it, but don't "dump" them. Just end it. "Dumping" someone makes it sound like, "I'm mad as!@#$%^&*, and I ain't gonna take it no more!" It makes the other person look like they're a cigarette butt being tossed out. It says you never want anything to do with them, ever again. EVER! And if that's really the case, it sounds to me like maybe you gave your heart away way too soon. If you feel you got taken advantage of, and now you're sorry you let that happen, understand that that's *your* fault, not theirs. Don't take it out on them.

When to End a Relationship

OK, so when and how do you end a relationship? It can be a mistake to spend a lot of time with someone who really doesn't "fit" with you, so how do you know when it's time to end it?

- When time together seems pointless, and lacks meaning and direction.
- When arguing seems to dominate your conversations.
- When your relationship is based on need.
- When sports or activities become consistently more important than the relationship.
- When your friends recognize the fact that you don't seem happy anymore.
- When the other person is constantly hurting you.
- When they have cheated on you.
- When they don't remember the little things anymore.
- When you are mentally, sexually, or physically being abused.
- When they keep pushing for sex.
- When you find they are addicted to drugs, drinking, or sex.
- When you find yourself constantly apologizing for *their* behavior.

If You Are the One Ending It

If you are the one ending the relationship, there are a few things to be aware of before you end it.

- Be aware of how you would feel if that person was "breaking up" with you. Put yourself in their shoes.
- Set a time and place to get together. Never end a relationship over the phone, unless it's an abusive relationship. Talk to them in a public place, not at your house or theirs, and never in a car or bedroom. Have your own transportation so you can leave on your own.
- Keep the conversation short, because they may try to talk you out of it or make you feel guilty.
- Look them in the eye and try not to cry. But just in case, have Kleenex with you. (Good luck!)
- Be honest, and go straight to the point. Make ending the relationship the focal point of your conversation.
- Own up to your own failures without pointing out theirs. Remember, this is about you moving on, not about listing everything that went wrong.
- Let them know you've had great times together, that you'll never forget them, and that you'll always have great memories.
- Tell them you want the best for them and for yourself, and that staying together will not accomplish that.
- Be clear about what your expectations are for the future (how you will act when you see each other at school, calling each other on the phone, etc.).
- Decide what you'll say to people who ask what's going on. Promise to never bad-mouth them.
- Thank them for the time you've had together.
- Allow them time to respond to what you have said, but don't feel obligated to explain all your reasons for the breakup. This is not a time for debate or argument.
- Do not hug or kiss afterward. It gives a mixed message of hope for the future.

Ending the Relationship: How to Say It

Let me give you an example of what you might actually say if you're ending a relationship with someone.

Chris, I've asked you here today because I need to tell you something. I've been thinking about this for quite a while, and I know this probably isn't going to be a surprise to you either, but I have come to the conclusion that even though I care a lot about you, I know that we need to end our relationship. I feel like we've both allowed other things to take priority over our relationship (sports, drama, parties, etc.), but I need more than that, and I know you can't give it. I want the best for you, too, and I know being together won't give you that. We've had some great times together, and I have a lot of great memories. I will never forget you.

I know it's going to be hard seeing you at school because I still have feelings for you, so I just want to say I won't ignore you when I see you, but I also know I can't spend time with you. For the same reason, I need to ask you, please don't call me on the phone. That will only make it harder on us both.

When people ask me what has happened, the only thing I will tell them is that we have decided to end our relationship; that we are no longer going out, but nothing more. I refuse to say anything bad about you or what's happened between us. I care about you too much to do that.

I want to thank you for all we've experienced together. Thank you for giving me what you could. I will never forget you.

I know I've just dumped a lot on you at once . . . are you OK?

(Allow them time to talk)

Thanks for listening. I've got to go. I've got my own ride. I'll see you at school tomorrow.

Getting Over a Guy/Girl

You can almost count on the fact that sometime in your life you will have to end a relationship with someone you really like, and it can be devastating. It can be almost like a divorce, but trust

me, you will survive. So once you actually end a relationship, how do you "get over" the person?

Let me make a suggestion. Don't TRY! That's right, don't try to get over them! Why should you? If that person was good to you, you probably have great memories of your time together. Why would you want to throw those memories away? I have great memories of being with some of my old girlfriends. I enjoy looking back on my high school days and remembering all the fun we had together. I still see some of them around town, and we still laugh about it all.

But if you have just ended a relationship with a person and you need to get on with your life, what do you do? First, "getting over" them does not mean forgetting all about them. *That can't be done.* Your brain doesn't work that way. The real objective here is to *move on with your life* and stop obsessing about them. What's cool about your brain is that it can't think about two things at the same time. Let me give you an example. OK . . . I want you to do these two things at the same time. Ready?

1. Solve $\dfrac{92 \times 73}{14}$ =?

2. Play ping-pong

Go! . . . How are you doing? Yeah, right! It can't be done. At least it can't be done well. And that's the point. If you are trying to get over a person, you can't do it by thinking about them all the time. If you keep pictures of a guy on your wall next to the single rose he gave you, tied to the tickets from the prom . . . yadda, yadda, yadda . . . it won't work. You will never quit thinking about him. You'll never "get over" him. So go put those things away. Don't *throw* them away, just put them out of your sight . . . for now.

Move On

Move on by becoming involved again in sports, or other activities, at school, church, or clubs. The more idle time you have, the

more you will tend to mentally wander back to the person you are trying leave behind.

You might want to ask someone else out for this next weekend, or spend time with a group of your friends. Be aware though, when you go out again you will instinctively be comparing the new date to the old, and there you are again, thinking about your past boyfriend or girlfriend. This is especially true if *they* ended the relationship with *you*, not the other way around.

There's something else you might want to consider, too. Ask yourself, "Do I kinda . . . well . . . do I kinda *like* the painful feelings?" Now wait . . . don't go so fast here. Think about it. The pain you experience when you end a relationship with somebody has that *melancholy* feel to it. If you're really honest . . . you may have to admit you kinda *like* that feeling, and you might not really *want* to get over it, 'cause *then* what would you do? Then you'd have nothing. No one would feel bad for you any more. So you hold on to the pain, nursing it along as if that will somehow feed your needy soul. People will keep feeling sorry for you, and you can justify your behavior and emotions and never have to change. But what a terrible way to have to live! Don't do it. Move on!

Section Three
SEX

Chapter 6. Sex
(Oh boy! The chapter most guys turn to first!)

Who's Getting It Most?

So let's talk about sex. All right!!! Whenever someone starts talking about the subject of sex, I kinda have this question in the back of my mind: Of all the people who are "doing it" I wonder who has the best (or most) sex? Whoever it is, well, that's what I want!

Now I always thought if you're talkin' wild sex, or fun sex, or most often, I'd have bet on college students. I mean they look like they probably have the best chance at it, since they're away from home and no one can tell them what they can or can't do. So, it's probably them. But then I read a study that said married couples have sex *five times more often* than college students do! Whooaa! OK, then maybe it's high school seniors. You sure hear all the stories and see the movies about high school so . . . well, maybe. Then I found out that in high school everyone *thinks* that everybody *else* is doing it. (But you know *you're* not, at least not like what you see in those movies, you're not.) The truth is that

the majority of kids who have ever been sexually active in high school actually had only one or two real sexual encounters. A lot of times they explain, "It just sorta happened," and that was the first and last time they did it. Or maybe they went for it a few times, but then either broke up or just never did it again. Here's something I bet you didn't know. "Half of sexually experienced young women wait almost 18 months between the time they first have intercourse and the time they have a second sexual partner; for another 25 percent, the gap is almost two years."[1] I know everyone thinks their friends are all hookin' up like crazy, but it's not as common as you think.

OK, so who else could be having the most sex? You might be thinking, "If it's not high school seniors, it's not college students, and it's certainly not me . . . Nooooo, it can't be my parents! Not a chance!" When I was in high school I was pretty sure that once my parents had me, they never did it again until my brother was conceived. (And since he's five years younger than me they must have screwed *that* up, too!) (If my brother is reading this . . . just kidding.) Anyway, I always figured sex probably gets boring once you're married 'cause it's the same person over and over again. *Wrong!*

Best Sex Comes in Marriage

Most of the rest of this book is about planning for, and building, the best relationship and the best sex life you could ever possibly have, and that, by the way, will be with your future marriage partner. Best relationships (marriage) and best sex—those two things absolutely go together. You can't separate them, and here's why.

Let's say you've been married to someone for five years. And it's someone you really love by *my* definition of love (choosing the highest good for the other person). And let's say the average married couple makes love somewhere around two times per week. Since you've been married for five years, that figures out to be about 650 times! (Not counting your honeymoon 'cause that would add

---

[1] *Sex and America's Teenagers* (New York: The Alan Guttmacher Institute, 1994), p. 24.

another 5,000 times or so.) So here's a question. After five years of being married (650 times), do you think you'll pretty much know what your partner likes when it comes to sex? I mean will you know *where* they like to make love (kitchen floor, garage, picnic table . . .), *where* they like to be touched (no comment), *what* they like you to wear, or not wear (socks, ski mask)? In other words, will you know what really turns them on by now? YEAH!!! Why? 'Cause you've got an unbelievable amount of experience with the *same person over and over again,* and you've learned to "read" them like a book. Of course, you won't know *everything* by then, but you'll know *a lot* of it. On the other hand, will you pretty much know what they *don't* like? (You're gonna try some things when you're first married that, afterwards, will make you ask, "Good grief, what were we thinkin'?" You know, things like doing it while swinging from the kitchen light fixture, and stuff.) Anyway, after 650 times, do you think you'll both know how to sexually fulfill each other's dreams? *OOOhhhhh, yeeaaaahhh!* And because you each *want* to please each other so much (very best, highest good) are you seriously going to tell me sex is gonna get old? Not a chance!

Sex Gets Better and Better!

In marriage sex gets better and better. What single people don't understand is that after a few years of being married, sex is no longer the *center of the relationship* like it was at first. It's still totally important (Man, I think about it all the time . . . !), but it isn't that constant drive—mostly because other things in the relationship have become more important. (Eating comes to mind!) After a while you learn not to get all bummed out 'cause you can't "do it" for the fifth time, in three hours, while hanging from the hall closet rod. The more years of sex you get under your belt (Ha, ha . . . Get it? Sex under . . . Anyway . . .), the more you know about your partner, and the more you know how to please them.

A one-night-stand with someone you don't even know isn't gonna be anywhere close to the best sex. Movies say it is, but it's not! So I want to ask an important question—one you're gonna

have to think about for a while. *Could a couple of one-night stands be the very thing that destroys what could have been the best sex ever?* The answer is a definite YES! More on that in a minute.

If Sex Is So Fun, Why Wait?

Look, sex is fun, and always will be. That's why people do it! Obviously rape or forced sex are a totally different thing, but sex between two willing people is just unbelievable. (And whether you believe it or not, your parents *ARE* still doing it . . .) So I want to go on record here as saying sex is a good thing, and it's an extremely important thing . . . and darn fun!!!! Now it seems pretty obvious what your next question will be. "Well, if married sex is so great, then ALL sex should be great. Why give up what's great NOW for something that's supposed to be great LATER, but is so stinkin' far away and unknown? Besides, what if I marry some dipstick who's not as good at sex as the person I've got now? Or what if I *never* get married, or die, and never get to have sex? And even if it's not the *best* sex, the worst day of sex is better than the best day of anything else, right? So why wait?"

Those are all good questions, but hey, we've got to get out of the shallow end of the pool and look a little deeper here. Let me set the stage for the next few chapters about sex and relationships.

Which Is Greater, 50 or 5,200? (Duh!)

Just for the fun of it, let's say you're gonna be in high school for five years, starting as a freshman. (I'm giving you an extra year in case you screw it up, OK?) And let's say the average person in high school does "the deed" five times in those five years. Oh yeah, some people are like rabbits, humpin' everything that moves. But I'm talkin' averages here. Or if you think it's more than that . . . let's be generous . . . let's say the average sexually active student does it 50 times while in high school. But just so you know, I'm being *really* generous! (A little over 50 percent of all high school students from ninth to 12th grades have never had any sex at all. Another 13.6 percent have had sex, but are currently abstinent. That leaves 36.3 percent that are currently sexually active and 63.6 percent that have never had sex or are currently sexually abstinent.

And 35.1 percent will graduate as virgins.[2]) So let's say, *generously speaking,*

Five years of high school = 50 times of sex.

But now let's also say you're gonna get married someday, and, just like your grandparents, you're gonna be married for 50 years. Don't laugh. A lot of grandparents have been married that long, and if they can do it, so can you! (By the way, staying married to someone for 40 or 50 years . . . now *THAT'S what it means to go all the way!* When a guy says, "Hey, I went all the way with this girl last night," no, he didn't. He hardly even got started!) So the deal is, you could be happily married to someone for 50 years and could be making love the whole time! Well, not the *whole* time. You gotta come up for air . . . you know what I mean. You could be married for years to someone you really love, and who really loves you, and you could be enjoying a sexual relationship the whole time. Like I said before, the average married couple does it around twice a week. (*The Case for Marriage* reports a study that found "43 percent of the married men reported that they had sex at least twice a week."[3] Overall it's less than twice per week, but you're probably thinkin', "If it was me I'd be doin' it *at least* that much." Right?) OK, so after 50 years of being married and doing it twice a week, do you know how many times you've made love? (Are you ready for this?) About 5,200 times!!!! Fifty years of marriage equals 5,200 times of sex.

Now if you were forced to choose one of these two options, which one would you choose? You can't have both; you *have* to choose one or the other.

Five-year high school plan = 50 (or fewer) times of sex
OR
50-year marriage plan = at *least* 5,200 times of sex

---

[2] "Youth Risk Behavior Surveillance," *Morbidity and Mortality Weekly Report,* CDC, Vol. 49, No. SS-5, June 9, 2000.
[3] Robert T. Michael, John H. Gagnon, Edward O. Laumann, Gina Kolata, *Sex in America* (New York: Time Warner, 1995), p. 114.

I know you're thinking, "But why do I have to pick just one? Why can't I have both?" Well, you *might* be able to, but then again *you might not*. Here's why.

What's It Gonna Cost?

Let's say you picked the five-year plan; the "get-it-when-you-can-in-high-school" option. But let's also say that during those five years you did something to your body, or your mind, or both, that messed you up so badly that when you finally *did* get married, you had already destroyed 50 years of making love to the person you love the most. You just lost 50 years of great sex.

Which option would you choose now? That seems like an easy call. But look at how many people are choosing the five-year plan and messing up their future love life! And they don't even know they're doing it. So the question comes down to this: Is fooling around in high school, for as few as five to 50 times, worth the risk of destroying your future marriage (and other people's marriages), and 50 years of great sex (5,200 times)?

Can that happen? Read on.

Dear Brad,

At 13 I became sexually active thinking sex was supposed to be part of relationships. Now I'm a 16-year-old sophomore who is 5 months pregnant wishing my world was different. I believe sex does ruin relationships. The father of my child and I were together almost 7 months and I feel as though I don't even know him. Using your definition of love I loved him, but sex became our whole relationship and look where I am now. Pregnant, alone, and as I look at it, I've already messed up my future marriage. I hope you talk to kids as early as 12 or 13, to prevent these teen pregnancies and heartaches.

Mary

Dear Brad,

I really enjoyed your talk. What you said about everyone should wait for the person he/she is going to be with for the rest of their life is true. But I didn't. I first had sex at age 13. I was at the end of 7th grade. I had known him since 6th grade. We were going out for only a couple of weeks when one day, on a day we got an early dismissal, it happened. It wasn't even what I expected, it was boring and non-caring. I thought it was gonna be so special. When I look back, it was the crowd I was hanging out with. All them were having sex and it seemed like I was the only virgin. Oh yeah, we broke up about a week after it happened. Some people don't think the crowd they are with will influence them, but take it from me it definitely happens. I just wanted to see what it was like that's all. I wasn't a slut before that, but after I was called that, and it still haunts me. My boyfriend now of 13 months jokes with me about doing it at 13 years old. It gets to me bad though. What saddens me the most is that when I have children, they might ask me when my first time was. I can't bear to tell them. I just want everyone to know that you should wait. Sex isn't worth getting hurt over and you do get hurt emotionally. Also, when you get in a relationship later on you have to tell your partner everyone you have been with. It's really hard to go through with. If I could go back in time I would in an instant and change so many things. I came to a point where I hated myself for it. I try and advise some of my friends now who are still virgins to wait, wait, wait! It's the smartest thing to do.

Unsigned

Dear Brad,

My questions are about sex. I still feel it's dirty and wrong. But I like it and enjoy it. I feel like I would still feel this way even after I am married.

Thank you.

Sharon

Dear Brad

I've done some things that I am terribly ashamed about. I lay awake nights wishing I had just said no, crying myself to sleep.

Unsigned

When people read letters or stories like the ones above they automatically think, "Hey, all that stuff will never happen to me." But *everybody* says that. Just to show you that it can happen, two days ago—*just two days ago*—I opened the newspaper and there, center page, was a photo of a guy I had known for years, but hadn't seen for a while. He was a good-lookin' guy, quite a bit younger than me, and he had just died . . . of AIDS. He got it in high school and didn't find out until years later. Do you think that as he was dying he wished he'd never been sexually active in high school? Do you think he would give up what he was doing *then* to have what I have *now*? You bet he would! Not only did he give up his *sex* life—he gave up his *entire* life.

When Will You Be Ready for Sex?

How will you know when you're ready for sex? I want to answer that by telling you about a book called *How to Be Popular with Boys,* given to me by a high school girl. I'd never read a girls' book before so I figured this was gonna be fun. One of the chapters was about how to know if you're ready for sex, and the author gave this advice:

Wait until you're involved in a loving, genuine relationship with a boy. How can you tell if you are or not? Here are some distinguishing characteristics to guide you. You have a genuine relationship when:

1. You've made a commitment to see only each other.
2. You talk and try to understand each other's thoughts, feelings, likes and dislikes, fears and hopes, joys and sorrows, moods, needs, etc.

3. You love each other for your faults as well as strengths.
4. You feel warmth and affection as well as desire for each other, and you express it through kissing, holding hands, teasing, hugging, laughing, etc.
5. You can share an ordinary day's activities: studying, eating, watching TV, raking leaves, running errands, etc.
6. You can express anger, disappointment; you can cry in front of this person and find comfort.
7. You miss each other when you're separated.
8. You consider yourselves best friends.
9. You can make up after a falling-out.
10. You trust his love for you and it makes you feel secure, safe, and happy. [4]

Now at first glance, all that sounded pretty right-on and all, but the more I looked at that list, the more I—well, the more I thought about my dog! See, the deal is I really like my dog. She's a beagle. Big, brown eyes; long, soft ears; loves to play. She's really cute. (Dumber'n a box of rocks, but she does love to play.) As I read that list of "Ways to Know You're Ready," it dawned on me! *I could apply every one of those things to my dog!* Suddenly the whole chapter became ridiculous! As much as I love her (trust me here), I have no desire to "do it" with my dog. But if the author of that book is right, then I guess I would be ready! Let's look at that list again. You think about your boyfriend or girlfriend, and I'll think about my dog. Her name is Abby. Ready?

BOOK: You've made a commitment to see only each other.
ME: I don't want anybody else's dog. I just want my own. She's cool.

BOOK: You talk and try to understand each other's thoughts, feelings, likes and dislikes, fears and hopes, joys and sorrows, moods, needs.
ME: Gee, Abby, do you have to go outside? Are you hungry?

---

[4] Stacy Rubis, *How to Be Popular with Boys* (New York: Crown Publishers Inc., 1984), p. 96.

BOOK: You love each other for your faults as well as strengths.
ME: I love my dog even though when she poops on the carpet I wanna kill her!

BOOK: You feel warmth and affection as well as desire for each other, and you express it through kissing, holding hands, teasing, hugging, laughing, etc.
ME: Man, I'll be honest here, I've kissed my dog. (Not on the lips, although she's tried to, lots of times.) I've held her while watching TV. I even shake hands with her. Does that mean I'm ready to have sex with my dog? *I don't think so!*

BOOK: You can share an ordinary day's activities: studying, eating, watching TV, raking leaves, running errands, etc.
ME: She plays in the garden or yard while I mow lawns. We go for walks together.

BOOK: You can express anger, disappointment; you can cry in front of this person and find comfort.
ME: I can yell at her for tearing up the toilet paper, but when I've had a bad day, she will come and lick my face and let me hold her.

BOOK: You miss each other when you're separated.
ME: She's the first one to greet me when I get home from a long trip. (She's also the first one to pee on my shoe.)

BOOK: You consider yourselves best friends.
ME: A man's best friend is his . . . DOG! *They're talkin' about my dog!*

BOOK: You can make up after a falling-out.
ME: Oh, I'm sorry I stepped on you. I didn't mean to hurt you.

BOOK: You trust his love for you and it makes you feel secure, safe, and happy.
ME: If my wife takes a walk around the block, who does she take with her? Abby! Why? 'Cause it makes her feel safe. (And Abby needs the exercise . . . a lot!)

So according to the writer of that book I'm ready to have sex with my dog! Well, great. I can hardly wait to get home.

Let me tell you, it goes a lot deeper than that. If that list is really the truth, not only could I say those things about my dog, I could also say them about my parents, grandparents, my next-door neighbor, or my best friend, for crying out loud! Am I gonna have sex with any of them? Give me a break!

How Will You *Really* Know You're Ready for Sex?

So how DO you know when you're ready? That's what we're gonna get into in the next few chapters, and some of the answers are gonna surprise you. Most of them will be different than anything you've heard before. I want to give you nine reasons why I think people need to wait to have sex until they're married. Or . . . let me put it another way. I want to give you nine reasons why I think people need to STOP HAVING SEX until they're married. I know you may already have had sex, so let me say a couple of things to you before we go any further.

Number 1: I'm not against sex. THANK YOU!! Do I sound *that* stupid? (Don't answer that!) Look, I'm not saying, "Don't do it." I'm actually saying . . . DO IT! . . . Once you're married . . .

Then make up for lost time!!! Yeessss!

Stay in bed for six years! I don't care. I did! (Well, not quite six years, but I gave it my best shot.) The point is, I'm not against sex. Sex isn't bad or wrong at all. It's a fantastic, powerful thing. Who doesn't want that? The question isn't, "Should I?" the question is, "When should I?"

Number 2: Because I'm saying that you ought to wait, you should be asking me if I waited. And the answer is yeah, I did. When I was in the seventh grade (and I didn't do anything before that), I promised myself that I wouldn't go to bed with a girl, fool around with her, take her clothes off . . . nothin'! . . . before I was married to her. Oh I hugged and kissed a lot but I never had sex, oral or otherwise, until I got married, and neither did my wife.

Did I think about it and struggle with it? OH, YEAH! Lots! But I waited, and I've never been sorry.

I know some of you guys are thinkin', "Man, wasn't that hard?" Yeah, it was, but I have some very close friends who went the exact opposite direction I did. If you think *my* way was hard, try theirs. They'd give anything to have what I have now, sex and all. Some of them are on their second or third marriage, and some have kids who don't want anything to do with them. Some have diseases they can't get rid of. Some are so depressed they can hardly make it through the day. Many are in counseling. A few are dead. And you think *my way* was hard? My question to you is this. Which kind of life do you hope to have? You do have a choice, you know. My way was, and still is, the easiest.

No, It's Not Too Late

But there's one more thing I want to say to you before I end this chapter. Again, this is for those of you who have already been sexually active. You're probably thinking, "Well, hey! It's too late for me, so what's the point? I'm not a virgin, so I guess it won't matter what you say." Listen, I'm writing this book for people just like you! This is a chance for you to rethink all this stuff. Your friends, or even your parents, may have told you that it's OK to do what you've been doing sexually—that it's no big deal—or that everyone else is doing it, so go ahead. But if it's no big deal, why are so many kids so screwed up when it comes to relationships, especially when it involves sex? Why are they no longer together? And why is it that when you look around your own town or school, you see some people who always seem to find happiness, but others who only find consequences? Which will *you* find?

Live for Tomorrow, Starting Today!

You're going to have to ask yourself some tough questions in the next few pages, but that's OK . . . don't back off. I'll help you find some of the answers. The key is to remember that everything you do today affects tomorrow. Everything! Are you choosing the

best, most loving thing for your future wife or husband, and for yourself? What you choose today affects their future, too, whether you like it or not. The longer you go the wrong direction in your life, the longer it takes, and harder it is to come back and go the right direction. The more *wrong* you do, the more UNdoing you will have to face.

At the end of these next few chapters, if you still say you're not going to wait, well, OK. It's your life and your decision, and I'll respect your right to choose. But somewhere down the road, when a few of those consequences start catching up with you, at least remember that there was somebody who told you the truth.

Chapter 7. Why Wait?
You've Got to Know the Whole Person

Dear Mr. Henning,

Let me tell you a short version of the last two years. I met this guy I thought he loved me and I loved him. I got pregnant in June of '95. I wanted to keep it and I thought he did to. Boy was I wrong. He paid someone to beat me up so I would lose the baby. I did. A year and a half later the guy I gave everything up to be with is now in jail for murder. Since then, it's been downhill. I still don't know how I have made it this far. You helped me in more ways than you know. Thank you very, very much.

Sue

Brad,

I have a story that I heard once and I think that you could use it in your talk. A boyfriend and girlfriend in high school decided that they wanted to live together. They were always and constantly very affectionate toward one another and both said they loved each other. A friend and counselor to them knew that it was not a good idea to live together. So he asked them to do him a favor. He challenged them to not touch each other for 10 days. No holding hands, hugging, kissing, etc. All they could

do was talk. Within two days, each person came to him and said they couldn't stand each other. The guy said, "She doesn't know one thing about baseball! She's been to every one of my games and can't tell me where first base is!" The girl's comment went like this. "He is so conceited, never talks about anything but himself!"

This story is true and I can see it in some of my friend's relationships and it's really sad. Once again, thanks for coming.

Gretchen

The Experiment

During one of my years in college I met a girl who told me about a experiment that she had been involved in. An ad in the college newspaper read something like this:

WANTED: 50 college men to participate in psychological experiment. No experience necessary. $25 paid to each of first 50 applicants.

There was nothing else in the ad. No explanation . . . nothin'. So 50 guys showed up (college guys are notorious for being broke, so they'll do anything for money) and here's what happened. They reported to a building and waited in the hallway outside the experiment room. The girl told me that this room had absolutely no outside light: no windows, no skylights, or anything. When the light was turned off the room was totally black. It was fixed up to look like an ordinary living room with furniture, rugs, lamps, tables, and pictures on the walls. Sitting in the corner, kitty-corner from the doorway, was this girl I had met. She was a gorgeous blonde, and she was wearing a long dark skirt and a white blouse. (Did I mention she was gorgeous?) Putting it all together it looked something like this:

Girl

Randomly, they picked one guy from the group, walked him through the foyer and across to the "living room" door. With the guy standing just inside the doorway, they flipped on the light for exactly 10 seconds, flipped it off, and walked him out through the foyer. Then, in another room, they handed him a clipboard and said, "List everything you saw in the room." (Remember, none of these guys knew beforehand what they were gonna have to do.) So the first guy started making his list. "Well . . . There's a girl (and she was gorgeous . . . smile), a chair, rug, table, lamp, picture . . ." and on and on. He remembered almost everything in the room. Pretty amazing! That was Guy Number One.

Then they brought in Guy Number Two. He went through the same drill: through the foyer, open the door, flip on the light for 10 seconds, flip it off. Then they handed *that* guy a clipboard and told him to list everything he saw in the room. The only difference between the first guy and the second guy was that *the girl sitting in the corner had raised her skirt juuuust a little bit.*

They did the third guy. He came in and she had raised her skirt a little more . . . then the fourth guy. . . . With each new guy she raised her skirt just a little bit more. By the 50th guy, the skirt was GONE! She was totally bare from the waist down, sitting on the chair, facing into the corner. The 50th guy came in, they flipped on the light for 10 seconds, flipped it off, walked the guy out, and handed him the clipboard. "List everything you saw in the room." Like a total bonehead he muttered, "THERE'S A GIRL IN THERE!" "Well, yeah, but what *else* was in there?" Not a clue! He couldn't remember one thing, other than the fact she didn't have anything on!!!

So here's the point. *The more sex that entered the room* (shorter and shorter skirt) *the less of anything else the guy would see.* Or, in other words, *the more sex he saw, the less observant he got.*

Now I'll come back to my story in just a second, but I have to add something here that will help you see what I'm getting at. Most people don't realize that men and women come at the sex stuff from two *totally different* directions. Let me explain by giving you an illustration.

A Thong Bikini . . .

Picture yourself in a room filled with people, both guys and girls. Suddenly, in through the door at one side of the room, comes this really gorgeous girl wearing a bikini . . . no, wait . . . a *thong bikini.* She saunters across the room and eventually exits through a door on the other side. Now tell me, what would all the guys in that room probably be doing while she's walking by? You got it. They'd be hootin' and hollerin', whistling, dancing the "pelvic tilt" on top of their chairs, and waving their arms like they were trying to stop a freight train. Some would try to follow her out the door hoping to get her phone number, while the rest of the guys cheered them on. It would be pandemonium!

. . . Or a Speedo

But then, let's say a couple of minutes later, after she's gone, a guy in one of those Speedo swimsuit thingies comes through the

door, and . . . what would . . . hey, wait a minute, why are you suddenly feeling sick here? (I can just hear the girls gagging. . . .)

Bbbblllaaaaaaaaaahhhhhh!!!!!

"That's so gross!!!! That is really gross! Like . . . gross!"

Now it's not that girls don't like sex, 'cause they do, and it's not that they won't look, 'cause they will. But, believe it or not, guys in Speedos usually turn girls *off*, not on. On the other hand, there won't be one guy in the crowd who would look at the girl in the bikini and say, "That girl in the bikini . . . that's gross!! That's just so gross! Did you see that? Gross!" NOPE . . . NOT A CHANCE! Us guys would make ourselves look like a bunch of goobers, while the girls would just get sick. Most girls will tell you they'd rather see a guy in *boxers* than in a Speedo, which means *more* of his body is *covered up*. To most girls, the Speedo is too obvious a sexual statement and therefore less attractive. The guys all hope the girl's gonna take the bikini *off*. Whooooooaa!! They want to see even *more* skin! Total opposites.

What Guys See

Guys get turned on by what they SEE. That's the main reason pornography is aimed almost entirely at guys. So girls, when you wear your bikini and parade around in front of him, what do you think is gonna happen? MELTDOWN!!!! His brain is functionally about the same as linoleum. Girls, when you wear stuff like that, just what is it that you expect him to look at . . . YOUR EYES? A girl wears a bikini and thinks, "Hey, I lost that extra five pounds, and I look great." In a letter, one girl told me, "I just thought it made me look nice and would get me a little attention." But HE isn't thinkin' that at all! He's thinkin', "Hey man, she's naked under there." And so where, exactly, is he looking? Exactly? Hmmmmm?

Where They *Look*

One of the funniest things I ever saw on TV was an experiment using a Pepsi ad to see what guys look at when they see girls in

bikinis. They made a video showing a tall, bikini-clad brunette, carrying a six-pack of Pepsi, walking in slow motion down the beach. They put the video in a viewing machine in the back of a van and drove down the California beaches, asking guys to preview the ad and evaluate it. One guy at a time would get in the van, look into the machine "eyeholes," and watch the ad. What he didn't know was the machine was "reading" what his eyes were *really* looking at. Each eye registered a little dot on the screen that showed *exactly* what that eye was focused on. The guy watching the ad couldn't see the dots on the screen, but the man recording the results could. After a whole day of testing, not one guy *ever* looked at the six-pack of Pepsi! Want to make any guesses where they *did* look?

Sexual Peaks

Hey girls, at what age do they say guys sexually peak? (I did an assembly once where a girl yelled out, "Four!") Actually it's around 16 to 19 years of age. That's right. Guys' bodies are at their prime condition (even for fathering a kid) at about 16 to 19. Hey girls, WELCOME TO HIGH SCHOOL! I think that's why, when people talk to high school guys about abstinence before marriage, the guys kinda freak out. They're thinkin', "Well, hey, if that's true . . . you don't want me to miss my *peak*, do you?" It's like they think if they turn 20 and they haven't "done it" yet,

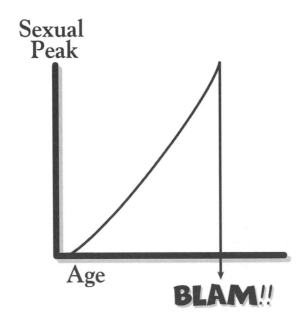

"AAAAaaaaaaaahhhhhhh!" Blam!

("Aw, man, I missed my peak!")

In reality a guy wouldn't even know he missed his peak, but it's one more thing for some guys to worry about.

But listen to this. Do you know when they say women sexually peak? Around 34 to 37 years of age. Some doctors I've talked to say women don't even have a sexual peak. Of course most doctors say it depends on what you *mean* by sexual peak, but . . . yeah, 34 to 37 is pretty much the right age. So if a guy says to a girl, "Well, how about it? You don't want me to miss my peak, do you?" I always tell the girls to reply, "Hey, no way, go for it! Gosh, I wouldn't want you to miss your peak! Heck no!" But then tell him, "But when you get married and your *wife* reaches *her* peak, she gets equal time with anyone *she* wants. Deal? I mean, after all, you wouldn't

want her to miss HER peak, now would you?" Would a guy *ever* go for that? Never!

While He Was Sleeping

There's a couple of other things you girls need to know here, and . . . uh . . . this may shock you. Did you know that the average guy, while he's asleep *(he ain't even awake)*, gets turned on between three and four times . . . EVERY NIGHT? That's right. He's not thinkin' anything, he's not dreamin' about anything. He's just asleep. He has no control over it. In fact, I don't know if you know this, but most guys wake up in the morning READY! Us guys even have little terms for that particular event (morning missile, morning wood, etc.).

The Dreaded "Blue Disease"

Now just 'cause a guy gets turned on, does that mean he has to do something about it? No. But some guys will still try to convince you that they do. They'll tell you they're gonna get that "blue" disease (blue balls) if they don't "do it." A friend of mine, when he and his buddies were in high school, called it DSB (Deadly Sperm Buildup).

One time a guy actually stopped a whole assembly and argued with me for five minutes about the "fact" that if a guy gets turned on he *has* to have sex or it will physically hurt him. I said, "No, that's actually not true." But he kept right on arguing. I told him if it WAS true he would need to have sex three to four times every night, 'cause that's how often he gets turned on when he's asleep! That didn't shut him up. He kept arguing with me until I finally couldn't stand it and I let him have it. "Look, *you* know it's not true and *I* know it's not true. You're just runnin' a scam on girls! Now sit down!" He sputtered, "THAT'S NOT . . . well (smile) . . . OK!" and sat down. The place went ballistic! (I guess you hafta at least give the guy credit for tryin'.)

Is *That* All He Thinks About?

Girls, this next thing may scare the stew out of you. (I was gonna say "scare the pants off you," but that's probably not a good way to put it in this particular chapter.) Did you know the average guy between the ages of 12 and 19 thinks about sex 20 times per hour??????[1] That's right . . . 20 times per hour!!!!!!!!!!!!! MTV's *Singled Out Guide to Dating* says there are clinical studies that say it's every seven seconds . . . **Naaah!**[2] I don't believe *that*. But you get the drift. *Sex in America* reports that in a survey of men and women ranging in age from 18 to 59, 54 percent of the men thought about sex "every day" or "several times a day." Only 19 percent of the women thought about sex that often. A whopping 14 percent of women thought about sex "never, or less than once a month." Only 4 percent of men said that.[3] (By the way, only 16 percent of the participants in that particular survey were ages 18–24.) When *Mademoiselle* surveyed some 2,000 women, they reported that 54 percent thought about sex every day, and 7 percent thought about it every single hour.[4] Now if you guys are done laughing, we'll go on, OK?

I've had girls almost fall out of their chairs when I tell them "20 times per hour," but the guys are thinkin', **"That's way low, man! It's way more than that!"** If you're still not believing this, listen to one girl's letter.

Dear Brad,

I thought the thing about guys thinking about sex 20 times an hour was pretty unreal, so I got on the phone after school and called up some of my guy friends. First I asked them if they thought they were normal, average guys. They said yes and I told

---

[1] Dr. Warren Farrell, *Why Men Are the Way They Are* (New York: Berkley Books, 1986), p. 118.

[2] J. D. Heiman and Lynn Harris, *Singled Out Guide to Dating* (New York: MTV Books/PocketBooks/Melcher Media, 1996), p. 8.

[3] Robert T. Michael, John H. Gagnon, Edward O. Laumann, Gina Kolata, *Sex in America* (New York: Time Warner, 1995), p. 156.

[4] Valerie Frankel, "Sex Happens, Sex Lives, Sex Rocks, Sex Sucks", *Mademoiselle*, November 1994, p. 119.

them about the 20 times an hour thing. My friend Ben said, "Hell no, woman! I think about it A LOT more than that!"

Or this letter from a guy.

You didn't have to make us guys look so bad. Only 20 times an hour . . . that's nothing. In a boring class all I think about is sex, sex, sex . . .

Mark

One guy wrote me and said he thought it was 65 times per hour. But another guy wrote, "That's not true. It's only one time an hour . . . but it lasts the whole hour!"

I had a ninth-grade guy tell me one time, "There isn't three minutes go by in any day that I don't think about doin' it with some girl." What does that figure out to be? Twenty times per hour!

Are these guys average? Probably. Are these guys out of control? Not necessarily. Can they be thinking sexual thoughts, be turned on, and still control their actions? Yeah.

List Everything You See . . .

Now let's bring all this together. Come back to the experiment with the blonde girl in the living room, but let's change the illustration just a little bit so you can see my point. Instead of a room filled with furniture and stuff, let's say this picture is now a "relationship," where sex is happening . . . right here in the back seat of this car.

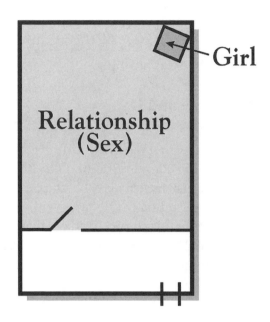

You and your boyfriend or girlfriend just had sex, and, as you're pulling your clothes back on, I come up to your car and knock on the window. I hand the guy my clipboard, and say to him, "Hey, guy, now that you've had sex in the back seat there, take this clipboard and make a list of everything you see in your *relationship.*" (Remember, the picture isn't a room with furniture anymore, it's a *relationship.*) You know what the guy will say?

Guy: Man, she's HOT!
Me: OK . . . what else?

Guy: She's really good lookin'!
Me: OK . . . true . . . but what else?

Guy: She's got a body that won't quit!
Me: Right, but what else?

Guy: Aaaahhhhhh. . . .

SEX IS THE ONLY THING HE SEES IN THE "ROOM." The more sex that enters the room (relationship), the less he'll see of anything else in the relationship.

First Date . . . Second Date

Here's another example. Let's say a guy went out last Friday night and on his very first date with this girl he had sex with her. (He's fast.) Now this coming Friday night he's planned a *second* date with the same girl. Last Friday—first date—they had sex. This coming Friday—second date. OK, what will the guy be thinking about *all week long* for this coming Friday's date? THE RELATION-SHIP? BOWLING? No way! "Man, she did THAT on the first date . . . what's she gonna do on the *second* date?" Will he be thinking about the girl and the relationship, or will he be thinking about sex? Heck yeah! Sex!

Here's the deal. Sex is so powerful and so fun (and that's how it's supposed to be) that it's all he'll be thinking about, all week long. He won't be thinkin' about the relationship, the girl's needs, goals, likes, dislikes, feelings, family, future, friends, or anything else. He's too wrapped up in the sex thing to think about her. It's all about him and the fun he's having.

Brad,

I have been involved in a sexual relationship. But the problem was that once we began to have sex our relationship went down hill. It was like a roller coaster, if I said "no" things were OK but when I said "yes" they were so bad. Going up and down setting my feelings and emotions wild. Trying to do anything I could to make him happy as he possible could be but he did nothing to make me happy. Don't get me wrong the sex was good but on the other hand, the worst thing that could possibly have happened to our relationship. Six months later when our relationship ended I was heartbroken and the two things that hurt most was that I knew he didn't love me like I loved him and that our relationship ended because of sex.

Tina

Why Guys *Really* Do It

Seventeen magazine quoted an unbelievable statistic from *Psychology Today* that said 94 percent of the guys who are having sex with their girlfriends are doing it for some reason other than love.[5] In fact, love wasn't in the top four reasons why guys do it. Of men of all ages, only 25 percent (one out of four) had sexual intercourse because of affection for their partner.[6]

Communication and Sex

Ladies, have you ever heard a girl say something like, "How can I get my boyfriend to talk with me? He just won't tell me what he's thinking or feeling. How can I get him to communicate better?" You ever heard that? If you think you are having a hard time getting him to communicate *now,* just add sex to the equation and it will become five times harder to get him to talk. Why? 'Cause what will he be thinkin' about? How to communicate? The relationship? No. He'll be thinking about sex and how to get more of it! Do you think that kind of guy will be honest with you the next time you ask him, "Hey, Steve, what are you thinking about?" No, 'cause if he *was* honest and told you what he was thinking, you'd think he was a sleazeball! That's exactly where guys learn to lie to girls. Most guys know they can't tell the truth because it would only get them in trouble, so they tell girls whatever they want to hear. Are all guys like that? No, but a lot are.

You've Got to Know the Whole Person

If I could give you just one reason to wait for sex until marriage, my number one reason would be this: 'cause you've got to know the whole person. Sex is fun, I'll grant you, but it's *so* fun it's blinding. Sex before marriage is the quickest way I know to destroy a relationship. In his book *Why Wait?*, Josh McDowell describes it like this:

---

[5] Josh McDowell, *Research Almanac & Statistical Digest*, 1990, p. 5, First published in Psychology Today May 1989.
[6] Robert T. Michael, John H. Gagnon, Edward O. Laumann, Gina Kolata, *Sex in America* (New York: Time Warner, 1995), p. 93.

Boy meets girl. Boy and girl find each other attractive and want to know each other better, so they set aside an evening. Do they talk and discuss? No. They spend (16) dollars to sit side by side in a movie theater and stare at the screen.

On the screen: Boy meets girl. Boy and girl find each other attractive and want to know each other better, so they set aside an evening. Do they talk and discuss? No. They remove their clothes and have sex to the sound of violins. The movie has a happy ending.

After the movie, real-life boy and girl still want to get to know each other. On top of that, their hormones are roaring. They have just been surrounded by a movie that said, "Sex is a great way to get to know someone." Their minds reel with flashes of skin, beautiful music, and happy endings. They look deeply into each other's eyes and have sex in the car.

Boy thinks girl is easy. Boy dumps girl. Girl wonders what went wrong.[7]

"We Know *Everything* About Each Other!"

Several years ago I got a letter from a sophomore girl in my hometown. She heard me say, "Sex before marriage will destroy your relationship." She totally disagreed and wrote me this letter.

Brad,

I only have one question to ask you. My boyfriend and I already have a sexual relationship. We have talked about sex and the pros and cons and have taken all of the appropriate procedures. We have a very good relationship in every way. We are best friends, I really mean that. Neither one of us are sexually oriented. We always talk about many different things and know practically everything about each other. We are not married. We are together

---

[7] Josh McDowell, *Why Wait?* (San Bernardino: Here's Life Publishers, Inc., 1987), p. 39.

only by choice. But forever. So my question is, how could stopping having sex, something we both enjoy, make our lives better? I enjoyed your speech, It gave me something to think about.

> Love,
> Karen

P.S. Write back please.

Some of you reading this right now are thinking the same thing that girl was thinking. "Hey, big deal. We love each other and we'll be together forever, so why not?" Why not? Let me tell you the end of the story and you'll see why not.

Instead of writing that girl back, I put her letter in my file, and I waited. Month after month I asked the girl's friends and her teacher if she was still with that guy, and she was . . . right up until her senior year. When I heard from the teacher that she had just broken up with him, I went to my file, grabbed her letter, and ran to the school. I found her in the hall and, hiding the letter behind my back, I tapped her on the shoulder and said, "Hey, I hear you broke up with your boyfriend." She whipped around and snapped, "Yeah, and if I find him I'm gonna kill him!" Whooaahh!!! "What happened?" I asked. "Well, I really liked him, but he was the only guy I'd ever gone out with, and I told him I just wanted to meet some other guys." She told me he got so mad that he went over to her house, yanked a lamp out of the wall, tore the shade off of it, and beat her to a bloody pulp! She stood there, telling me all this, with two black eyes and her arms all bruised. I think she even had stitches in her forehead. The guy had almost killed her.

When she finished her story I pulled her letter out from behind my back, and I read it back to her.

We have a very good relationship . . .
We're best friends . . .
We know practically everything about each other . . .
We're together FOREVER . . .

I stopped near the end of the letter and said, "You ended your letter by asking me a question. You never would have believed my answer then, but I know you will now. Your question was, 'How could stopping having sex, something we both enjoy, make our lives better?' My answer is, because you never would have been fooled into believing that love and sex were the same thing. You thought they were, and it almost got you killed."

The girl just stood there, and with tears in her eyes she said, "You're right!"

Now am I saying sex is bad? No, not at all. But most people are being fooled into thinking love and sex are the same thing. They aren't. Sex is so fun it's blinding. It can fool you into thinking you really know and love another person, when you're really just experiencing sexual feelings. It feels like it's love, but, like I said, you can be totally fooled. I mean, think about it. How many couples do you know who were sure they were in love and were going to be together forever, who now hate each other? Great sex, but how come it ended? How come the deep regret? At the beginning of the relationship they never would have pictured their lover dumping them or beating them to within an inch of their life, but it happens anyway.

. . . It's *Just* Sex!

Every part of who we are is affected by what happens to us sexually, and we carry those effects in our minds and bodies forever. Sex is far more than two bodies doin' stuff to each other. If that's all it was, being raped would be no big deal. "After all, it was *just sex*." But rape *is* a big deal. A girl (or a guy) who has been raped never forgets it 'cause it affects the entire person. Sex impacts us physically, mentally, socially, emotionally, and spiritually. Now picture being married to a person with a very colorful sexual past with lots of hurts and struggles. Without help to get over that past, it could be 30 or 40 years of relational and sexual hell.

10-Week Experiment

To all of you who still feel that none of those things will ever happen to you, okay, I understand why you'd say that. But here's an experiment that can help to tell you whether or not sex is hurting your relationship. For the next 10 weeks: NO SEX. NOTHING! Three minutes of every day you can kiss your partner, but you can't touch, or grab any body parts along the way. (And that includes taking clothes off, touching, oral sex, everything.) You can only kiss for three minutes a day, for 10 weeks. Let's find out just how much you *really* know about each other.

Now I've had hundreds and hundreds of high school couples try the 10-Week Experiment, but I know of only 10 or 12 couples who actually made it. I'm sure there are more, but those are the ones I've heard from. Here's a letter from one girl who tried it, but didn't make it.

Dear Mr. Henning,

My boyfriend and I are/were _very_ sexually active. After your talk we tried your 10-week thing and couldn't even last a weekend! We weren't even aware that we had nothing in common. On Sunday morning he broke up with me. He said he's really horny and can't handle it. This is the third day and I cry every hour. You've destroyed my life. I love him deeply. Write me back as soon as possible and help me get through this.

Lisa

Could You Trust Him?

When I went back and looked at my calendar, I found that I did my talk at their school on Friday afternoon. He broke up with her on Sunday morning. He couldn't even handle it for three days!? My gosh! No big deal, you say? Really? Girls, let's say you married this guy and then he gets a great job . . . *as a traveling salesman*? (Or long-haul trucker? Professional athlete?) Girls, could you trust him? No way!

One girl wrote and said she wanted me to know that she and her boyfriend were going to try the 10-week thing. I kept her letter and after nine weeks I wrote back to see how they were doing. She wrote me a second time.

Dear Brad,

Wow . . . I'm surprised you remembered . . . We still have 9 days to go and . . . we made it! I'm so proud of him! And me too. Sometimes it was really difficult. But not only did he keep his promise to me, we've actually become better relationship partners in the process. We are both much more respectful than we were 10 weeks ago and I enjoy his company all the more. We both learned that there is so much more to know about a person than just what they have on under their clothes. He and I are very much still together. We have our own little world that grows larger with each moment we spend together. He seems to have the idea in his head that he has to earn my affection with smiles, chocolate and love. But he doesn't realize that he's won it over 10 fold. Thanks for writing, Brad. You've probably saved us both a lot of pain.

> Most affectionately,
> Jamie

Now compare that letter to this one.

Dear Mr. Henning,

I'm familiar with a lot of what you said about love and sex and everything because I've been with my boyfriend two years, and we've been through a lot. Probably more than I will in the rest of my life. At first, we started out our relationship, and I thought it was perfect. So we thought. Actually, at that point in the beginning we probably did know just about all there is to know about each other. But like you said, things change. After six months of this perfect relationship, we had sex for the first time. Right after that happened, everything else just disappeared. We stopped talking about things that mattered with each other,

and we stopped respecting each other basically and whenever we did anything with each other, we always found a time and a place for sex. After a few months of this I got really depressed, because I knew he was only using me. He told me he wasn't of course, and he said it was natural for me to feel that way, and he even said he loved me. But, nothing he said helped the way I felt inside. It just kept getting worse. . . .

I can't give you the rest of the letter (I want to protect her) but she ended up saying that he totally controlled her, and wouldn't let her go or do anything by herself at all. She got so depressed she almost committed suicide, and she finally left him.

If you had your choice between the relationships described in the last two letters, which would you choose?

Am I Safe Here?

Sex before marriage undermines trust, which undermines the relationship. When sex is in the picture, the focus of the relationship is in the wrong place. If you don't really know the other person's character (and you won't unless you spend a lot of quality time finding that out), you can never totally give yourself to them. You can't give yourself to someone if you don't trust what they will do next. The question, "Am I safe here?" will always be in the back of your mind.

"Safe" Sex?

Can you have "safe sex" without good character? No. In one study 34 percent of the men and 10 percent of the women admitted to telling a lie to get sex. In the same study 47 percent of the men and 42 percent of the women admitted they would lie to get an attractive partner into bed.[8] In another study, 47 percent of the men and 60 percent of the women said they had been lied to for purposes of sex.[9] Almost half of both men and women said they

---

[8] *National On-Campus Report,* May 7, 1990, p. 5.
[9] "Sex, Lies and Risk of AIDS," *USA Today,* March 15, 1991, 1D.

would understate to a new partner the number of previous partners they had been with. And get this! Twenty percent of men would even lie about having HIV.[10]

So just how important are honesty, trust, and character in a relationship? THEY MEAN EVERYTHING! If you haven't taken time—a LOT of time—to discover if your partner has these character traits, it could even get you killed. And what would be the Number One biggest distraction in finding out if they are honest, trustworthy, and have good character? SEX!

If your partner can't be sexually disciplined *before* marriage, what makes you think they can stay in control of themselves *after* you're married and they're on a business trip without you? By the way, if you think I'm only talking about guys here, think again. I know lots of girls who are sexually out of control, too.

Sex After Marriage

"But wait," some of you would say. "If sex *before* marriage is killing relationships, why doesn't sex *after* marriage do the same thing?" Good question! The reason is, sex before marriage keeps people's minds focused on . . . well, sex—not on the relationship. When they finally get married, the relationship is totally lopsided and geared mostly towards sex. After a year or so, reality sets in. They discover that their genitals aren't the center of the universe, but they don't know what *is*, so their marriage heads for the rocks. But if a couple spent their premarriage time focusing on their relationship instead of on sex, then, after the wedding, sex would simply be the frosting on the cake. And it's *good* frosting! After the first year or so of marriage, when sex becomes less the center of the relationship (not less important, just less the center), the relationship itself takes center stage. Because it was healthy *before* you got married, your relationship is still healthy *after*.

---

[10] "Sex, Lies and HIV," *New England Journal of Medicine*, Vol. 322, No. 11, p. 744.

But Are We "Sexually Compatible"?

Some people would still argue, "Yeah, but how will you know if you're sexually compatible if you don't have sex before marriage?" Now what does that *really* mean? Are they worried they won't "fit" or somethin'? Most people who use that line just want to play around. They're on a quest, lookin' for the perfect sexual partner, and they're tryin' everyone on for size. Are those same people just as concerned about personality, or mental or spiritual compatibility? Do they ever talk about *that*? Never!

Think about your grandparents again. What's kept them together all these years? Sex? Partly. But I can tell you, if they're still together after 40 or 50 years it's because they are compatible *relationally.* I'll bet they've had to work hard at it too. (And I'll even bet they still like the frosting!)

Car . . . or Driver?

Before I end this chapter I want to give you one more thing. When my daughter was 5, she had surgery because of a heart problem. As parents we were scared to death, and for the entire time we hardly ever left her side. After several days of hospital food and no sleep, we started to go crazy trying to keep our minds occupied. My wife happened to spot a book left behind by some other family, so she picked it up and began reading. *Against All Odds* was the story of a young guy who was in a car wreck and was paralyzed from the neck down. He went through months of physical therapy and was essentially back to normal when a second accident paralyzed him *again* from the neck down. As he lay in bed contemplating the mess he was in, he realized how differently he saw life now, and how, for the first time, he was seeing his body in a whole new way.

> The idea was new to me. I had thought I understood the separation of mind and body, but the full extent of that separation had just become apparent to me. Tom Helms was perfectly all right. Nothing had changed in my life. I was exactly as I had always been. I felt the same. My hunger was the same. I still thought

of girls as I always had and wanted them in the same way. I still saw beauty and ugliness and was moved by them. I felt the same fears, the same anger, the same compassion, the same needs, the same sorrow, the same joy. Absolutely nothing had changed for me except that someone had stolen my body. Somebody had picked me up and set me down outside my body. And it was this thought that intrigued me. Nothing was wrong with me. I wasn't paralyzed. The body lying in bed was—but I wasn't. I had always thought of that body as being me, but now I knew it wasn't. It had very little to do with me really, except for the fact that I was trapped in it. It was like being in a car that would not run anymore. In fact, it had no more to do with me than my car did. Thinking about it now, it seemed to me that a car was exactly what it was—a method of getting from one place to another. My car had stopped running, and I was locked inside. The truth of the thought fascinated me. I immediately applied it to everyone and saw life in a ridiculous panorama. Instead of a body, each person was born into a car and spent his life trapped in it. There were all kinds of cars—grand touring models, sleek sports models, average cars, and super cars. Some were shiny and new, some old and rusty, some ran swiftly and smoothly and were capable of intricate maneuvers, while others clunked and sputtered along, threatening to quit at any moment. Some unlucky souls got defective models at birth, but they were stuck with them and had to make life's journey the best way they could. You could never trade in your car. If you wrecked it, that was just too bad, you did not get a new one. There were body shops along the way, but they were limited in what they could do. They could repair some things and patch others, but there weren't very many parts that they could replace. If you lost a wheel, for instance, you simply had to limp along. When a car was beyond repair, finished, the driver left it to be buried in a junkyard and went to some place where there were no cars. No one was sure where this was.

It was a strange world I saw, but the most curious thing, it seemed to me, was the value system that had grown up around the cars. Almost everything was geared to the cars and almost nothing to the drivers. Drivers were liked or disliked, their company sought or avoided, according to the size, shape or color of their

car. Drivers got very excited if a car had big bumpers or moved a certain way. There were actual cases of cars that met, fell in love, and got married without ever having looked inside to see who was driving, only to find later that they did not like the driver of the car at all. Even the color of the cars had great significance. It didn't matter who was driving, certain-colored cars were inferior and that was the way of it. The car was the thing. One simply did not have time to go around looking into cars to see who was driving. It was unpleasant and confusing. There did not seem to be any reason or logic behind it. Some small cars were driven by giants; and dull, uninteresting drivers, at times, had huge, grand cars. Some spectacularly beautiful, complicated people went around in rusty wrecks.[11]

Have you been dating people because you like their "car" or because you want to get to know the "driver"? Are you assuming that the "latest model with all the bells and whistles" comes with a "driver" who knows how to drive? And where are they driving to? Sex before marriage is dangerous mainly because it literally makes the person inside the car less important than the car.

Your Best Chance

Sex is worth waiting for. Two independently happy, mentally stable people who save sex for marriage have a far greater chance of being relationally happy and sexually fulfilled for the rest of their lives than couples who don't. The next few chapters will tell you why. In fact, waiting for sex may partly be why they *are* mentally stable.

---

[11] Tom Helms, *Against All Odds* (New York: Thomas Y. Crowell Company, 1978)

Chapter 8. Why Wait?
You Have to Build Trust in the
Relationship

"To be trusted is a greater compliment than to be loved."
—J. Macdonald

Dear Brad,

There is this guy that I know named Jeramy and we aren't going out but we've been fooling around for a while. He keeps telling me he loves me and expects a kiss after each time he says it which makes me question if he's lying or not. (So) I talked to him on the internet, pretending to be a girl who wanted to meet him at the mall this upcoming Saturday and he told me he wanted to meet me and do all this stuff with me which makes me feel all played now.

Jenny

I still fall for unavailable men . . . men who don't want my heart. As a result, this year has been just as painful for me as every other time it happened.

> Monica Lewinsky,
> ex–White House intern[1]

Be Honest NOW

Do you trust your boyfriend or girlfriend? Do you *really*? If your boyfriend had to work on a school project this evening, together with several obviously good-looking girls, would you trust him? Or if your girlfriend was involved in play practice with a bunch of guys from school almost every night this week, would you trust her? If you aren't sure, then you aren't ready for a long-term relationship, and you're certainly not ready for marriage or sex. To know if you can trust someone *in marriage*, you have to see if they can be trusted *before marriage*.

Building Trust

Trust has to be built into a relationship, and one of the main ways to do that is through sex—or maybe I should say *waiting* for sex. When we got married both my wife and I were virgins. We had each made a promise, first to ourselves and then to our future spouse, that we would be faithful to wait until marriage. We both kept our promises. It was hard, but worth it. I knew if I could trust her to be in control sexually, I could trust her in almost *any* situation.

But trust, if it's the real thing, has to be tested, especially before marriage, 'cause, sure as anything, it will be tested afterward.

Let me give you an example. A few years into our marriage I got the chance to go to a foreign country for two weeks. Since our daughter was only a few months old at the time, my wife had to stay home. I got off the plane, went through customs, then jumped in a cab to head to the hotel. The first thing the cabdriver said to

---

[1] *Tacoma News Tribune*, August 22, 1999.

me was, "Hey, you want ladies? Five bucks . . . you can have my sister!" What? His sister for five bucks!!???? I couldn't believe it. (I always wondered if the guy's sister knew what he was doing.) I said no, thanks. As we drove to the hotel he kept pointing to girls on the street, saying he could get them for me for 10 bucks or less. After I got home from that trip and told my wife what happened, do you think she'd let me go back to that place? The answer is YES. You know why? She trusts me. And why does she trust me? 'Cause when we first started dating I told her I was going to wait sexually for marriage, and I kept my promise. She learned to trust what I said because I backed it up with my actions. Believe me! It doesn't get harder than loving your girlfriend, being totally sexually drawn to her, knowing you're going to get married soon . . . BUT WAITING ANYWAY! I knew if I showed her I could control myself in *that* situation, then she could trust me in almost any situation; even being in a foreign country with a taxi-drivin' pimp.

Since then I've traveled all over the country, speaking to thousands of people about all the stuff I'm telling you. One place I visited was a sorority house at a major university in the state of Washington. I spoke to 60 of the most beautiful girls (every one of them was a blonde) I'd ever seen in one place . . . and my wife wasn't anywhere around. She knew where I was going, but could she trust me? Yup! And where was my wife while I was in front of all those girls? How should I know? She could have been any-where, doin' whatever, and I would never have known it. Do we trust each other? Yes. How did we learn to trust each other? We did it by showing sexual control *before* we got married. If you can be patient and control yourself *before* marriage, you can control yourself anytime, anywhere. And yeah, it is hard! That's the point!!! If waiting sexually before marriage was easy, what would it prove to wait? Nothing. Anyone can be trusted when things are easy. It's when things get tough that trust is really challenged. Let me show you what happens when you DON'T build trust.

What Is He Doing Tonight?

Let's say there's a couple at your school who think they're in love, and whenever they're together they're "going for it:" in the hallway, at the game, in the park, by their locker . . . IN their locker . . . (whatever). They're going for it while the rest of us are totally grossed out. (It's always gross unless it's you, right?) Anyway, it's like they have to "prove their love" to the whole world. But OK, pretend this couple finally gets married, and now they think they can go for it any time they want. By the way, you think that's true? When I got married I thought, "Man, I can have it any time I want it," until one night my wife said, "NO!" I said, "What? C'mon! I have a license that says I can do it whenever I want." "Well, I never signed THAT!" Bummer!

So anyway, this couple is now married and the guy gets a great job . . . as a *traveling salesman!* But first he has to go to California for a two-week training class. Well, he gets there thinking, "This is gonna be a piece of cake!" and he figures he can hang out at the beach and watch all the girls for a few days. But at the first day of training he finds out the company that hired him really means business, and he's going to have to work his butt off! All day and all night, every day, he studies until he finally falls asleep in his book. He's scared 'cause he knows he can't blow this. He has a wife and baby now, a car payment, insurance, rent. . . . But because he's so scared of blowin' it, he doesn't want to call home and worry his wife. So he puts off making the call. All of a sudden he realizes it's been almost a week since he last spoke to her! She's home wonderin' what the heck is going on, 'cause he hasn't called, *and she's furious!* She starts thinking back to when they were dating and how fun it used to be. She remembers how they used to kiss and hug, and how they used to go for it in the back seat of his car. Then it dawns on her, "Ya know, *before* we got married he always had to have sex. He could never keep his hands off me. He could never say no to himself 'cause he just wasn't disciplined enough. And now that I think about it, he hasn't changed all that much since we got married! Did getting married miraculously turn him into this self-disciplined person?" Hardly! She begins to wonder what movies he's watching in his hotel room at night; what magazines

he has been looking at. (*Playboy?*) And she wonders if there are any women in that class he's taking. Is he spending time at the beach with any of those "California girls"? DOES SHE TRUST HIM? NO WAY! And not only does she not trust him . . . she's mad! Since she's not hearing from him, "OK . . . fine! Then I'm not callin' either!"

Good Character Doesn't Come with the Ring

Your character doesn't miraculously change just 'cause you got a ring and went through a wedding ceremony. And you can't trust someone just because they *say* they can be trusted. The person who expects to be trusted, without proof of their character, is kidding themselves. When someone blows it and trust is destroyed, what does it take to rebuild that trust? A lot of time, communication, sincere apology, and forgiveness. But the hardest part of re-establishing that trust is proving it, by consistently good behavior, over a looooong period of time.

Girls, Help Us Out Here!

I'll be the first to admit it. Us guys need help in the area of self-control, because without self-control we could never be trusted. We need help mostly from you girls. I'm not saying it's anybody's fault but our own, but so much of the time you girls aren't helping us by the things you do and the way you dress.

Girls have got to understand that guys are *designed* so that *they have to be turned on* (have an erection) in order to have sex, and what a guy *sees* is what turns him on. What a guy SEES is the first link in the process of sexual fulfillment and procreation. It's what *prepares* him for sex. If there's nothing to see, he's usually not turned on. Of course he can get turned on by touch, smell, sounds, etc. (Think about it. Do blind guys ever get turned on? Yeah!), but the easiest way to stimulate him sexually is visually. Now if he's not turned on, no erection. No erection, no sex. No sex, no procreation, and therefore no ongoing society.

Obviously in junior or senior high, guys aren't ready to fill the role of "daddy," but when you girls display your bodies and make yourselves sexually available *before* marriage, you're triggering a

process that should take place only IN marriage. You're turning a guy on, only to tell him to stop before the logical "conclusion," or you're giving him sex and then finding yourself with a baby you can't take care of. Girls can make it really hard for the guys who WANT to wait, while they make it easy for the other guys to be totally undisciplined and totally selfish. If a guy knows he can get sex outside of marriage, why should he learn to control himself? Control himself for what? He doesn't get the point.

Whose Problem Is It?

Some girls will say, "Hey! It's your problem, not mine." But how would you like it, girls, if your boyfriend started chowin' down on your favorite food right in front of you, knowing you're on a diet and you can't eat it? What if he said, "It's your problem, not mine." Yeah? Well, that's how HE feels when you wear stuff that screams, "Come get me!" and then you expect him to be the perfect gentleman.

Not long ago I was walking down the street with my wife, when, out of nowhere, along came these two women, dressed *to kill*. They knew they had the goods, and they were usin' it. I was caught totally off guard. My heart started pounding and I couldn't quit staring. My wife just laughed at me. (Oh . . . you think that's funny? "Here, have another donut. Ohhhhhhh . . . gosh . . . you're on a diet? Too bad! Chomp, chomp." How funny's THAT?) Could I control myself? Yeah. Did these women make it harder? Yeah. Is it fair? No!

Stuff like this happens to guys all the time, and sometimes it's totally embarrassing. Once I actually got turned on by a mannequin in a store window! (Yeah, well, I thought it was a real girl posing in the window.) The longer I stared at her, the cuter she got . . . great figure, nice legs, low-cut dress . . . *but she wasn't even real!* I about died when I figured it out.

You Can't Possibly Understand!

Do women struggle with that kind of stuff? Some do. Yet, as much as a woman enjoys sexual contact with a man (they say she

can actually reach a higher sexual climax than he can), she can also more easily do without sex altogether, and many times she'd rather. A leading women's magazine polled its readers with this question: "If you had to choose between being cuddled by your husband or having sex with him, which would you choose?" Hands down, they chose cuddling! And in a *Mademoiselle* poll, one in four women said flatly that sex, for sex's sake alone, has zero appeal. Would guys say that? Not really! Since sex doesn't *drive* a woman like it does a man, she thinks, "Hey, just get control of yourself!" Sounds easy to her. She's more concerned about being close, sharing her life, her dreams, her needs, the children, and the future. In the process of sharing her life, sex becomes a natural expression of that closeness. Not for the average guy. He's just horny and hopin' to get laid!

Girls Who Give Mixed Messages

LUANN reprinted by permission of United Feature Syndicate, Inc.

Girls sometimes say, "I will *never* be able to trust a guy. They're so out of control! Why can't guys just grow up?" But again, are you helping him to grow up? Guys *can* control themselves, but it's not easy. If you girls go around wearing low-cut sweaters, skimpy tank tops, and bikinis, or if you wear a prom dress that looks like a negligee, don't act surprised or disgusted when a guy can't keep his eyes or his hands off your body. Yeah, he needs to stay in control, but his body has a natural response to yours. It's supposed to be like that.

When a guy sees a girl's body it's *supposed* to turn him on . . . and it does. The problem is that sex is being pushed at him *everywhere he looks:* at movies, parties, friends' houses, at the beach, magazines, TV, the Internet, and now his own girlfriend. Every minute of every day, every guy fights an incredible battle. The whole time his body is screaming "YES" but he knows he's supposed to say "no." At the same time his body is cranking out some 750,000 sperm every 15 minutes (and they're all looking for somethin' to do), while her body is producing one egg every 28 days (yawn). Is it any wonder that guys seem so sexually "antsy," so sexually driven, compared to women? "Hey, hey, over here! I've got 750,000 sperm waitin' for some action here!" If you think about it, it's a miracle any guy ever stays in control.

Let me be brutally honest with you. Tight little spaghetti-strap tops and hip-hugging pants that reveal too much of you or your underwear are not just a turn-on for YOUR guy, they're a turn-on to ANY guy who sees you. That includes the married man next door, your male teachers, your dad, me, everyone! No matter how committed us guys are to being good, we will still respond to that kind of visual stuff. We will have to deal with it just because you want to be in style. In any single day the way *you* dress will affect the minds of dozens, maybe hundreds of guys. Makes you feel pretty powerful, doesn't it? (Wait till you read chapter 17.) You have the power either to help a guy be in control of himself, or to push him over the edge. Which will it be?

Soooooo . . . now that you know this, if you keep dressing in a way that can't help but turn guys on, you're saying that you don't care anything about what you're doing to the guys around you. You don't care that your body is putting thoughts in the minds of guys who really are trying to be good.

Chapter 9. Why Wait?
No Comparisons Later

Dear Mr. Henning

I really enjoyed your little talk. I heard it in ninth grade but I must have forgotten a lot because it still interested me. A lot of the things you said were true I think because it does bother me that my girlfriend is not a virgin. Just like you said because sometimes it just pisses me off to think about her with that guy. No matter what I do I think I will always think about it every once in a while.

Jason

Brad Henning,

I have been with my boyfriend for about seventeen months. And I wouldn't trade him for the world. But his past does bother me more than I want to admit. I asked him once how many girls he has been with, sexually I mean. He didn't want to answer and I kept asking and he says he can't remember, "over ten." He says he can't remember any of the girls, or what they did. The fact that he has slept with so many girls haunts me all the time. I told myself it didn't matter and that he has changed. Yes he has changed but I really don't know what to do with what my

mind keeps remembering. I have only seen his ex-girlfriends in pictures but every time I see them I can actually imagine him having sex with her. And that bothers me more than anything in the world. Don't get me wrong, I love him to death, and we plan to get married next summer. I can't imagine being without him or ever seeing him with another woman. Mr. Henning, tell me how do I make these thoughts disappear. I hate thinking about them but especially when you showed up (in) our health class, it brought back all the thoughts. The funny thing is that when we bring up my past, kissing a guy is so wrong and he hates to hear that I have ever been with another guy. But I am supposed to be this virgin saint and he thinks he's a "guy" and it's not the same. I always imagined myself with a virgin but I guess not everybody gets that lucky these days. . . .Oh yeah, (in) your speech you bring up the fact that's it's so important for girls to be virgins but it's just as important for guys too!!! Please help me clear my mind. Tell me what I should do to make these thoughts disappear!!

Amy

P.S. I am still a virgin and I will be till the day I get married!

Here's just a part of a very long letter from a guy who had some sort of sexual relationship with his girlfriend. They had just broken up. He ends the last paragraph by saying:

. . . I wonder sometimes though if the simple feelings, emotions, and sexual experiences I expressed with her then, will affect me later in life. It sounded like you seem to think so, but sometimes I think to myself that this was a time when my curiosity controlled me. I guess I'm satisfied with this reasoning and pray my future wife will too.

But then he continues by writing:

Long after the breakup and the piecing of my broken heart back together again, I find myself in another relationship now. This

particular relationship hasn't been the normal "let's hook up" relationship though. I met this girl during the beginning of my senior year and instantly connected with her. I seriously thought it was love at first sight. But I'm not the type of person who develops an infatuation by mere beauty, so I knew it really wasn't love at first sight. But, after developing a serious friendship with her, I knew it was something more . . . I guess I think it was love. I'd like to say too, that I believe in your definition of love. I truly feel I am "choosing the highest good" for this person. Yet, there is one problem I'm faced with. After becoming what I considered to be best friends with her, we ended up revealing secrets that we thought we could never share with anyone. It was a test of pure trust within each other. It was from this test that I later learned she was not a virgin anymore. It was the first time I'd ever met someone who I had deep feelings for and had lost their virginity. At first I didn't know how to feel about it, but later on I tried ignoring the thoughts I would have of her with another guy in bed. I also had to deal with the fact that she had been with more than one guy. I need to say that I'm not the type of person to hold grudges or point fingers at people, but knowing she wasn't a virgin made me feel uncomfortable around her for quite some time. As time passed by we learned to accept and deal with each other's past faults and actions. I didn't want to accept the fact that she wasn't a virgin in my mind though, and that has been the hardest part for me . . . even to today. I've tried to ignore the fact that she isn't a virgin and still try to maintain a high level of intimacy with her, but I feel like there is only "leftovers" if you will, in our relationship. I feel like I should just move on, yet something inside me tells me that I really do love this person.

How Your Mind Works

Your mind is a tricky thing. It can be your best friend, but sometimes it's your worst enemy. Let me prove it to you. I'll give you $100 if, for the next three minutes, you won't think about . . . MONKEYS! GO!

Well, how'd you do? Not so good? That's right. 'Cause as soon as I said the word *monkeys,* you immediately pictured this stupid monkey, swinging through the trees, eatin' a banana.

Now watch this. I'll give you $100 if, for the next three minutes, you won't think about . . . THE LAST PERSON YOU WENT TO BED WITH . . . GO!

OK, so how'd you do this time? Now for all you virgins out there who think I owe you $100 (Way to go, by the way!), just hang on a minute. There isn't any way you could lose, so that's not a fair bet. But for those of you who are no longer virgins (and I'm not trying to rank on you), don't even *try* to tell me you're not thinkin' about that person. You know it, and so do I. You can't just "quit thinking" about the past, good or bad. Your mind doesn't work that way.

I know guys who can remember vividly, clear back to their high school days, *Playboy*-type pictures of naked women, movies with nudity in them, or high school girls they saw naked, and all that could have been 20 or 30 years ago. Man, it's right there, embedded in their brains!

In Her Dress . . . or *out* of Her Dress?

Girls, remember when I told you the story about going to the senior prom with your boyfriend, and that really cute girl wore the same dress as you? Remember how you felt? How far away did you want to stay from that girl? Yeah, as far as possible! Why? 'Cause you didn't want to be standing side by side with her while everyone was comparing you to her . . . especially if it was your boyfriend doing the comparing.

But what's it gonna be like to be married to a guy who's been to bed with, oh, say, 10 . . . 20 girls before you? He's not comparing you to those girls IN their dresses, he's comparing you to those girls OUT of their dresses!!!! How are you gonna handle THAT?!

Or let's say you go to a school dance with your boyfriend and in the door comes a girl who, six months before, was in bed with your boyfriend. How would *that* make you feel? How would it make *him* feel? Or guys, how would you feel if you were at a party with your girlfriend and you saw her old boyfriend, sitting in the corner with a bunch of his friends, pointing at her, laughing and

grinning, 'cause he just told them stories about what he used to do to her? Does that kind of thing really happen? You know it does. All the time. So are you telling me it wouldn't bother you, or that it's no big deal?

Sex and Mental Images

The problem with all the "great sexual experiences" people say they have *before* marriage is that once you get married the images can stay with you and can even come back to haunt you. You can't help it. You'll find yourself comparing your husband or wife to all the past relationships and experiences you've had, and once the comparisons start, trust can begin to be undermined. When you go through hard times in your marriage (and you *will* go through them) the sexual memories can come flooding back and you could be in trouble. You begin to wonder if you had it better "back then." Even when everything is going great, some dumb little thing happens, and bingo! An image from your past pops into your mind and you feel like a traitor. Or maybe one day your spouse glances *a little too long* at some other person and you begin to wonder what they are thinkin'.

I was talking to a group of kids once, and the guy leader who worked with them was sitting in the back of the room with his wife of six months. When I started to talk about the potential problem of having comparisons once you're married, the guy burst into tears and ran out of the room, followed by his suspicious wife. It turned out he had been very sexually active before they got married, and now he can't stop thinking about all the other girls he had been with. He wants to quit, but he can't. Is that fair to her? Not at all. All the time I hear high school guys say that they're *already* struggling, and they're not even close to being married.

Let me give you another example. After a parent meeting one night, I had a dad follow me out to the parking lot to help me load all my equipment into my truck. As I was tossing my stuff in the back I turned to thank him for his help—and I saw tears in his eyes. When I asked him if he was OK, he proceeded to tell me the story

about when he was in college. He worked his way through school by being a summer lifeguard at a lake close by. In the process he met another lifeguard who taught him a "system" to get any girl he ever wanted to go to bed with him, and, he said, it never failed. He told me, "As God is my witness, in a three-month period (90 days) I went to bed with over two hundred girls." I almost choked. That's more than two girls a day! I asked him, "Are you married?" He said, "Yeah, and to a wonderful lady. Both of us were pretty wild back then, but we've both totally changed. But now, every time we make love all I can think about are those two hundred girls." I was stunned.

A friend of mine, when he was in college, got drunk and went to a Playboy Club where he went to bed with two Playboy Bunnies at the same time. When I met him years later, he was married to a great lady, who was gaining just a little bit of weight. Guess what he thinks about when he makes love to his wife? That's right . . . BUNNIES! Do you think he can be honest and confide in his wife about his struggles? How could he do that without devastating her?

A few years back, a guy came into my office lookin' like someone had just run over him with a truck. He sat down and began to tell me about his high school and college days, and how he had slept with every girl he ever dated. He said he never missed one. I couldn't believe I was hearing this. I'd known this guy for years and I knew his wife, but I'd had no idea about his past dating life, and I certainly didn't know why he was telling me any of this. Then he dropped a bomb. "Every once in a while I run into one of those girls in town, and all the memories come flooding back into my mind. They've even asked me to come back to their place with them." I said, "You're not having an affair, are you?" "No, that's not the problem. The problem is, for as long as I can remember, every time I make love to my wife, all I can see in my mind are all those other girls. Some of them had better bodies than my wife and some of them were better lovers than my wife. But I don't want any of those girls or the memories they bring, 'cause I love my wife! So how do I make it all go away?" He was crying so hard that he literally fell out of the chair onto the floor in my office.

Now help me here. What was I supposed to say? "Oh, just don't think about it!" That's brilliant! Have *you* ever tried that advice? Yeah, and it doesn't work! Want me to prove it one more time? Sing the song, "It's a Small World After All" . . . *but only once.*

People Change . . . Memories Don't

Another problem with the memories (of past partners) is that the mental pictures of past partners never change. How can you compete with an image that stays young and sexy, while you get older and time takes its toll? Ladies, what if you've been married a couple years and you've had your first kid, but you still haven't quite got your figure back? Can you trust your husband to be faithful, even if he sees one of his old girlfriends walking by in a bikini?

What She Doesn't Know Can't Hurt You

Or guys, you know how you used to check each other out in the locker room to see who's got the biggest "package?" Well, what would it be like if you finally found some girl who would go to bed with you but, because she's been with so many other guys, when she sees your "little package" for the first time she starts laughing. "That's the smallest . . . oh, sorry." Would you want to run and hide, or what? Girls, has it dawned on you just why most guys want to marry virgins? No comparisons!

It *Does* Make a Difference

I once got a letter from a senior guy who was dating a senior girl. He was a virgin but she wasn't. One night she felt so bad about not being a virgin that she told him the whole story—but she refused to tell him who it was she had gone to bed with. It so shook him up that he broke up with her, and later he wrote, telling me about it. He said he couldn't stand the thoughts of her being in bed with someone else. So he dumped her. What he never found out was that she had had sex *with his best friend.* He still doesn't know.

I have an article from our local newspaper entitled, "Ghost of Ex-Boyfriend Blocks Woman from Giving Herself to Husband."[1] The woman, because of past premarital flings, can't seem to give herself sexually to her husband, and, as you can imagine, it's causing all kinds of problems in their marriage.

I have "Dear Abby" columns that say almost the exact same thing; that past sexual partners are influencing marriages for the worse. Abby's advice of, "Don't dwell on the past so much," seems like a shallow answer, even though it's partly true. The problem is, OK, don't think about monkeys either . . . GO!

Compared to *What?*

Like I said before, I was a virgin on my honeymoon night and so was my wife. Yeah, you laugh. . . . It's not that I didn't have opportunities, guys . . . I just wasn't gonna do it. I figured it would mess me up, not to mention what would happen to the girls I would have had sex with. Somewhere around the seventh grade I had made a promise to myself that I would stay a virgin till the day I got married, and I kept my promise. And three states away, my future wife was making that same promise. When I got married . . . you know, our honeymoon night . . . that was the first time for me.

Now this next part didn't really happen, but let's say, after having sex with my wife for the very first time, I looked at her and said, "Hey, how'd I do? You know . . . I mean . . . how'd I do?" You know what she would have said? She would have said, "Compared to what? I don't have anything to compare you to. You were AWESOME!!!"

(Dang right I was!!!!)

The Best Wedding Present

Do you realize what a relief it would be to never, *ever,* have to struggle with being compared to anything or anybody else? What a great gift it would be to be able to say to your new wife or husband,

---

[1] *Tacoma News Tribune,* November 19, 1997, FM-2, first published in Ladies' Home Journal

"I've been waiting my whole life to give you something, and now it's time. YA WANT IT GIFT-WRAPPED OR ALL BY ITSELF???!!!!!"
OH YEAAAAAH!!!!

Now THAT'S great sex!!!!!

If You're No Longer a Virgin . . .

I know a lot of you reading this book are no longer virgins. Thanks for taking the chance on reading this anyway. I know some of you must be feeling bad at this point, and I'm sorry for that, 'cause I'm not purposely trying to do that. I want you to know I'm not pointing my finger at you or thinking you're an idiot or something. Nor am I saying your life is going to be a mess from here on out. What I *am* saying is this. There are things you can do now, while you're young, that can give you a much better chance at having a successful future with your wife or husband, and to not do those things could be a huge mistake. It's your life and your body, and you have to decide *right now*, not just later, what you're going to do with it. If you like having sex now 'cause it's fun (and I know it is, 'cause you wouldn't be doing it if it wasn't), realize you're taking a huge risk of hurting not only *your* body and mind, but your future partner's body and mind as well. And because of that, you may be destroying the best sex you ever could've had. More about that in the next chapter.

So What Do You Do?

So if you're no longer a virgin, is it too late? Not necessarily, and here's why I say that. Let me tell you about a guy I met in a school near my home. During high school this guy was sexually active and quite the party animal. After hearing my talk he realized that what he was doing had the potential to destroy his future marriage, and that his actions *now* could deeply hurt his future wife. That idea really bothered him and he couldn't seem to get it out of his mind. So one summer day, during a slack time at work, he sat down and wrote a letter to his future wife. Now you have to understand—he wasn't even dating any particular girl at the time

he was doing this. So as he's telling me all this I'm thinkin', "This guy's nuts!" I said, "This is to your future wife? You're not even *dating* anyone. What did you say in the letter?" And here's pretty much what he said. He wrote,

> Dear_____

Well, he doesn't have any idea who it is he's gonna marry, so he left the name blank and just put a line there.

> My name is (_____) and I go to this school and I have this job during the summer, etc., etc.

Then in the last paragraph he said something like this:

> The reason I'm writing you this letter, even though I don't know who you are, is because I want to tell you how much I love you (Choosing the highest good for the other person). When I was in high school I did some things I wish I had never done, but I want you to know that from this day on I'm keeping myself physically, mentally, socially, emotionally, and spiritually . . . just for you.

He signed his name and the date, put the letter in an envelope, along with two pictures of himself, and someday in the future he planned on giving that letter to his bride on their wedding night. Well I was floored! I'd never heard of anything like that before, and I was blown away. No one told him to do it; he just did it!

Over the next few years he and I kept in touch and became good friends. About three years ago he got married, and he asked me to be in his wedding. My job was to read something during the ceremony, and while I was up there on the platform, reading away, I glanced up at him. Standing next to his bride, he reached into the inside pocket of his tux, and with a big grin on his face he pulled out an old wrinkled envelope, just enough for me to see. It was the letter he had written almost 10 years before!

Several weeks later he wrote to thank me for being in his wedding. His wife wrote the first part, then he wrote this:

> Thanks for your support! And thanks for being a part of our wedding! (My wife) cried and continues to re-read The Letter. It was so nice to see what I wrote and see the pictures I included! I think she was in shock for 30 minutes!

Man, I've never seen anything like that before or since. I'd never met a guy who actually knew what it was like to have sex with a girl but was still willing to stop, because he loved his future wife *that much* . . . someone he didn't even know. You guys, that's love!!!!! Do you think she believes and trusts him, even though he was no longer a virgin? Why? Because he was willing to prove his love and commitment by changing his mind and stopping in his tracks . . . before anything else happened. He saw what was right and did it. AND SO CAN YOU!

A Challenge

I've told that story all over the country and have had many people take the challenge of writing their own letter to their future wife or husband. One time, after hearing that story, a ninth grade guy (still a virgin) wrote to his future bride. He put two pictures of himself in the envelope, one of which was with his ninth grade girlfriend. (Brilliant!) Well, that guy got married a few weeks after the first guy I told you about. During the wedding ceremony the minister, a good friend of mine, told the audience that the groom had a special gift he wanted to give to his bride. The guy pulled out the letter and handed it to his bride, and, while everyone waited, she read the letter for the first time. All she could do was cry. What's really cool is that the ninth-grade girlfriend in the picture—she was in the audience . . . and she was cheering him on! Neither one of them was embarrassed because of the past. No one had any weird mental images to overcome, and all were supportive of the new married couple.

My wife and I live in the town where I graduated from high school, and I still see some of my old girlfriends from time to time 'cause they still live here. I even know some of their husbands and kids. It's fun. I have no regrets about how I treated them. I'll admit I made some stupid mistakes, but still no regrets. I can look their husband in the eye and say, "I never did anything to hurt you or your wife in all the time I spent with her. I want you to know I think you're married to a great lady!"

Your Marriage Starts Right Now!

The success of your marriage is being determined by what you are doing RIGHT NOW, way before the marriage even begins. Don't you hope someone, somewhere, is making the right decisions about you? So, how about it? How about you doing that same thing for them . . . right now?

Do unto others as you would have them do unto you.
—(Matt 7:12)

Chapter 10. Why Wait?
So Best Sex Is Not Destroyed

Dear Brad,

It was pretty late one night and I was out with some friends and we were drinking and doing pot and smoking and my girlfriend wanted to have sex so we went in the room and one thing led to another and we were almost there when I upchucked all over her breasts and private area and I was glad I did because that would have been a big mistake. Thank you.

Your friend,
Steve

Yeah, well, maybe Steve was glad, but I bet the girl doesn't look back on that night with fond memories. After she gets married, do you think that memory could ever crop up in her mind at some very inappropriate time? Count on it!!!

This chapter is probably going to be the hardest chapter for any of you to believe, 'cause you're thinkin', "Wait a minute! If this guy's telling me the sex I just had isn't as good as the sex I'm gonna get when I'm married, I'm gonna laugh my head off! In fact I'll tell ya what, if what I just had in the back seat of my car was BAD sex, whoooooaaaa!!! I'll take my chances!!!"

Trust me here, I would never in a million years try to convince you that the sex you just had wasn't good. Good grief! I know that! The problem is you may have just traded "a little good sex" for "a lot of GREAT sex"! Let me see if I can explain this.

Sex in America

One of the largest studies ever done on the sexual practices of Americans was published in a book called *Sex in America*. After interviewing 4,367 people, ages 18 to 59, these are some of the conclusions the authors came to.

> The young single people who flit from partner to partner and seem to be having a sex life that is satisfying beyond most people's dreams are, it seems, mostly a media creation. *In real life, the unheralded, seldom discussed world of married sex is actually the one that satisfies people the most.*[1] (emphasis mine)

But this was the killer statement:

> *The lowest rates of (sexual) satisfaction were among men and women who were neither married nor living with someone—the very group thought to be having the hottest sex.*[2] (emphasis mine)

Of the 4,367 people interviewed, 1,743 were not married and not living with anyone, and "about half of these people had only one sexual partner in the past year."[3] Citing another study, they said "sexually active" young men, ages 15–19, did not have sex in at least six of the previous 12 months.[4] As they analyzed the data it became very obvious that "the group that has the most sex is not the young and the footloose but the married."[5] And it's the married couples who reported being the most *physically* pleased

---

[1] Robert T. Michael, John H. Gagnon, Edward O. Laumann, Gina Kolata, *Sex in America* (New York: Time Warner, 1995), p. 131.
[2] *Ibid.*, p. 124.
[3] *Ibid.*, p. 70.
[4] *Ibid.*, p. 94.
[5] *Ibid.*, p. 112.

and *emotionally* satisfied.[6] Couples living together, but not married, were almost as high in sexual satisfaction, but as you will see a little later, they suffered from other problems.

So, just to summarize, guys aged 15–19 didn't have sex for at least half of the year and when they did, it was with one girl. During that same time married people had more sex and had more pleasure than the high school guys experienced.

> The least satisfied (sexually) were those who were not married, not living with anyone, and who had at least two sexual partners. *Physical and emotional satisfaction started to decline when people had more than one sexual partner.*[7] (emphasis mine)

> Never-married and non-cohabiting (not living with someone outside of marriage) women have much higher rates of never having orgasms—11 percent—compared to the rate for all other women—2 percent.[8]

Compared to singles, married couples are far more sexual—mainly because they're together far more often and obviously have more access to a partner, a place, and a time. Think about what a single guy has to go through, for instance, to find a willing sexual partner. If he's not dating anyone but still wants to have a romp in the sack, he first has to get all cleaned up to go find someone. Then he has to decide *where* it is he's going to look. If he does find a potentially interested person he will probably have to string her along for what may take hours, pathetically trying to sell himself as a "good catch." He'll play his "I'm cool" schtick as best he can, hoping all the while that he can talk her into a one-night stand—which, by the way, any girl worth having would never fall for. If he gets lucky and "scores," he dumps her the next day because he doesn't want to settle down. He wants his freedom. That's the point. That's why he's going to all this trouble. Which means he has to start the whole process of "freedom" over again the next weekend.

---

[6] Robert T. Michael, John H. Gagnon, Edward O. Laumann, Gina Kolata, *Sex in America* (New York: Time Warner, 1995), p. 124.

[7] *Ibid.*, p. 125.

[8] *Ibid.*, p. 127.

Statistically, there's no question that married couples have the most sex and the most climaxes doing it. Of all the people interviewed they are the happiest about their sex lives, and are better at it because their sexual experience is with the same person over time. Add to this the fact that if they were virgins when they got married, they don't have to struggle with diseases, memories, guilt, bad reputations, previous children, or a slew of other hidden issues. Because they focused more on their relationship and far less on sexual issues while they were dating, they have a far better chance of having a long and successful marriage. If it's a happy and successful marriage, then it's a SEXUALLY HAPPY MARRIAGE, TOO!!!!

Good Sex?

When you finally get married to the person you have been waiting for all this time, you want to be as free from problems as you can be. Then, when it comes to sex, you'll have the most satisfying and bonding time possible. You'll want to focus entirely on the joy of being together. Pure, sexual pleasure! I mean think about it! Does *this* look like great sex to you?

- "Now, before we do this, is there anything you need to be telling me about your past or anything?"
- "I love you too. That's why I know the sexually transmitted disease I have won't keep us apart."
- "Yeah, I know it's forty below zero and the car heater doesn't work, but so what? It'll be like in the movies . . . fun!"
- "Gee Mary, we've got ten minutes before your mom gets home from work. . . ."
- "Oh, come on, Steve! I thought *you* had the condom!"
- "Whad'ya mean my boobs aren't as big as Mary's?!"
- "Of course I'll stay with you if you get pregnant. I didn't really *love* those other girls (who got pregnant)."
- "Matt, I think I'm pregnant!"
- "Yes we do have a very meaningful relationship, Sue, I mean Mary. Sorry."

- "I just spent some time with one of your old girlfriends and she told me. . . ."

Best Sex

Now let me tell you what I think BEST SEX is. Best sex is being able to say, "Hey, we've got a three-day weekend and I was thinking. . . ." Or if your wife comes home and shouts, "I'm pregnant!" you can shout back, "FANTASTIC!!!!!!!" How cool would it be to say, "Condoms? Who needs condoms any more?" (Yeah, you still might have to deal with contraceptives, but there are times . . . !) Great sex is having no worries, threats, comparisons, diseases, guilt, or fear. Just pure sex with the person you are married to for life. Doesn't get better than that!

No Big Deal?

A lot of people don't feel that way, though. They say sex just isn't that big of a deal. Why take it so seriously? Listen to this girl's letter:

Brad,

I think everything you said was to a great value of mine, but really though having sex isn't a big deal as long as you use protection. I mean it's not like you can only have sex if you love the person. I had sex with this guy and I didn't even go with him. We just decided to do it! Nobody cares. Really all sex is something that I do for pleasure. Why would you just have sex with someone you love? Who really cares!!!! Just because we're young still, and people think that at that age you're too young to do it because we don't know what were doing, well that's wrong cause I know exactly what I was doing. I personally think it was one of the best things that has ever happened to me! Recently I had sex with my boyfriend we've been going out for 2 years. We don't love each other, but we care about each other a lot. We have sex all the time, but it's for fun. We don't plan on breaking up anytime soon.

Anna

Anna says sex just isn't that big a deal. I betcha most of the people in the media, especially Hollywood, would agree with her. But just how solid are *their* relationships, and how do most of them end up? Are they really happy? Do their marriages last? For two years I bet anyone who would take me up on it, that a certain married couple in Hollywood wouldn't be together five years down the road. I saw the way they lived and the kinds of movies they were in—the roles they chose to play—and I knew their marriage wouldn't last. Just like Anna, sex seemed to them to be no big deal. Sure enough . . . they recently broke up. Now I'm taking bets on several other couples in the Hollywood. Any takers? In fact, you want to bet me on Anna's chances with her boyfriend or her future husband?

As I said before, sex is far more than two bodies frolicking under the sheets. Sex is connected to every part of you: your mind, body, soul, emotions, and spirit. In fact when a woman has sex with a guy, her body releases a hormone that "bonds" her to him emotionally. It's the same hormone that's involved when a mother nurses her baby. The mother and baby "bond," and become deeply connected emotionally. If a woman has sex only with her husband, this hormonal process helps to make their marriage emotionally stronger, just like the bond between the nursing mother and her baby. But if a woman is sexually involved with a number of guys, that same hormonal process is really messing with her emotions. If you act as if sex is just "cavorting body parts," and, at the same time, your emotions are saying, "Bond, baby, bond!" then your whole "person" is fighting against itself. Sex can become "physically and emotionally confusing" and far less satisfying than it was created and intended to be.

What Are Your Options?

Some people will argue, "But what if I never get married? Are you saying I can't have sex?" If you choose to never get married, fine, don't get married. It's your choice. I certainly wouldn't have a problem with that decision. But does that give you the right, or excuse, to steal from someone else's marriage by having sex with

their future husband or wife? No. That's wrong! Sex is right only when there's total commitment on the part of both people—for life!

It's true that married couples make love somewhere around one or two times a week, week after week, year after year, potentially for 50 years or more. But if you're not married, your sexual options narrow down to these four:

Option 1. Living with Someone

If you are living with someone, statistically you will have about as much sex as if you were married. There's a problem, though. How long do most couples who are living together *stay* together? The average isn't that long. It's about two years. If you break up, the sex ends, and that puts you into the next category: dating.

(Meanwhile, the married couples keep right on having sex.)

Option 2. Dating Someone

The average person who is dating has only one sexual partner per year and over half of the year they are without any partner at all. If they are sexually active during those six months, they tend to make love three to four times per month, much less than the average married couple. Then, for the next six months, nothing!

(Meanwhile, the married couples keep right on having sex.)

Option 3. Being Alone

If you're not married, not living with someone, and not dating anyone, that means you're alone and not having any sex at all.

(Meanwhile, the married couples keep right on having sex.)

Option 4. Buying Someone

If you're sexually desperate (and being desperate isn't all that sexy) you can go buy a prostitute for whatever price you can

negotiate, but the next day you're back to square one: being single (Option 3). The only thing you may have gained is a disease, guilt and a whole lot of regret. If that's the case, you are now less desirable to the majority of singles out there who, if they had a choice, would rather date and marry someone who doesn't have a disease. Isn't that what you'd want, a disease-free partner? Of course!

(Meanwhile, the married couples keep right on having sex.)

Putting It All Together

People have a desperate need to be loved, but don't always know if they really *are* loved. Sex can make you *feel* like you are loved, so it may keep the truth from hitting you in the face. Unfortunately, it also keeps you from getting the very thing you so desperately want . . . TRUE LOVE. You'll find that you don't dare get too close to your sexual partners, 'cause they might begin making demands on you or see you for who you really are. So you move on as quickly as possible. Which means the very act of sex is now the thing that's keeping you from experiencing genuine love and closeness. You may live with someone for a while, date a bit and maybe even try the prostitute thing, but you'll find yourself disillusioned about the opposite sex, and the "action" you *are* getting won't seem all that fulfilling to you anymore.

Sex becomes an *inoculation* against having the real thing; moving you from one partner to another, never staying too long in one place. The sex itself may be great, but, at the same time, there's this gnawing feeling that all is not right. So you try to keep yourself from thinking too much, 'cause not thinking keeps you from asking yourself the right questions, which keeps you in "relational kindergarten." You don't dare enjoy your feelings too much because that would mean the other person could control you. If they did control you and then dumped you, you would get deeply hurt. Even if *you* reject *them* by dumping them first, somehow it still feels more like they rejected you, and you begin to wonder if anybody would ever want you for a marriage partner. For women, the longer they wait to get married, the more difficulty they will have finding a suit-

able partner. The more sexual partners they have, the less sexually satisfied they are. The less satisfied they are, the more depressed they get—and the more they feel like giving up. And dissatisfied, depressed, numb, unthinking people aren't all that attractive. This whole time they have been looking for sex in all the wrong places, trying to find partners who will trust them enough to give them what they want. The more time that passes, the less available sex becomes and the less sex they are actually having.

(Meanwhile, the married couples keep right on having a great relationship and GREAT sex!)

Moral of the Story

You've traded "A LOT OF GREAT SEX in a meaningful relationship" for "A LITTLE GOOD SEX with almost no relationship!!!"

Marriage vs. Living Together

> Marriage is yes or no, not maybe. Living together is like "playing house," but it's not building a home.
> —Dr. Nathan W. Ackerman

Living together before marriage might seem like a good idea, but is it, really? Some say, "Hey, doesn't practice make perfect?" Well, actually, no. At least not in this case. A lot of people look at living together as a first step toward marriage—a kind of "try it and see if you like it" deal. The problem is that most of those relationships never make it to the altar. Marcia Lasswell, a Los Angeles therapist and president of the American Association of Marriage and Family Therapists, says, "Most couples who live together do not go on to marry later. . . .Women pushed by their biological clocks and hoping to marry are wasting time living with men who aren't yet ready."[9] One study found that "cohabiting people with

---

[9] Lunn Smith, "Living Together Has Lost Allure for Some," The News Tribune, February 11, 1996.

no plans to marry were significantly less committed to their partners than husbands and wives were to each other. Men who were cohabiting scored lower on commitment than anyone else in the survey."[10] One woman admitted, "Living together was a mistake, because I lost four years of dating other people. If we're not committed enough to get married, but live together, it eliminates all other possibilities." And as one writer put it, living together but not marrying is like "living in a permanent audition."[11]

Couples who live together tend to withhold from their partners what married couples generously and freely give—*commitment!* Marriage makes a big difference in the expectations each person brings to the relationship. A wife, for instance, who wants a baby or who gets pregnant, is in a much better situation than a live-in girlfriend in the same condition.

Living together is a lot like being married, but mostly in negative ways. It seems to have most of the disadvantages and almost none of the advantages of marriage. Couples who live together before marriage usually give the excuse, "We don't want to become like some old married couple that gets bogged down in the family 'routine.'" It almost sounds like they're afraid of becoming like their parents, but it happens just the same. They go to work, come home, cook dinner, and wash dishes. They might watch a little TV, but then they hit the sack, too tired for sex. In the process they may lose many of their old friends because they spend all their available time alone with their boyfriend or girlfriend.

> Because they do not feel certain their future lives will be spent with their current partners and because they do not feel as responsible for their partners' well-being, lovers who live together do not exhibit the same healthy behaviors as husbands and wives.[12]

---

[10] Linda J. Waite and Maggie Callagher, *The Case for Marriage* (New York: Doubleday, 2000), p. 85.

[11] Katie Roiphe, "Leap of Faith," *Family Circle,* April 1, 2000, p. 116.

[12] Linda J. Waite and Maggie Callagher, *The Case for Marriage* (New York: Doubleday, 2000), p. 63.

I just read a great book, *The Case for Marriage,* by Linda J. Waite and Maggie Gallagher. I know it must sound like a boring book, but it wasn't at all. Here's just a few of the facts they give about marriage versus living together:

- People who only live together but don't marry value their relationship far less, and those relationships last a fraction of the time marriages do. The average marriage lasts around 25 years, and 60 percent of all first-time marriages will last for life.[13]
- According to the latest data, 40 percent of married (couples) said they are very happy with their life in general, compared to just under a quarter (22 percent) of those who were single or who were cohabiting."[14]
- Married women—regardless of whether they worked or had children—reported greater purpose and meaning in life, and neither work nor children, in the absence of marriage, increased women's feelings of purpose and meaning.[15]
- A married man's lifespan is almost 10 years longer than that of a man who isn't married.[16]
- "Compared to married people, the non-married . . . have higher mortality rates than the married: about 50 percent higher among women and 250 percent among men."[17]

But what about sex? Don't people who are living together have the same benefits as married couples when it comes to sex? At first glance it looks like they do, but let's look a little closer.

Married couples are far less likely to cheat on each other and are far more sexually satisfied, both physically and emotionally, than are couples who are not married.[18]

---

[13] Linda J. Waite and Maggie Callagher, *The Case for Marriage* (New York: Doubleday, 2000), p. 25.

[14] *Ibid.,* p. 67.

[15] *Ibid.,* p. 76.

[16] *Ibid.,* p. 48.

[17] *Ibid.,* p. 47.

[18] Robert T. Michael, John H. Gagnon, Edward O. Laumann, Gina Kolata, *Sex in America* (New York: Time Warner, 1995), p. 24.

Sex is usually what makes people want to live together without marriage. That's why some call it "Sex without strings, relationships without rings." They argue, "We don't need a piece of paper to prove our love," but it's not love that's the main attraction, it's sex. "We just want to find out if we're sexually 'compatible.'" (In other words, do you like doing it as much as I do? If not, . . .)

Sex in marriage is extremely important, but it's not the center of the relationship like it is with couples who just live together. When comparing single, cohabiting, or married men, it's the cohabiting men who are having the most sex. The downside is those same guys enjoy it FAR less!

- "Married people enjoy sex more not only because their sex partners are more available, less distracted, more eager, and more able to please, but also because marriage adds *meaning* to the sexual act."[19]
- Forty-eight percent of husbands say sex with their partner is extremely satisfying emotionally, compared to just 37 percent of cohabiting men.
- Fifty percent of married men find sex physically satisfying, compared to 39 percent of cohabiting men.[20]
- Forty-two percent of married women interviewed in the *National Sex Survey* said they found sex extremely satisfying both emotionally and physically, compared to just 31 percent of single women who had a sex partner.[21]
- When it comes to sex, emotional satisfaction, and love, the gap is even larger: "Forty-one percent of men who said they had sex to express love were extremely satisfied emotionally, versus 7 percent of those who did not give this reason.

---

[19] Robert T. Michael, John H. Gagnon, Edward O. Laumann, Gina Kolata, *Sex in America* (New York: Time Warner, 1995), p. 94.
[20] *Ibid.,* p. 83.
[21] *Ibid.,* p. 82.

Thirty-eight percent of women who gave this reason were extremely satisfied emotionally, compared to 13 percent who did not give this reason."[22]

Men who are cohabiting are far less committed to their relationship than married men. That's why cohabiting men are almost four times more likely to report infidelity in the past year than married husbands are. Cohabiting women are eight times more likely to cheat.[23] What does that say about live-in relationships?

Sex in cohabiting relationships becomes a way to avoid intimacy, not gain it. That can also happen in marriage, but the difference is that with the cohabiting couples there's no real commitment pressing them to grow together and learn to be responsible, to communicate, or to change.

The absence of true commitment seems to be rooted in the very principle that people who live together—unlike people who go through a marriage ceremony—don't "make promises" to each other. But by avoiding promises, you avoid the need to keep them, or even to *try* to keep them. And if you don't have to keep promises, why, that simply means that you don't really have to work at whatever may be wrong or missing in your relationship. Without this responsibility, living together cannot begin to reflect the values or the challenges—or the satisfactions—of actual marriage.[24]

By getting married instead of living together, a couple builds a relationship that produces a deep sense of safety. There's less anxiety about sexual abilities, and less fear of getting dumped or left behind when the relationship goes through hard stuff.

---

[22] Robert T. Michael, John H. Gagnon, Edward O. Laumann, Gina Kolata, *Sex in America* (New York: Time Warner, 1995), p. 90.

[23] *Ibid.*, p. 93.

[24] Norman M. Lobsenz, "Marriage vs. Living Together," *Modern Bride*, April/May 1973, p. 209.

Is Sex the Only Problem in Living Together?

Even though sex is the main issue for cohabiting couples, other important issues enter into the mix. Like money. Cohabiting couples tend to keep their assets separate, sharing money only when bills need to be paid. If a child is born and mom needs to stay home with the baby, the man starts feeling like she isn't financially pulling her weight. She feels he's insensitive. After all it's *their* kid, not just hers. And, of course, when these issues come up, it's easy for either of them to fall back on the old argument: "What's keeping me here? We're not married!" And they call it quits. It feels like there's always an ace up the sleeve protecting them from having to do whatever it is they don't really want to do. So when things get tough, one or the other bails out, and the relationship's over.

Another issue is kids. Condom breaks, she forgets to take a pill . . . Bingo! Many times unmarried couples have children between them and, given the fact that these relationships don't last, the results can be tragic. According to *The National Longitudinal Survey of Youth,*

> Children born of parents who are not married will, on average, spend 51 percent of their lifetime in poverty, while children whose parents are married, and stay married, will spend 7 percent of their lifetime in poverty.[25]

After the Relationship Ends

The biggest problem, though, isn't the relationship ending, it's what the couple faces *after* the relationship ends. They've always said they wanted their relationship to remain open and free, but when it ends it's as if they were getting a divorce, only worse. The legal issues are certainly easier, with no courts and lawyers to fight through, but emotionally it's just as devastating. One counselor explained,

---

[25] "The Truth about Abstinence Education," *CitizenLink,* March 14, 2001, p. 12.

I think it's because the couple starts out with such high ideals, such honest motives, and with the spoken or unspoken understanding that each is still free, still his or her own person. Then when a partner wants out and the other doesn't or when one wants to get married and the other doesn't they realize they are not emotionally free after all. That can be a terrible shock, a severe disillusionment. It's usually the girl who pays the heaviest emotional price. And counseling, we find, doesn't work well because the couple lacks the commitment to work toward a solution.[26]

Again, what is lacking in these relationships is commitment! Physical, intellectual, and emotional commitment. Dr. James W. Ramey, head of The Center for the Study of Innovative Lifestyles, put it this way:

For any relationship to survive each of the two people in it must value the bond between them more highly than anything else. That is what takes place in a good marriage.[27]

But couples who just live together usually don't have that bond. Counselors will tell you, "Yeah, they're together, but they're not really together. They're each totally selfish." Because they reserve the right to bail out at any time, they don't have to work hard at whatever may be wrong or missing in their relationship. With that underlying attitude, those couples can't even begin to live up to what a married couple can. Married people's values, goals, commitments, and happiness far exceed the others'.

If married people really are healthier, happier, and having better sex than anyone else, doesn't it make sense to do everything you can to protect your own future marriage? If a little sex *now* can threaten the "Best Sex" and the best relationship *later*, isn't it worth it to wait?

---

[26] Norman M. Lobsenz, "Marriage vs. Living Together," *Modern Bride*, April/May 1973, p. 209.
[27] *Ibid.*, p. 209.

Chapter 11. Why Wait?
No Pregnancy or Abortions

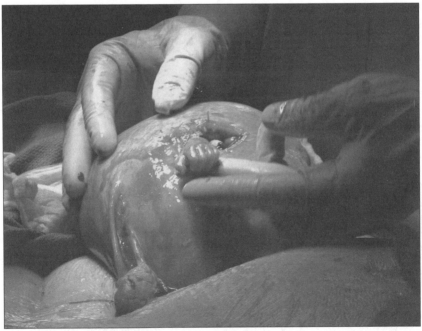

Michael Clancy photograph of Samuel Alexander Armas
SABA Press, New York, N.Y.

His name is Samuel. When Samuel was 21 weeks old, ultra-
sound pictures showed he had spina bifida. His parents opted
for prebirth surgery. During that surgery a small incision was

239

made in the uterus; the surgeon reached inside to learn the baby's position and gently touched the baby's hand. It grasped the surgeon's finger.

We All Started Out . . .

Little babies are so cute! Walk into any room with a 4-week-old baby in your arms and watch everyone come running. At least the girls will. They all want to hold it, kiss it, touch its pudgy little hands and feet. (And then it pukes on you!!!)

Babies are cool. They're "little people." Someday they'll learn to walk and talk, they'll go to school, hold jobs, learn to give and receive love, and someday get married and even have their own babies. What an amazing world! (Who said there's no God?) But panic and fear can quickly swallow up the wonder of that new life if the baby is not the result of a loving marriage.

The "Problem" of Pregnancy

Pregnancy, outside of marriage at least, seems to be something people fear and want to avoid at all costs. "I'm pregnant!" Think about it. When you hear those words, what's your immediate response? Joy? Panic? Fear? Is it something to be glad about, or to be devastated by? For many in America, pregnancy has become something to feel bad about. It's something girls want to prevent, or, if it happens, to hide and deal with in the dark. It's evidence to be suppressed—a problem to be solved. And boy, do we know how to solve it! We've got pills, patches, procedures, and products of all kinds that will keep multimillion-dollar companies in the chips forever, all because "we don't want the dang thing!" Instead of someone to hold and love, to kiss and nurse, a baby is now seen as the enemy of passion, love, and pleasure.

Syndicated columnist Mona Charen wrote about a young college couple, Brian Peterson and Amy Grossberg who, after she had given birth, tried to fix their "problem" by placing the baby in a plastic bag and heaving it into a dumpster.

Grossberg had written to her boyfriend of her regret that the pregnancy had interfered with their sex life. "I wish I could have my nice body back," she whined. "As soon as everything gets better, I'll be my sweet, normal self. We'll be able to uh-uuh lots. I really miss it." About the pregnancy, she wrote, "All I want is for it to go away." (She declined an abortion for fear her mother would discover it.)[1]

In other words, she was sorry the pregnancy had interfered with her and her boyfriend's love life, that her body wasn't as sexy as before the "problem," and that, after all, sex was far more important than a baby, so "get rid of the dang thing."

Unfortunately, the two lovebirds didn't know about the necessity of delivering the afterbirth (placenta), so later, when she began hemorrhaging, she was immediately rushed to the hospital. Charen writes, "That's when the big question was asked, 'Where's the baby?'" If there's a placenta there has to be a baby. Grossberg was sentenced to 24 months in jail and her boyfriend to 30 months plus 300 hours of community service. In the last paragraph of her article Charen makes this amazing statement:

> The feelings of the mother, not the child made in the image and likeness of God, determine the baby's value. In Janesville, Wis., a 37-year-old man was sentenced to 12 years in prison—for killing cats. They were wanted cats.[2]

Just for the record, you can call what's inside a woman's womb a "thing" or a "product of conception," but any way you define it, it is intended to be and has the potential to be a complete human being! IT IS A LIFE! Look at the picture of baby Samuel again and tell me whether it's just a "thing to be disposed of" or a real, live baby waiting for its entrance into the world.

---

[1] Mona Charen, "When Abortion is OK, Infanticide Becomes Logical," *Tacoma New Tribune*, July 16, 1998.
[2] *Ibid.*

The *Roe v. Wade* "Two-Step"

When the Supreme Court ruled to legalize abortion (*Roe v. Wade*), they began the process by deciding not to define what is meant by "human being." I can hear them saying, "Gee, since everyone has such a different idea of what human life is, we won't decide either." If the opinion of nine justices is correct, everyone can now decide for themselves what a human life is and isn't, and you can take whatever steps you want to deal with it. How convenient! But the end result of that kind of thinking is the kind of confusion that Amy and Brian got caught in. If you kill the "fetus" *inside* the womb it's no problem (as long as you have $250). If you kill the baby when it's only halfway out (partial-birth abortion) you're still okay. But if the "baby" is thrown into a dumpster a minute *after it's outside the womb*: two years in the clink. It seems that protection of life is only an issue of timing. Do that same thing when the baby's 5 years old and you go to prison for life. Timing. It's all in the timing.

"A Very Positive Thing in a Woman's Life . . ."

Abortion. I know of few other issues that bring to the surface more emotions than this one. I've talked to hundreds of girls who have had abortions, and I don't know of *one* who hasn't struggled deeply with thoughts, fears, and guilt because of it. Sometimes the emotional struggle goes on for years. Many pretend to be free of emotional scars or turmoil of any kind, but are they?

When I do my talks in schools I usually read a letter from a girl who wrote to me describing what it was like for her to find out she was pregnant and to go through an abortion. That's all I usually say about the subject. I'm going to give you that letter in just a minute. But at this one school, as I was about halfway through reading that letter, a girl grabbed her books and, in an emotional huff, stormed out of the room. The class didn't know what to make of it, and neither did I, so we just kept going. The next day the girl wrote me a powerful letter explaining why she ran out. She told me that she had had an abortion and that it was "the best thing

that ever happened to me," that "without it, my life couldn't have gone on," and "it has never emotionally bothered me in the least." But if she was never "bothered in the least," why did she storm out? She couldn't even sit in a class where the topic of abortion had been brought up.

At another school I was asked to speak in a classroom for AIDs Awareness Day. The administration had it set up so that students could choose between an adult-led presentation (mine) or a student-led presentation (if you got a parental permission slip). Now you have to understand there was a big controversy about the student-led presentation. I stood strongly for abstinence before marriage, and the students took the "kids-are-gonna-do-it- anyway-so-give-them-condoms-and-this-is-how-to-use-them" approach. They also talked about the fact that if you did get pregnant, one of the obvious options would be abortion. There were a lot of other issues involved, but anyway, two girls from the student-led program came to visit my presentation to see what I was saying. They were both nice enough, but they were obviously listening for any areas of disagreement.

When I started to read the letter from the girl who got her abortion, one of those two girls burst into tears and literally ran out of the room. (I don't want you to think this happens every time I do this talk, but it has happened a number of times.) A few minutes later her friend left to go be with her. After the class was over, the second girl came back to tell me how much she had enjoyed my presentation. I thanked her and then asked what had happened to her friend. She explained that the girl had had an abortion a year or two earlier and had never really thought about it until I began reading that letter. It had suddenly hit her—what she had done. She had never even thought about it before that time, but when she heard her own story in another person's words, she had been absolutely overwhelmed with emotion. She never saw it coming. If this realization hadn't happened in my class, it probably would have hit her somewhere else, when she least expected it.

Right to Life or Right to Sex?

It seems like the risk of getting pregnant outside of marriage and possibly having an abortion would be an obvious motivation for people to be sexually abstinent before marriage, but for millions of women that doesn't seem to be the case. Even though they know that pregnancy is ALWAYS a possible result of sex, and even though they know they are not ready to raise a baby, they go ahead and have sex anyway. After all, a half-hour visit to a clinic can take care of any "problems" that may result. To them, sex has become more important than *killing babies*. Did I say that too strongly for you? Well, I wasn't the one who said it. A woman defending her own abortion said it.

I was speaking at a parent night, and when I addressed the subject of abortion and what it can do to a young girl, this woman jumped to her feet and began defending abortion. She argued that it was a very positive, great option. In fact, she said, it was the best thing that ever could have happened to her! After the meeting was over she came up to me and confided that she was a psychotherapist (counselor), and that when she was in college she had had an abortion. She said, and I quote, "I want you to know that *killing my baby was the most difficult decision I have ever had to make in my life.*" Again I was stunned. I said, "Ma'am, if you are a counselor, like you say you are, and a client told you what you have just said to me, that *killing* her baby was the most difficult decision she ever made but that she did it anyway, would you be at all concerned or worried about her mental health?" I didn't get much of a reply.

The "Abortion Letter"

So here is the letter I told you about. It's just one of hundreds I've received, but this letter is one that I've never gotten over. I don't know who this girl is, or where she is, to this day. I only know the school she attended and the teacher who had her in class. I've read her story over and over again, all over the country, for the last nine or 10 years. I don't think this girl has any idea of how many kids' lives she has changed simply by sharing her story with me.

Dear Brad,

I got to be very honest with you, but you really scared the poo-poo out of me. You made me really think about everything. I just really think that you should talk to kids at a younger age like 13 years of age 'cause I'll tell you why. Well, I was in the eighth grade—I was 14 years old when I lost my virginity to a guy whom I had a crush on and would almost do anything he wanted and I really think he knew that too. But I thought if I gave it up to him he would like me but it lasted about one month and I never heard from him again. I was really crushed by this. I didn't think your first time should be like that and wish to god till this day I would have waited till I was married.

Well now I have a boyfriend for a year now. I think in that short of time we have been through so much, both good and bad. I've already had my first abortion Oct. 23, 1993. I (will) really never forget that day. It was a Saturday and me and my boyfriend had been thinking about it ever since I found out I was (pregnant). There was a lot of thinking . . . one week we wanted to keep it the next we didn't. It was such a hard thing to go through . . . I never want to have to be in that situation. Well, that Saturday morning I woke up at 6:00 am went to his house to pick him up . . . it was very dark out. As he got into the car we just looked at each other . . . we both didn't really talk the whole way up there . . . I think in our minds we both were asking ourselves if we were doing the right thing and I was also getting really nervous asking myself was it going to hurt, would I chicken out, was I going to regret it. As we got there and turned off the car he turned to me and said, "Are you sure you wanna go ahead with it?" I just sat there. I didn't want to but I kinda knew it was best for us. He told me either way he'd be with me. Well as we walked in there he stopped walking and looked down at my stomach and kissed it and rubbed it very slowly. Then we began walking. I was the first appointment so no one was there except the staff. He gave them the money . . . it was two hundred and fifty dollars. Then the nurse walked in and told us to come back. We sat down. She asked how long I thought I was, well Planned Parenthood told me I was 10 weeks. She told us that I could be over 10. So we went back to this room and took off my pants

and panties. My boyfriend came in with me which the nurse was surprised 'cause a lot of them could chicken out! She gave me a shot in my thigh, then she began . . . it hurt so bad the worst pain ever . . . I was ripping off my boyfriend's face . . . it took about 5 minutes. After it was done she said I was 13 1/2 weeks along so it would be another 200 dollars. After lying in bed for 15 minutes we left the room slowly but both very quiet. She had told me I'd done very well, that there had been 13 years-old olds in there. I couldn't believe it. As we walked out to leave there was a girl that was giving the secretary money for hers . . . she just looked at me and put her head down. I looked like crap . . . my hair was messed up. Everyone in the waiting room just put their heads down. As me and my boyfriend walked out he gave me a big hug and I looked back and the people were all looking. I felt secure with my boyfriend there. A lot of them didn't have any with them. We drove home once again quiet. I was in shock I guess you could say. That night after I woke up and we decided I needed to eat so we went to a restaurant. As we sat there and ate a little 2 year-old boy came up to our table and stared at us. I started to cry a little and could tell my boyfriend did too. It is so hard to see little kids and babies knowing I killed mine. Me and my boyfriend try not to think about it but it's so hard. We both got to get on with our lives but we will always remember what we went through. It has also brought us so much closer but I know I never wanna go through it again. My parents don't know. I'm sure I'll tell them when I'm older.

I found out from this girl's teacher that two weeks after the abortion her boyfriend (you know, the one that made her feel so secure) dumped her. He just left. He never said goodbye, never called, never wrote, and never came back. I was told that he moved to another state. Since she was totally alone, she finally told her mom and dad. They kicked her out of the house. She went to the hospital in my town every week for almost two months because of the complications from the abortion. And to top it all off she's now an anorexic.

Will She Ever Get Over It?

So how long is it gonna take for her to get over all that's happened to her? Did her abortion turn out to be (as one woman describe it to me) "a great alternative to having an unwanted baby, a very positive thing in the life of a woman"?

Think back a minute to the chapter telling you about how girls tend to remember things that were said about them, or things that guys have done to them. Was I pretty accurate when I said that girls don't forget those things and that the hurt sometimes lasts for years, or even forever? OK, then. Let me ask you a question. Do you think a girl who has gone through an abortion, like the girl in the letter, will ever get over all the memories? Will she be able to say, "That's the last time I'm ever gonna think about it!"? Probably not. Can she get help? Absolutely. I'll tell you where in just a minute.

"But We Did Everything Right!"

I told you I've had girls so affected just by hearing that letter that they've run out of the room. Here's a girl who emotionally fell apart over hearing the letter. She made it through the first part, but couldn't handle the rest, and she ran out. A few days later she wrote me a great letter, and this is the last paragraph of that letter:

> When you were reading the letter about the abortion I had to leave class because I know the story about abortions all too well. I have had three abortions and did use protection each and every time I had sexual intercourse. Just like you said condoms are not 100% effective.
>
> Thanks a lot,
> The girl in the front row

This girl did everything right. She did what everyone told her to do. She practiced "safe sex" by using a condom "each and every time," but she still got pregnant.

What About the Guys?

Are girls the only ones affected by abortion? Not hardly! Listen to this guy's letter. He waited until after my assembly was over and everyone had left the room. He came up in tears, didn't say anything except, "Thanks, man," handed me this letter, and walked out. I never saw him again.

> Dear teach,
>
> All I have to say is thank you! I'm a 16 year-old junior and less than two weeks ago I just found out that my girlfriend is pregnant. It was just another score. I don't love her, she was fine, I liked her, my friends said I couldn't get her, well I proved them wrong huh? Her mom is making her get an abortion. I think it's for the best but I'll think about it every day wishing you talked to me a couple weeks earlier. . . . Oh, and condoms don't work every time cause I was wearing one. It broke and now life sucks. I on this day vow to wait until I get married to ever have sex again.
>
> > Thank you,
> > James
>
> P.S. Keep spreading the word you make kids think!!

He's another person who did everything that people had told him would make him "safe" sexually, and it didn't work.

Statistics

Statistics can have a way of cementing an idea into your mind like nothing else can. They represent "the real thing." They represent the pain and agony in the lives of millions and millions of people. If for no other reason, read it just for them. Read slowly and carefully, letting each one sink in.

- Each year, almost 1 million teenage women—11 percent of all women ages 15–19 and 22 percent of those who have had sexual intercourse—become pregnant.[3]
- Among sexually experienced teenagers, annual pregnancy rates are as follows:
  14-year-olds: 9 percent (contraception not known). *Almost one in 10 got pregnant.*
  15- to 17-year-olds: 18 percent (72 percent used contraception). *Almost one in five got pregnant.*
  18- to 19-year-olds: 22 percent (84 percent used contraception). *Almost one in four got pregnant.*[4]
- "Within a year . . . a sexually active teenager who does not use a contraceptive has a 90 percent chance of becoming pregnant."[5]
- Twenty-five percent of all young women have been pregnant by the time they turn 18 and 50 percent by age 21. Eighty-five percent of the pregnancies were unintended.
- About half of adolescent pregnancies end in birth, slightly over a third in abortion, and the rest in miscarriage.[6]
- Adolescents account for roughly a quarter of all abortions performed annually.[7]
- Fifty-three percent of 15- to 19-year-old teenagers who experience unintended pregnancies have an abortion.[8]
- Over 40 percent of mothers aged 15–17 had sexual partners three to five years older; almost one in five had partners six or more years older. With teen mothers in the 15–17 age range, 49.2 percent of the fathers were between ages 20 and 29 years of age.[9]

---

[3] *Facts in Brief* (New York: The Alan Guttmacher Institute), 1996.
[4] *Sex and America's Teenagers* (New York: The Alan Guttmacher Institute, 1994), p. 41.
[5] *Ibid.*, p. 30.
[6] *Sex and America's Teenagers* (New York: The Alan Guttmacher Institute, 1994), p. 44.
[7] *Ibid.*, p. 44.
[8] *Ibid.*, p. 44.
[9] *Family Planning Perspectives*, July/August 1995.

- The younger the adolescent mother, the greater the age gap with her male partner.[10]
- Out-of-wedlock births account for nearly seven in 10 of all births to adolescent women.[11]

Abortion: "Heart" Surgery

Abortion isn't just the antiseptic removal of "products of conception." It isn't as simple as removing a wart or a tumor. Eighty-one percent of women who have had abortions can't quit thinking about the aborted child. Seventy-three percent have flashbacks to the abortion experience, and 69 percent experience feelings of "craziness." Around 54 percent struggle with nightmares related to the experience, and a staggering 35 percent have visions or dreams of visitations from the aborted child. Seventy-two percent of women who had abortions say they had no religious beliefs at the time of the abortion, but 96 percent, in retrospect, regard abortion as the taking of life, or murder.[12] Another study showed that "sixty-two percent had become 'suicidal' following the procedure, 20 percent had actually made suicide attempts, 30 percent began drinking heavily, 40 percent experienced nightmares, and 20 percent had undergone a 'nervous breakdown.'"[13]

Is it worth waiting sexually for marriage? For just a minute think about it only from the viewpoint of guilt and memories. Is it worth risking feelings and emotions you may never get over, knowing you're pregnant with a baby and then ending that pregnancy by abortion? Will you have to try to convince yourself it wasn't really a baby at all, only an "untimely product of conception" as one national spokeswoman called it?

---

[10] California Resident Live Births, 1990, by Age of Father, by Age of Mother, California Vital Statistics Section, Department of Health Services, 1992.

[11] *Sex and America's Teenagers* (New York: The Alan Guttmacher Institute), 1994, p. 53.

[12] Josh McDowell, *Right from Wrong* (Dallas: Word Publishing), 1994, pp. 158–159.

[13] George Grant, *Grand Illusions* (Franklin, Tennessee: Adroit Press), p. 183.

If You Need Help . . .

If you've had an abortion and you're struggling with memories, dreams, or flashbacks, or you're still pregnant and wondering what to do, there are several places I'd suggest you go to for help. One place would be the Crisis Pregnancy Clinic (also known as Care Net) in your area; call 1-800-395-4357 to their national center to find the closest one (or www.care-net.org). Many churches and synagogues have professional counselors on staff who know how to help you walk through the issues, but call first and ask something like, "If someone was struggling with issues from having an abortion, how would you suggest she find help?" Don't tell them it's you yet. Have a piece of paper and pen ready to write down a phone number or address. If it doesn't work out at one place, don't give up. Try another place, but don't go it alone.

Kids Tell Their Stories

I want to end this chapter by sharing with you a poem and a few of the letters kids have written to me. I have received hundreds of them, and I keep every one of them. Somehow it would feel wrong to throw any of them away, 'cause each one represents so much. These are real people who have had to make very difficult decisions. They aren't easy to read, but each one tells a story that needs to be heard. So here they are. If you don't have the stomach to read them I would totally understand. You may want to just move on to the next chapter.

The girl who sent me this poem told me that her cousin had actually written the first two lines but couldn't finish it; so she did. She titled it simply, ABORTION.

ABORTION

It's early yet, the month is one,
You can't see me I've just begun.
I'm so small I don't have to hide,
I'm just a little seed inside.
Four weeks later the month is two,
I'm so small but still a part of you.

Mommy you'll love me, wait and see.
You will be so proud of me.
Time is passing the month is three.
Now anybody is able to see me.
I've got black hair my eyes are brown.
Mom, your gonna love having me around.
It's getting late the month is five.
Mom didn't want me so I'm no longer alive.
Abortion is the name they give it.
It takes your life before you live it.
I want to be born the month is six.
It's already been done it can't be fixed.
I guess mommy didn't want me because she threw me away.
She'll never forget me I'm in her mind to stay.
I've got a new home the month is seven.
God has welcomed me back to heaven.
You would have loved me but now I'm gone.
Now only my memory carries on.
If I were around the month would be eight.
I know mommy would have loved me but now it's too late.
Goodbye mommy the month is nine.
If I would have been born things would have been fine.
Even though I'm in heaven I still cry.
Oh mommy, why did you make me die?

The reason the girl who started the poem didn't finish the poem was because, after her abortion, she felt so guilty she shot herself in the head, and died.

WHY WAIT?

Brad,

I just wanted to tell you "thanks" for speaking at my school. Many of the things you said were true although I do disagree with some.

I wanted to say that I wish I had heard you before. When you spoke at my school I was beginning my 35th week of pregnancy. I am due just 3 days after my graduation. I hope I am able to attend my graduation.

Being pregnant has been hard for me. I have had to make some tough decisions, yet it was so easy for me to decide to have unprotected sex. I have lost the companionship of several family members and friends. All for one night of sex. I didn't even love the guy. In fact, I hardly knew him.

WHY WAIT?

Dear Brad,

Every time I hear the word abortion my insides hurt and my heart yearns for the child that I lost. I could have been a good mother but I wouldn't have been able to be a good mother at 16. My friend asked me why I was so upset and I knew I couldn't tell her about the abortion. For one thing it cost my boyfriend $350, for another thing I couldn't take the guilt. It was one year ago today. On February 14, my boyfriend started treating me like trash and all he wanted was sex. I could not handle the pain he caused and every time I would go running to my friend for help. I am so grateful to this day that I had her as my friend because without the loving support she gave I would have either gone mad or killed myself. My best friend had to do that (abortion) 3 yrs ago when she was 16. I had to go to counseling also because I was there holding her hand when she had it done.

WHY WAIT?

Dear Brad,
Hi, I was in your talk about sex, relationships and love . . . Well when you read the note about the abortion, well I'm almost two months pregnant and I was on birth control and we used a condom. Well I still ended up pregnant. I can't tell my parents because they'll kick me out of the house. And I'm only 15. The baby's dad is with his girlfriend which is 5 months pregnant. I

never knew about her. He's nowhere around now. So I decided to take the three pills called the morning after pills. We'll I've only taken one pill so far and now I regret it. I'm beating my self up inside and now I don't want to take the other two pills anymore.

I want to thank you.
Brenda

WHY WAIT?

Dear Brad,

I know that I will never have sex until I am married for two reasons. Number one, I have taken some vows with my church to never be sexually active until marriage. Another reason is because of my friend. She got pregnant when she was 14. When she turned 15 she went to get an abortion. The first time she couldn't do it and she left. But she went back two weeks later and had her abortion. "It was the greatest pain I have ever had," she said. Five days later she shot herself in the head. Her last five days were spent crying and hating herself. She wrote me a note. "I was going to name her ____. She was going to be so beautiful, then I had to kill her." She was very depressed about the whole situation and told her mom she wished she had never had sex. I know if she hadn't she would still be here. I have always wondered what I could have said or done to make a difference. Probably not much. I am not a very good advice giver.

Pam

WHY WAIT?

Chapter 12. Why Wait?
No Diseases

To You:

Yes, that's me, the girl with the STD. I may be the girl sitting in front of you, or behind you. Or, I may even be at your side. I may be the best friend that never told you because I was afraid that you might think of me as a slut. I come from a really small town where everyone knows everything, but no one knows that I have a disease. I am only 17 years old and have slept with three different guys in just two years. I started having sex when I was only 15. Now I have an STD that will never go away. Its called Genital Warts. I got it from my last boyfriend. We are both having to learn how to deal with it. At least he's still with me. It has not been easy. I found out I also have cervical cancer and, according to the doctors, that makes my chance of having a child more difficult. But what's actually the hardest for me to deal with are all the questions in my mind. Questions like, "Why did this have to happen to me?" It's questions that I can't find answers for and probably never will.

The reason I'm telling you all this is because I hope you will never have to experience the pain that I have. Believe me, you don't ever want to know what it's like to be up nights crying like I do, or being scared to death to go to the doctor again so he can tell you what else is wrong with your body, all because of a few nights with that "special person"!

PLEASE THINK ABOUT THIS! IF YOU DON'T, IT MAY NOT
BE JUST MY BOYFRIEND AND I GOING THROUGH THIS . . .
IT WILL BE YOU!
GOOD LUCK WITH YOUR LIFE. MAY IT TURN OUT THE
VERY BEST FOR YOU AND THE ONES YOU CARE ABOUT
MOST.

THE GIRL JUST LIKE YOU
January 15, 1999

Dis-ease

Have you ever looked up the word "disease" in the dictionary? Look it up. I'll wait. . . . The word starts with "dis"—which is
Latin for "apart" or "away" (like the word *disembark)*. Ease means
freedom from pain. So disease means there's no freedom or sepa-
ration from pain. Welcome to the world of sexually transmitted
diseases.

Some people now call them sexually transmitted infections
(STIs) instead of sexually transmitted diseases (STDs), but whether
it's a disease or an infection, you don't want either of them. Can
you imagine being the girl in the letter and having to deal with that
stuff for the rest of your life? Did having sex make her life easier or
harder? More sexually exciting, or less? So why don't people run as
far and as fast as they can from sexually transmitted diseases and
infections? The answer is sexual pleasure! Now I'm all for sexual
pleasure, but I'd like to enjoy it for as much of my life as possible.
The girl in the letter had pleasure a few times, but that pleasure
will never balance out the pain that she's going to be dealing with
for the rest of her life.

I once told some kids that I knew of a way to keep any one of
them from getting a sexually transmitted disease. They laughed and
said *nobody* could do that . . . but they were wrong. All it would
take is three things:

1. Don't have sex before marriage;
2. Marry a person who also waited and be faithful to each
   other;
3. Don't do drugs.

That's it! If you don't want to get a sexually transmitted disease . . . there's your answer! It's very simple, and it's exactly what I did. I have never, *ever*, had to worry about getting an STD or infection in my life. Trust me! It's a nice feeling.

But for those of you who haven't waited, or *won't* wait sexually, the chances of your getting a sexually transmitted disease are incredibly high. And if you think I'm just trying to scare you . . . YOU'RE RIGHT!!! RIGHT DOWN TO YOUR SOCKS!!!!

> . . . in a single act of unprotected intercourse with an infected partner, a woman has a 1 percent risk of acquiring HIV, a 30 percent risk of getting genital herpes, and a 50 percent chance of contracting gonorrhea; a man's risk of infection ranges from 1 percent for HIV to 30 percent for genital herpes.[1]

The latest statistics say that in the United States, 25.6% of *all* American women now have genital herpes.[2] For men, it's around one out of five. Some say by the time you graduate from college that last statistic will have grown to about TWO out of five. The problem is *nobody believes it.* And to put this into perspective, herpes is just *one* of the TWENTY to TWENTY-FIVE sexually transmitted diseases you can get!

Every day 8,000 teenagers in America get a sexually transmitted disease.[3] Roughly 13 percent of American young people between the ages of 13 and 19 get an STD annually. About 25 percent of sexually experienced adolescents become infected (with an STD) each year. It's estimated that some 56 million Americans (more than one in five) are infected with a *viral* STD (not counting baterial STDs) other than HIV, and 1 million are believed to have the virus that causes AIDS.[4] Approximately two-thirds of all people

---

[1] *Sex and America's Teenagers* (New York: The Alan Guttmacher Institute), 1994, p. 30.

[2] "Herpes Simplex Virus Type 2 in the United States," *New England Journal of Medicine*, October 16, 1997: 1105–1111

[3] Ibid.

[4] *Sex and America's Teenagers* (New York: The Alan Guttmacher Institute), 1994, p. 38.

who acquire STDs are under the age of 25. Scared yet? If you're like most kids . . . probably not.

Why People Don't Believe the Statistics

You know why most people don't believe those statistics? Two reasons. Number One: People who have a disease won't tell anyone. Let me ask you, do you personally know anyone in your school who has an STD? (Let's not count AIDS, and don't count yourself or a family member.) So, do you know anyone? Most people don't, so they automatically assume no one has one. The reason you don't know anyone is because, well . . . if *you* had a sexually transmitted disease, would *you* tell your friends? "Hi! I'm Brad . . . I have herpes!" No way! If you had a disease and could go to a hospital or clinic and get a shot or something to take care of it, would you come back to school and yell, "Hey, I got my *shot!*" and then start singin', "I feeeeel good!"? No, you wouldn't do that, 'cause you wouldn't want *anyone* to know about your disease. That's what the girl in the letter at the beginning of this chapter said. She didn't want anyone to know 'cause she knew if they did, the rumors would start flying and everyone would treat her like she was a freak. That's not fair, of course, but that's what happens. *That's* also why you don't know anyone in your school who has an STD.

Number Two: Most people don't believe the statistics because a huge number of the people who *do* have a disease *don't know they have it.* You can actually have a disease and not have any symptoms at all, at least at the beginning. Seventy-five percent of herpes-infected people, for instance, have never had an outbreak of herpes—but they've got it.[5] Some people with an STD won't know about their disease for sometimes up to 20 years or more, and, unless they get tested, some may *never* know they have it. But for all those 20 years they will be passing that disease to everyone they come in sexual contact with. If you were to ask them if they had a disease they'd just laugh at you.

---

[5] Joe S. McIlhaney, MD, *Sexuality and Sexually Transmitted Diseases* (Baker Book House, 1990), p. 114.

Now if you're like me, you're probably asking how a disease with no symptoms can be such a big deal. If you can't even tell you've got it, then who cares?! The rest of this chapter will answer that question.

"You Can Trust Me!"

Some people will believe anything anybody tells them, so when their friends say they have been tested and don't have a disease, they believe every word. Somehow "being tested" makes them feel safe. But there's a problem. Having just one test doesn't necessarily mean you're clean. If you just contracted HIV, for instance, and a week later you took the test for HIV, it probably wouldn't show you had the disease. It's too early for the antibodies (that's what that particular test really looks for) to show up on the test 'cause your body hasn't swung into full battle against the disease. Do you have it? Yes. Could you pass it to someone else? Yes. Will you know you have it? NO! Not yet! So you go out and have sex with someone, thinking you don't have it ('cause the test said you were clean), and, bingo! Your new partner could be a statistic right along with you. Even if you got tested once, it's important that you wait for six months and *get tested again*. Then, if the test comes out "clear" AND YOU HAVEN'T HAD SEX, OR SHARED NEEDLES WITH ANYONE SINCE THE FIRST TEST, you're *probably* safe. But remember, every time you have sex with someone you run the risk of getting something new.

Would I Lie to You?

Another problem you might face if you're sexually active is that some people will actually LIE about having been tested or about having a disease. *The New England Journal of Medicine* reported one survey that found 32 percent of the men and 23 percent of the women questioned said they had concealed from a partner their sexual involvement with someone else. The survey also revealed that close to half of both the men and the women would *understate* to a new partner the number of *previous* partners they had had.

But, scariest of all, *20 percent of men and 4 percent of women said they would lie about having tested positive for HIV.*[6]

A National On-Campus Report said, "Of 422 respondents, 34 percent of the men and 10 percent of the women confessed to lying about past partners, while 47 percent and 42 percent, respectively, admitted they would lie to get an attractive date into bed."[7] *USA Today* stated that "forty-seven percent of the men and 60 percent of the women said they had been lied to for purposes of sex."[8] Now how does all this lying affect an ongoing relationship? *What ongoing relationship?* If two people can't trust each other to tell the truth about stuff like this, do they even HAVE a relationship? Heck, no!

So many unmarried, sexually active people are so willing to do or say anything to get a new partner into bed, that it becomes dangerous to trust *anyone* sexually!

> Reed was living with his current lover for a year—and had unprotected sex the entire time—before he mustered the courage to tell her he was HIV-positive. It turns out that his lover was also HIV-positive and also was afraid to tell the truth. "If two people who love each other can't be honest, then how can you be sure when it's for one night?" Reed asked.[9]

Sex for that couple was more important than life itself. *Each of them was knowingly risking the life of the other!* That's crazy!

The only way you can completely trust someone to be free of diseases is to have them go get tested before you are sexually involved with them. PERIOD! If you really love each other like you say you do, get tested. Then both of you should be committed to being sexually abstinent until marriage, and prove your commitment by your actions until the day you take your vows.

---

[6] William K. Kilpatrick, Why Johnny Can't Tell Right From Wrong (New York: Touchstone, 1992), 63. first reported in Susan Cochran and Vickie Mays, "Correspondence," New England Journal of Medicine (March 15, 1990), p. 774.
[7] *National On-Campus Report,* May 7, 1990, p. 5.
[8] *USA Today,* March 15, 1991.
[9] Debra Lynn Vial, "AIDS Takes Toll on Young Love," *Fairfax Journal Weekly,* December 18, 1991, A1.

So if someone wants to have sex with you and says, "Oh, you can trust me," can you *really* trust them? No! Why?

1. Because they might not know they have a disease (giving them the benefit of the doubt).
2. Because they may be lying (You don't *dare* give them the benefit of the doubt).

"Uh-Oh! What Do I Do Now?"

If you have been sexually involved with someone and you wonder if you might have a sexually transmitted disease, what should you do? Well, first off, don't panic. Slow down and let's talk this through. There's a good chance you'll be fine, but you have to think clearly about all this and not just HOPE it will all work out or go away. I had to take a senior guy to get checked for a disease once. He thought he had gotten herpes from a one-time fling with this girl he had met. It turned out to be jock itch. I hope you're as lucky.

If you have been sexually active with someone who is not a virgin or who is a drug user, then you are automatically at risk for a disease and you need to get tested *right now!* The longer you wait to get treated, the more chance you have of doing permanent damage to your body or theirs. Remember that you could have a disease and have absolutely no signs of it at all. Just because the person you were with *says* they have never been with anyone else, doesn't necessarily mean they were telling you the truth. You can hope all you want, but you can't know for sure unless you're tested.

You can take control of your body and the fear of uncertainty once and for all. My first suggestion is this: make up your mind right now that you're not going to be sexually involved ever again until you're married, and that you're only gonna date people who are willing to do the same. That will establish an actual date to begin dealing with all the rest of the disease issues. Next, get tested for any disease you may have been exposed to. Once you've been tested you're going to need to wait for a while (six months for AIDS) and then get tested again to make sure everything is clear.

"Where Do I Go?"

So where do you go to get tested? OK, there's several places I'd suggest. The best person to call would be your family doctor, because they will have your medical history. Or you can go to a walk-in medical clinic (CHEC or a place like that). You can also call your local hospital. Your county health department may do testing, or they can tell you where to go. Crisis Pregnancy Centers offer testing for some diseases and for pregnancy as well. They can tell you what to do and they'll help you walk through it. (You'll find them in the phone book.)

Now I know the last thing some of you want to do is tell your parents. I know that's a scary thought, but if one of my own kids was going through this I'd *absolutely* want to know so I could help. Yeah, I would be disappointed in them but I'd be even *more* disappointed if they went by themselves to get tested and didn't tell me. So even if your parents get mad at you, believe me, you'll feel a lot better having someone with you in this.

When You Call the Doctor

When you call the doctor's office here's what you can say:

Hello. (Don't give them your name yet.) I'm calling because I'm looking for a place to get tested for STDs. I'm _____ years old and my parents do (or don't) know about this. I'm not sure what to do, but I was told to start by calling you. Can you help me, or at least tell me where I can get help?

Have a piece of paper and a pencil ready for instructions and other phone numbers. If you decide to make an appointment, before giving them your name, make sure that they agree to total confidentiality. Say something like this:

I would like to make an appointment in the next few weeks, but I need to know if I can keep this confidential. Is that possible?

By law, if they say yes, they have to keep it that way. OK? If you don't want your parents to know, the doctor will keep your visit confidential, but the office will want to know up front how you're going to pay for the visit. They should be able to tell you in advance how much it will be. If you're hoping your parents' insurance is going to pay, remember that the insurance company will send a statement to your parents, so they *will* find out sooner or later. So be prepared.

Some Crisis Pregnancy Centers can do testing (confidentially) for free, but it's usually just for girls. They will first test a girl to see if she's pregnant. If she is, then they will refer her to her own doctor and he will do STD testing. If she is not pregnant, they can go ahead and test for some diseases and give her the results in a few days.

But let me say this one more time. I think you need to tell your parents. They have a right to know what's happening to their kids. If it turns out you do have a disease, they will ultimately find out anyway.

If your test results are negative (that means you're OK), good for you. If you are testing for HIV, you will still need a second test about six months later, just to make sure. One note here: Girls, there's no test for HPV (human papilloma virus). If you have been sexually active you need to get a Pap test every year, because if you do have HPV it can cause precancerous changes to your cervix. Caught early, cervical cancer can be treated, but if you put it off the results can be devastating.

If you test positive for any disease (meaning you are infected) then the doctor will tell you what you need to do from there. Usually that means more doctors' appointments and prescription medication, and someone will have to pay for that. Again, your parents are an important factor here. Some of these diseases are deadly serious, and most parents would rather face the disappointment than lose you because you didn't get help in time.

Condoms

A lot of research has been done to determine whether or not condoms are the way to go in helping to prevent pregnancy and STDs. I literally have stacks of "studies" that will tell you whatever you want to hear. Some say condoms are at least 98–99 percent effective "if used consistently with every act of intercourse," but other studies show condoms to be *much* less reliable. Which information is correct? You be the judge, but you'd better look VERY CAREFULLY!!! If you want to trust your life to a condom . . . well . . . OK, but personally, I wouldn't. Why? Here's a quote from *Sexual Health Update.*

> STD protection from condoms is limited. Condoms provide almost no protection from sexually transmitted HPV (human papillomavirus), the most common viral STD. HPV causes more than 90 percent of all truly abnormal Pap smears and cervical cancer. Condoms also give very unreliable protection for women's fertility, because they provide unreliable protection from chlamydia (the most common bacterial STD). While research does suggest that condoms can provide moderate risk reduction for some STDs (such as gonorrhea and herpes) and significant protection against HIV when used consistently and correctly, the fact is that condoms are often not used consistently and correctly. Even in the most reliable studies investigating condom effectiveness against HIV, almost half of the research couples did not use condoms consistently, even though they knew that their sexual partner had HIV.[10]

Tons more can be said about the subject of condoms and their effectiveness, but I don't have time here. (This book is getting too long as it is.) If you really want to research the subject, go to the Medical Institute for Sexual Health web site, *www.medinstitute.org,* and get ready for an eyeful.

---

[10] Why This Update Focuses on Contraception, *Sexual Health Update,* Vol. 7, no. 1 (Spring, 1999), p. 3.

Are You Willing to Gamble?

Now you can see how complicated life gets for people who don't wait sexually. But hey! You, on the other hand, may "luck out" and be one of the people who doesn't get caught—who doesn't get a disease—but there are millions and millions of people in the United States who aren't so lucky. Are you willing to gamble on the odds? Are you willing to risk your future marriage and sex life? Are you willing to risk your girlfriend's or boyfriend's future marriage? Are you willing to risk your ability to have kids and the health of those kids if you do have them? If you are, maybe you need to go back and reread the chapter on love again. And while you're at it, read the letter at the beginning of this chapter one more time before you move on. I hope it makes you think hard 'cause your life may depend on it.

Facts and Figures (Term Paper Heaven)

Here's some information and some statistics to help you see just how big a deal this Sexually Transmitted Disease thing really is. And for all of you doing term papers on diseases, welcome to "statistics heaven." Yes, I know how much you love hearing this kind of stuff in school, but we're talking Real Life here. People can't pretend it doesn't exist, 'cause it does!

Let me encourage you to read through this whole section. It may gross you out, but it will help you to see a real world going on out there—a world that most people don't really know exists. As I said before, *if you are sexually active the odds are one in four that you already have a disease.* Think of all your friends who are messing around. *Every fourth one of them. . . .*

Read this next section so you can see with fresh eyes the danger people have been trying to warn you about. I wish I could provide a few pictures (to help gross you out even more) but if I did I'd have to make this book X-rated. Believe me, the pictures I have would instantly convince you to never do "IT" again until you're married. Guys, just five slides would do it. If you could see the diseases a guy can get . . . Whoooooooa!

General Statistics

- Of the 52 diseases kept under surveillance in the United States, five out of the 10 most common reportable infectious diseases are chlamydia, gonorrhea, syphilis, hepatitis B, and AIDS. They account for 87 percent of all cases of infectious diseases in America.[11] (Think about that. If people quit messing around outside of marriage we would cut infectious disease by 87 percent!)
- "The annual direct and indirect costs of selected major STDs are approximately $10 billion or, if HIV infections are included, $17 billion."[12]
- There are more than 65 million Americans currently living with an *incurable* STD. Approximately 15 million people become infected with one or more STDs each year, and 25 percent of those infected are teenagers.[13]
- "In 1999, a re-examination of earlier data led to the conclusion that HPV infection was actually present in over 99 percent of cervical cancers."[14]
- One out of every three American women who are sterile cannot conceive because the fallopian tubes have been damaged by sexually transmitted diseases.[15]
- Teenagers have a high susceptibility to STDs. The lining of a teenage girl's cervix, for instance, is more susceptible to STDs than that of an older woman.

Now let's take a little closer look at each one of the most common sexually transmitted diseases. I'll give you a brief description of

---

[11] "Supporting Evidence From Recent Studies That Reveal the Necessity of Healthier, More Responsible Sexual Behavior and Education," *Sexual Health Update*, Vol. 5, no. 2 (Winter 1997), p. 1.

[12] *Ibid.*, p. 1.

[13] Centers for Disease Control and Prevention, *Tracking the Hidden Epidemics: Trends in STDs in the United States* (U.S. Department of Health and Human Services, March 5, 2001). Available at *www.cdc.gov/nchstp/dstd/Stats_Trends/Trends2000.pdf*

[14] Human Papilloma Virus (HPV)-What Is It?, *Sexual Health Update*, Vol. 8, no. 1 (Spring 2000), p. 1.

[15] *The Medical Institute Advisory*, December 16, 1997.

each disease as well as some statistics about them. The information in the descriptions of these diseases came mostly from the book *Sexuality and Sexually Transmitted Diseases*, by Dr. Joe McIlhaney, as well as many other sources.

Chlamydia

Chlamydia is an infection that affects both men and women. It is caused by an organism that is passed through sexual contact. A person can have this infection for months without knowing it, and during that time they can be passing it on to their partners. When the organism multiplies in a woman's reproductive organs it causes pelvic inflammatory disease (PID). This disease can cause the woman to become sterile or have a tubal pregnancy in the future. *This infection can be present and cause sterility even though the woman has no symptoms.* Simple chlamydia can be treated and cured by antibiotics, but PID requires more intensive treatment. If left untreated, chlamydia-related PID can cause abscesses in the uterus, ovaries, and fallopian tubes, which may make a full hysterectomy necessary. The liver can even be affected. Untreated chlamydia in men can cause sterility. Oral or anal sex with an infected partner can result in infections of the throat or rectum.

This is one nasty disease, and the following facts should help to make you believe just how serious it really is.

- Chlamydia is the most frequently reported infectious disease in the United States.
- About 3–5 million Americans become infected with chlamydia *each year*.
- As high as 85 percent of infected women and 40 percent of infected men are asymptomatic (have no symptoms).
- Almost all of the reported cases of chlamydia are among women, and 72 percent are found in young women ages 15–24.
- Women infected with chlamydia are 30–80 percent more likely to later develop cervical cancer.

- Up to 40 percent of women with chlamydia will develop PID (pelvic inflammatory disease).[16]
- PID caused by chlamydia can cause an ectopic or tubal pregnancy: a pregnancy where the egg lodges inside the fallopian tube instead of the uterus. The growing baby makes the fallopian tube rupture, causing massive internal bleeding and loss of the baby.
- Tubal pregnancy is the leading cause of first-trimester, pregnancy-related deaths in American women.
- Treatment has a high rate of success, but sometimes eliminates the problem only in one part of the body, allowing PID to continue in other parts with no obvious symptoms. So even if a woman has been successfully treated, she may still become infertile.[17]
- A baby born to an infected mother can become blind if not treated soon after birth. Chlamydia is the second leading cause of blindness worldwide, even though blindness caused by chlamydia is more rare in the United States.[18]
- A single infection produces approximately a 25 percent chance of infertility; a second infection causes about a 50 percent chance of infertility. After four infections a woman has almost a 100 percent chance of being sterile.[19]
- 40 percent of chlamydia cases are among 15- to 19-year-olds.[20]

---

[16] "Chlamydia Trachomatis – Why Should We Care?," *Sexual Health Update*, Vol. 7, no. 2 (Summer 1999):2, First published in National Institute of Allergy and Infectious Diseases. (1996, September).

[17] *Ibid.*, p. 3.

[18] *Ibid.*, p. 2.

[19] Joe S. McIlhaney, MD, *Sexuality and Sexually Transmitted Diseases* (Baker Book House, 1990), p. 98.

[20] STD trends in the United States, *The Medical Institute Advisory*, March 13,, 2001, p. 1.

- "In some studies, up to 30–40 percent of sexually active adolescent females studied have been infected" (with chlamydia).[21]
- About 50 percent of the cases of chlamydia reported by the CDC were in sexually active teenage boys and girls.[22]

Genital Herpes (HSV-2)

Herpes is a disease caused by a virus that is spread by direct skin-to-skin contact with an infected person. That means it can be spread by intercourse (vaginal, oral, or anal), kissing, or mutual masturbation. Herpes produces sores and blisters on and inside the sex organs of both men and women, as well as outbreaks on any part of the body. The most common symptom is pain, itching, or burning in the infected area. Blisters appear, then start to weep, and later scab over. This first (primary) outbreak lasts about three weeks. The person may have swollen lymph nodes, urination pain, and vaginal discharge. The virus doesn't stay just in the place you contracted it—it moves into the body and then "lives" near the spinal cord *for the rest of your life*. A person with herpes can pass it on to a partner even if they're not having an "outbreak," and even if they've *never* had any sores. In one study, the authors commented that "condom effectiveness against this STD is probably limited because genital herpes lesions 'can occur on areas of the body not covered by condoms.'"[23]

For most people herpes is not a dangerous disease, but it is embarrassing and uncomfortable and can be very painful. The first outbreak is usually the worst, and medications can make things

---

[21] "Sexual Abstinence Until Marriage – The Reports Confirm It's Best," *Sexual Health Update*, Vol. 5, no. 2 (Winter 1997): 1, First published in Eng, Thomas R. and William T. Butler, Editors, "The Hidden Epidemic – Confronting Sexually Transmitted Disease," 1997; National Academy Press, Washington, DC:39.

[22] "Sexual Abstinence Until Marriage – The Reports Confirm It's Best," *Sexual Health Update*, Vol. 5, no. 2, First published in "Morbidity and Mortality Weekly Report, 1996," CDC Infectious Disease List of 1995, 45:883–884.

[23] "Sexual Abstinence Until Marriage – The Reports Confirm It's Best," *Sexual Health Update*, Vol. 5, no. 2, (Winter 1997), first published in "Herpes Simplex Virus Type 2 in the United States," *The New England Journal of Medicine*, October 16, 1997: 1105–1111.

easier to deal with. Recurrences vary from person to person, but there is no way to predict how the disease will behave. Some fortunate people stop having outbreaks after a few years, but most people with herpes can expect to have several symptomatic recurrences each year (average four to five). There is no treatment that can cure herpes, but antiviral medications can shorten and prevent outbreaks for whatever period of time the person takes the medication. These medications are very expensive. If a baby is born to a herpes-infected woman it may become infected. While this is very rare, only 35 percent of infected babies live, and only 10 percent of them will be normal. People with weakened immune systems from AIDS or chemotherapy face greater risks from herpes.

- Nationwide, approximately 45 million Americans ages 12 and older, or one out of five of the total adolescent and adult population, are infected with HSV-2 (genital herpes).[24]
- "Today, genital herpes infects 25.6 percent of all American women and 45.9 percent of all African Americans more than 11 years of age."[25]
- Infection is more common in women (one out of four) than in men (one out of five).
- If a person has herpes they are three to five times more likely to contract HIV from a partner with HIV/AIDS.
- Only 9 percent of people testing positive for genital herpes are aware of their infection.[26]
- If a person has only two sexual partners over a lifetime, he or she still faces a 39 percent probability that one of the partners has genital herpes.[27]

---

[24] "A Beginner's Guide to Herpes Simplex Virus," *Sexual Health Update*, Vol. 9, no. 1 (Spring 2001).

[25] "Sexual Abstinence Until Marriage – The Reports Confirm It's Best," *Sexual Health Update*, Vol. 5, no. 2, (Winter 1997), First published in "Herpes Simplex Virus Type 2 in the United States," *The New England Journal of Medicine*, October 16, 1997: 1105–1111.

[26] "Genital Herpes is a Major Problem in the United States," *The Medical Institute Advisory*, February 16, 2000.

[27] "A Beginner's Guide to Herpes Simplex Virus," *Sexual Health Update*, Vol. 9, no. 1 (Spring 2001), p. 3.

- Condoms may not cover a herpes lesion when viral shedding occurs; therefore they may not prevent infection even if used correctly.
- It is estimated that 1 million Americans are newly infected each year and that forty-five million Americans age 12 and up have herpes simplex virus type 2.[28]

Human Papillomavirus (HPV)

This is a virus that causes soft warts on the genitals of both men and women. They form on the penis, scrotum, anus, and groin area in men and on the vulva, vagina, anus, and cervix in women. These warts aren't usually very uncomfortable (in fact, many women don't know they have them) and often the body's immune system can stop the infection in about a year. But that doesn't always happen, and the longer you have the infection, the greater the chance that it will cause precancerous or cancerous changes in cell structure. If HPV warts aren't treated, they can lead to cervical and vulvar cancer in women, and cancer of the penis in men. For years doctors have recommended that sexually active women have Pap smear tests done annually, because cervical cancer kills about 5,000 women per year.[29] And *"essentially all abnormal Pap smears indicating precancerous cells are a result of infection from this sexually transmitted virus."*[30]

Girls, this disease can be absolutely devastating to you. Of all the women who get cervical cancer, about 10 percent of them get cancer of the vulva. That's the area around the entrance to the vagina. Extensive vulvar cancer *requires* surgical removal of the entire vulvar area. This is major surgery and is *disfiguring*. What's amazing is, "The partner of a person with an HPV infection will contract

---

[28] "A Beginner's Guide to Herpes Simplex Virus," *Sexual Health Update*, Vol. 9, no. 1 (Spring 2001), p. 3.

[29] Ries LAG, Kosary CL, Kanakey BF, Miller BA, Clegg L, Edwards K (eds.), *SEER cancer statistics review, 1973–1996* (Bethesda, Md.: National Cancer Institute), 1999.

[30] Joe S. McIlhaney, MD, *Sexuality and Sexually Transmitted Diseases* (Baker Book House, 1990), p. 132.

the virus from 60 to 90 percent of the time . . . It is estimated that up to 30 percent of all sexually active women and men have this virus."[31] And to top things off, "Given that HPV infections can occur in and be transmitted by areas not covered or protected by the condom, correct use without breakage or slippage of the male latex condom could at most be expected to partially reduce the risk of HPV transmission."[32] What that says is, you can get (or give) HPV from areas of your body or your partner's body that aren't covered by a condom. Some studies show that condoms help prevent infection in men, but don't do much to prevent infection in women,[33] and women are the ones who suffer greater consequences from HPV. Translation: HPV is so contagious and so hard to prevent that you are crazy to have sex with anyone who has ever had sex with anyone else.

Ladies, if you have been sexually active you *absolutely* need to have a Pap smear done every year to watch for cervical cancer. Early treatment gives you a very good chance to defeat the disease. If you wait, or think you're not at risk because you don't have any symptoms, you could be taking a terrible chance.

Guys, you're at risk too. Every year "about 1,400 American men develop cancer of the penis . . . HPV infection of the anus can lead to anal cancer in both men and women . . . currently over 3,000 individuals develop anal cancer each year. . . . Anal cancer is usually treated by having a colostomy."[34] So if you have been sexually active and you notice anything unusual, even if it's just a little bump, go have it checked out by a doctor.

---

[31] Joe S. McIlhaney, MD, *Sexuality and Sexually Transmitted Diseases* (Baker Book House, 1990), p. 138–139.

[32] *Scientific Evidence on Condom Effectiveness for Sexually Transmitted Disease (STD) Prevention,* (National Institute of Allergy and Infectious Diseases, NIH, DHHS, July 20, 2001).

[33] "Human Papilloma Virus (HPV) – What Is It?," *Sexual Health Update*, Vol. 8, no. 1 (Spring 2000), first printed in Division of STD Prevention, Prevention of genital HPV infection and sequelae: Report of an external consultants' meeting, Department of Health and Human Services, Atlanta: Centers for Disease Control and Prevention (CDC), December 1999.

[34] "Human Papilloma Virus (HPV) – What Is It?," *Sexual Health Update*, Vol. 8, no. 1 (Spring 2000), p. 1

The thing that makes this disease so serious is that so many people have it. Several studies say that HPV is the most common STD among teen girls.[35] The more people you have sex with, the greater your risk of getting it, or being re-infected if you have already had it.

- About 5.5 million new infections occur each year and at least 20 million people are currently infected. HPV infects more people each year than any other STD. There is no cure.[36]
- "80 million Americans between 15 and 49 years of age have been infected by genital HPV at some point in their lives! This means that approximately 75 percent of sexually active individuals are now, or have previously been, infected with HPV."[37]
- It's estimated that 20 million Americans are presently infected with genital HPV.[38]
- HPV infects the skin and mucous membranes and is spread by direct sexual contact with an infected person, and potentially by hand-to-hand contact.[39]
- About 14,000 women in the United States develop cervical cancer each year.[40]

---

[35] Jamison JH, Kaplan DW, Hamman R, Eagar R, Beach R, Douglas JM Jr., "Spectrum of genital human papilloma virus infection in a female adolescent population," *Sex Transm Dis.* 1995; 22:236–243.

[36] American Social Health Association, *Sexually Transmitted Diseases in America: How Many Cases and at What Cost?* Menlo Park, CA: Kaiser Family Foundation; 1998.

[37] Koutsky LA, Kiviat NB, "Genital human papillomavirus." In: Holmes KK, Mardh PA, Sparling PF, et al, eds., *Sexually Transmitted Diseases*, Third ed. (New York: McGraw Hill Co.; 1999), p. 347–359.

[38] American Social Health Assoc. *Sexually Transmitted Diseases in America: How Many Cases and at What Cost?* (Menlo Park, Calif.: Kaiser Family Foundation, 1998).

[39] Sonnex C, et al. "Detection of human papillomavirus DNA on the fingers of patients with genital warts," *Sex Transm Inf.* 1999; 75:317–319.

[40] "Human Papilloma Virus (HPV) – What Is It?", *Sexual Health Update*, Volume 8, Number 1 (Spring 2000), 2, first printed in Ries LAG, Kosary CL, Hankey BF, Miller BA, Clegg L, Edwards K (eds). SEER cancer statistics review, 1973 – 1996. National Cancer Institute, Bethesda, MD, 1999.

- "Studies have shown an association between the presence of the HPV virus and the presence of cancers in the mouth. These infections may be transmitted by oral sex."[41]
- HPV causes venereal warts in over a million Americans per year and can be very painful to treat, even to the point of having to be surgically removed.
- The Centers for Disease Control (CDC) reported that barrier contraceptives (condoms) are less likely to be effective against HPV than for diseases like chlamydia or gonorrhea, which are spread by semen and are more limited to certain areas of the body.[42]

Gonorrhea

Gonorrhea is an STD caused by bacteria. It is almost always transmitted through sexual intercourse. One reason gonorrhea is so dangerous is that you can have it but not have any symptoms. In fact, about 80 percent of infected men and women can go for long periods of time without knowing they have the disease. But during that time they can pass it on to their sexual partners.

A woman may have symptoms a few days or a few months after sex with an infected man. She can be infected in any or all of her reproductive organs as well as her urinary system. If the infection causes PID, it can make all her pelvic organs (uterus, ovaries, fallopian tubes, and intestines) stick together. This kind of infection causes major problems with infertility. Scarring from the disease can cause pelvic pain every month and pain during intercourse. Sometimes the pain is so bad that a hysterectomy is necessary. The infection can affect the Bartholin's glands (the lubricating glands for a woman's vulva), which means surgery may be required. The

---

[41] "Human Papilloma Virus (HPV) – What Is It?", *Sexual Health Update*, Volume 8, Number 1 (Spring 2000), 2, first printed in Ke LD, Adler – Storthz K, Mitchell MF, Clayman GL, Chen Z, Expression of human papillomavirus E7 mRNA in human oral and cervical neoplasia and cell lines. Oral Oncol. 1999; 35: 415–420.

[42] Division of STD Prevention. "Prevention of genital HPV infection and sequelae: Report of an external consultant's meeting" (Department of Health and Human Services, Atlanta: Centers for Disease Control and Prevention, December 1999).

glands can continue to cause problems and pain even after the infection is gone, which can make intercourse painful.

If a man is infected, he might not have any symptoms at all, or he might have pain urinating or a discharge from the penis. If the infection is not treated it can cause scarring of the urethra, which causes urinary problems.

Gonorrhea can be treated with antibiotics, but new strains of the disease resist penicillin and even some of the new drugs. Since the newer medicines are about 10 times more expensive than penicillin, treatment usually starts with penicillin—but if that doesn't work, the newer drugs are given. By that time a woman may already be sterile. Like chlamydia, gonorrhea can cause damage to the fallopian tubes and create a greater chance of tubal pregnancy.

- An estimated 650,000 cases of gonorrhea infection occur in America per year and are highest among females ages 15–19 and males ages 20–24.
- "Reported gonorrhea rates increased by 9 percent between 1997 and 1999 with a 13 percent increase among adolescents."[43]
- Infection can be spread to the rectum and to the mouth through anal and oral sex.
- Gonorrhea causes pelvic inflammatory disease (PID).
- After one episode of gonorrhea, a woman has about a 12 percent chance of becoming infertile. After a second episode, the chances are 25 percent.[44]
- Gonorrhea can scar the urethra, requiring repeated dilatation of the man's urethra just so he can urinate and have an ejaculation.

---

[43] Centers for Disease Control and Prevention. Tracking the Hidden Epidemics: Trends in STDs in the United States. US Department of Health and Human Services. Available at http://www.cdc.gov/nchstp/dstd/Stats_Trends/Trends2000.pdf

[44] Joe S. McIlhaney, MD, *Sexuality and Sexually Transmitted Diseases* (Baker Book House, 1990), p. 120.

Syphilis

The good news about syphilis is that infections in the United States are at the lowest level since 1941. The bad news is that it's still out there. It's one of the top 10 infectious diseases found in America. A few years ago, in Rockdale County, Georgia, sexually active teens experienced a syphilis outbreak so large it caught the attention of national media.[45]

This disease needs a warm, moist place to live, so it is almost always spread through sexual contact or kissing. If a woman has sex *one time* with an infected man, she has over a 50 percent chance of getting the disease.

The disease goes through three stages. During the first stage a sore (chancre) will appear on the genital area, in the mouth, or on the lips. This happens within a few days or a few weeks of initial contact. These sores are painless most of the time, so many people don't pay too much attention to them. The second stage (also the most contagious stage) feels a lot like the flu: headache, fatigue, low-grade fever, rash, enlarged lymph nodes. There may also be raised, flat-topped, moist, gray growths on other parts of the body. These are highly contagious. The symptoms of the second stage will go away even without treatment, but the disease is still there, doing more damage. The last stage is called the latent period and can last up to 20 years. Usually there are no visible symptoms, and it's not very contagious, so the only way to know you have it is through a blood test. If syphilis reaches this last stage and no treatment is given, it can cause aneurysms and damage to the bones, central nervous system, and peripheral nerves. It can eventually cause insanity, paralysis, and fatal damage to the circulatory system.

The first two stages of syphilis don't seriously damage your body and can be treated with penicillin, stopping the disease. But if you are pregnant and have the disease, it can be extremely dangerous

---

[45] *The Lost Children of Rockdale County* (PBS Home Video/WGBH Educational Foundation, 1999).

or fatal to your baby. During the highly contagious stage, you have better than a 50 percent chance of passing it on to any partner.

Syphilis

- Can damage heart and blood vessels.
- Can produce severe brain damage.
- Is highly contagious in the first and second stages.
- Can be symptomless in the latent stage, making a person look cured.
- Is 100 percent cured by penicillin, but damage may occur before detection.

Hepatitis B

Hepatitis B is a disease of the liver that is spread through exchange of body fluids—blood, saliva, semen, and vaginal fluids. It often causes enough damage to the liver to be fatal. About 10 percent of people who get hepatitis B will get an infection that can cause cancer of the liver and cirrhosis of the liver. There is a vaccination against this disease, and many health care workers are routinely immunized to prevent infection.

There is no cure for this disease once you have it. "Many people recover from the infection, but some become carriers and have the infection for years with no symptoms."[46]

- Of the estimated 200,000 infections each year, 120,000 are acquired through sexual transmission. It's estimated that about 5 percent of the total U.S. population has been infected.[47]
- Hepatitis B kills 5,000–6,000 Americans per year.

---

[46] Joe S. McIlhaney, MD, *Sexuality and Sexually Transmitted Diseases* (Baker Book House, 1990), p. 153.

[47] Centers for Disease Control and Prevention, *Tracking the Hidden Epidemics: Trends in STDs in the United States* (U.S. Department of Health and Human Services, March 5, 2001). Available at www.cdc.gov/nchstp/dstd/Stats_Trends/Trends2000.pdf

- Seventy percent to 90 percent of infected babies become lifelong infectious carriers.
- Hepatitis B is the most common cause of liver cancer.

AIDS (Acquired Immune Deficiency Syndrome)

You've probably been hearing about AIDS since you were in the fifth grade, and by now you may even know someone who has it or has died from it. Here's a quick review of the disease, in case you've forgotten what you heard in school.

AIDS is an infection caused by the human immunodeficiency virus (HIV). The virus attacks cells of the immune system, and sometimes the cells in the brain and spinal cord. After a person is infected with HIV, the virus spreads through the body and slowly destroys the immune system. Your immune system helps your body fight off diseases—it's your total defense system. Without an immune system you could catch diseases from any germ that came your way.

If you are HIV-positive you are infected and will be contagious *for life*. You will go through a "silent" period where there may be no symptoms, and tests for the virus may even be negative.

> A person who is HIV-positive may feel perfectly healthy and be unaware of carrying the AIDS virus. Even a blood test can give a false sense of security, since it may fail to show positive from months to years after the infection. . . . HIV can permanently insert itself into the genes of blood cells but stay "hidden," so that the body does not produce antibodies for three years—and perhaps much longer—after the initial infection.[48]

People infected with HIV will eventually have full-blown AIDS: the condition in which the immune system is unable to fight off opportunistic infections. At some point one or more of these infections will be serious enough to cause death.

---

[48] Joe S. McIlhaney, MD, *Sexuality and Sexually Transmitted Diseases* (Baker Book House, 1990), p. 143.

AIDS is spread through the exchange of HIV-infected body fluids, so you can get it through intercourse (oral, anal, and vaginal), French kissing (possible, but unlikely), or using contaminated needles. Blood-to-blood contact with an infected person can result in infection. That's why health care professionals have to be so careful (gloves, masks, etc.). AIDS affects both men and women, whether heterosexual or homosexual. Before they began testing for AIDS, people who received blood transfusions were also at risk for the disease. In fact a friend of mine has AIDS because of a transfusion she received when she was having her baby. You can't catch it from casual contact (hugging), toilet seats, or mosquitoes. There has to be intimate contact or mingling of blood.

- AIDS always results in death.
- It's the leading cause of death for people ages 25–44 in United States
- Children born to infected mothers have a one-in-three chance of being infected.
- Twenty-five percent of all newly reported HIV infections are found in people under age 22.

Vaginitis

There are a couple of organisms that cause vaginitis: *Bacterial Vaginosis* and *Trichomonas*. The main symptoms are vaginal discharge and pain or itching of the vulva. This can get so uncomfortable that a woman is forced to see a doctor. It can also cause pain with intercourse. The only symptom that men have is a discharge from the penis, and sometimes slight burning when they urinate. These infections can be treated with prescription medications, although they can be persistent and require repeated treatments. They're also very uncomfortable. To get rid of the disease, *both partners need to be treated* or one will just re-infect the other.

- About 5 million cases of trichomoniasis (infection with *Trichomonas*) occur each year.[49]
- As many as 16 percent of pregnant women in the United States have bacterial vaginosis.[50]
- Trichomoniasis may cause premature delivery.[51]
- Vaginitis causes an increased risk of HIV infection in both men and women, if exposed to the virus.[52]

For More Information

- *www.cdc.gov/nchstp/dstd/Stats*
- *www.medinstitute.org*

[49] Centers for Disease Control and Prevention, *Tracking the Hidden Epidemics: Trends in STDs in the United States* (U.S. Department of Health and Human Services, March 5, 2001). Available at www.cdc.gov/nchstp/dstd/Stats_Trends/Trends2000.pdf

[50] *Ibid.*

[51] Cole and Duran, *Sex and Character* (Dallas, Panda Publications, 1998), 72.

[52] *Ibid.*, p. 72.

Chapter 13. Why Wait?
No Hurt, Guilt, or Fear (Now or Later)

Have you ever watched a movie with a plot so twisted that it kept you hangin' every minute? Even if you had to go to the bathroom, you didn't go 'cause you didn't want to miss something. The girl (it's always a girl) is totally alone in some haunted mansion–type place, when she hears a mournful cry from somewhere down the long dark hallway. She thought she was completely alone and safe in this haunted, run-down mansion until the moaning came from the "empty bedroom." (Now at this point, everybody in the theater knows that if this were happening to *them*, they'd beat feet out the front door, screaming so loud people in Brazil could hear them!!) But what does the girl in the movie do? She starts tiptoeing TOWARDS THE BEDROOM DOOR, armed with nothing but . . . a hairbrush! You, of course, *know* it's not going to work out for her, mainly because the music is getting louder and more and more intense. But down the hall she goes, ready to lash out with her hairbrush, through the flickering lights, closer and closer to the moaning. (Like, come on! Does she think it's a surprise party and she's going to fool her friends or something?) Finally she reaches the bedroom, puts her ear to the door, and suddenly, without warning, it bursts open!!! Surprise, surprise! It's the bad guy! He grabs her, and the rest of the movie is about the good guy trying

to save her. Why he *wants* to save this DUMB chick is beyond me, but that's the way the movie goes.

Watching those movies, we all know that we would never act like that. We'd be smarter, for sure. If *we* heard somebody moaning in the other room we would get the heck outta Dodge! That's because the natural response to fear is to get away as fast as possible.

Fear comes in all kinds of packages. Think of all the phobias you've heard of. Things like:

Necrophobia = fear of death
Arachnophobia = fear of spiders (Ever see *that* movie? Yuck!)
Agoraphobia = fear of crowds
Hydrophobia = fear of water
Claustrophobia = fear of enclosed places
Acrophobia = fear of heights
Yo-phobia = fear of rap music (It's a joke, OK?)

Then, of course, there's the fear of failure, fear of losing someone through death or divorce, fear of losing something important to you, or the fear of speaking in front of a class. We fear things like being raped or abandoned, losing a game, or failing a test. All of these fears are real, and some people's fears leave them absolutely petrified or sick to their stomachs and desperate to run. That can even happen when it comes to sex. Like this girl.

Dear Mr. Henning,

I was wondering if you could catch a disease or anything if it (the boy's part) goes half way in, not even half? Does it mean that I'm still a virgin or not? If I wanted to get checked to see if I did have something what do I say? I want to get tested for anything and everything. How much will it cost for all these tests? Do my parents have to know because if they were to find out they'd probably ground me for life. He used two condoms at first and then it broke so he put two more on and they broke so we used one more. It hurt so we stopped. Do you think I have a chance of

having anything? *I'm scared.* What if I'm dying and I don't know it? But I don't want this to happen again till I'm older. It was my first and last (time).

Unsigned

Look at this letter again, and let's make a list of all the fears she brings up directly or indirectly. She's afraid of:

1. Getting a disease
2. Not being a virgin anymore
3. Being ignorant
4. Going to get checked for diseases
5. Not knowing what to say to the doctor
6. The cost of getting tested
7. Her parents finding out
8. Getting grounded when her parents do find out
9. The condoms not working (And they didn't)
10. Not doing it right
11. The pain in the future
12. Possibly dying from a disease
13. Having it happen again

She did it only once, and look what happened to her. Was it worth it? If you wait to be sexually active until marriage you won't have to ever think about ANY of those things . . . EVER!!!!

What If . . . ?

Obviously, then, fear can come from sexual experiences, too. Those fears are just as real as any other fear and can damage a person for life. Can you imagine, for instance, having to tell your future husband or wife just before you get married that you have a sexually transmitted disease? What words are you gonna use? How do you think they're gonna take the news? Would that tend to bring fear into your life? Or would you just not tell them? Ladies, what if you had to tell your new husband that you were infertile

and couldn't have his children? Would you have any feelings of guilt, hurt, or pain even if he said it's all right? You *know* you would! And that's just the beginning. How about the sexual guilt and pain that comes . . .

When you had sex . . . only to be dumped the next day
When the person you are dating is a virgin but you're not
When you have to go to the doctor for an exam
When you have a disease and have to explain how you got it
When you get pregnant and don't know what to do
When you get an abortion and end your baby's life
When you get married and have to tell your spouse about your past
When you want to have sex but you are having an outbreak from your STD
When you see one of your old sexual partners at the mall
When you have to explain to your child why she doesn't have a daddy
When you have to explain to your own kids why *they* should wait, knowing you didn't
When you sneak behind your parents' backs to have sex

Want an example of that last one? Read this!

My boyfriend and I had decided we were ready to have sex. I was a little nervous, 'cause it was going to be my first time, and I wanted to know all the details about using condoms safely. So I made a trip to the drugstore, and the pharmacist was really nice about answering all of my questions and helping me choose a brand. Later that night, I headed over to my boy (friend's) house, and I thought I was going to drop dead when his mom opened the door——she was the pharmacist who had helped me pick out the condoms! She acted normal, but *I couldn't look her in the eye the rest of the evening.*

YM, September 1999

If It's No Big Deal, Why Are You Hiding?

Wait a minute! Why was this girl feeling so guilty? Because people feel guilty when they've done something (or, in her case, they're *about* to do something) that they know is wrong. You don't feel guilty if you're caught doing something *right*, do you? Could it be that people really *do* know right from wrong? If sex is supposed to be so natural and no big deal, why was she so uncomfortable? Why all the embarrassment?

Running Scared

When a girl or guy is sexually or relationally hurt or taken advantage of, what is their natural response? To RUN! But run to where? To just start running may mean you end up right back where you started, and that means you're ready for more hurt and guilt. Let me explain.

The girl who is sexually hurt in one relationship tries to protect herself from the pain in a second relationship by not getting too close too soon. She takes a little more time getting to know him before she "gives in." But more often than not she gets dumped again, and the hurt, pain, and guilt come flooding back.

After her second breakup she may wonder if she's making too big a deal out of the sex thing and that maybe she just needs to lighten up a bit. After all, that's what her friends keep telling her: "If you'd just loosen up a little everything would be OK." So she redefines what happened to her by telling herself it wasn't that big a deal. "You know, hey, it really is no big deal. I mean, guys are just like that. So what's the big deal?" By redefining the problem she thinks she's distancing herself from the pain and memories, but it doesn't work. Her next relationship turns out the same way. She gets dumped a third time. By refusing to look deeply into *what* she is doing and *why*, she dooms herself to a pattern of failure. The pain hits her right in the face as she circles back for yet another try at the same kind of sexual relationship.

Part of the pain comes from being thought of as a "thing," like a discarded toy, tossed aside for a newer, better model. It's wondering if each new guy really loves you, and if he will stick around

when things get hard. It's lack of trust and commitment. It's fear of the unknown.

Fear of Discovery

And what happens to the guy? Does he get off scot-free? Nope. When the guy finally gets the girl to give him the sex he was looking for, how come he dumps her? Since he got sex from her you'd think he'd stick around and try again, but that's not usually what happens. The reason he moves on so quickly is he's running just like she is. But he's running 'cause he doesn't want to be "found out." His fear is that a woman would get close enough to find out he's not what he says he is—that he's really just a self-centered "user" who has no idea what a woman's real needs are, and wouldn't know how to meet them even if he did. He just takes what he wants and runs. Sticking around too long would be suicide to him, so he beats her to the punch and dumps her first. But the more women he takes advantage of, the more he fears being discovered. He suspects that someday it's all going to blow up in his face, but he knows that if he wanted to change he'd have to eat humble pie, admit his mistakes, and eventually settle down . . . with one girl . . . and that's too dangerous. *Way* too dangerous! Until he makes a permanent commitment to one woman he's caught in a trap: his body is craving hers, but rejection makes him run as fast as he can.

Trapped!

This pattern can become as powerful as a drug addiction. Look at this next guy. He couldn't stop even though he wanted to.

Mr. Henning,

To you I am probably just a face in the crowd. I am a alcoholic/ drug addict in recovery. I have been sober for a year and a half now. Part of your presentation was like a punch in the gut. When you were talking about diseases I was reminded of my friend. She died last summer from pneumonia. She had AIDS. I've been scared for a while that I've got it too. She and I never slept together but

I've done some pretty dangerous things in the years before I got sober. I use to inject morphine and can't even remember how many sexual relationships I've had.

I would like to say that I haven't had sex since I got sober but that would be a lie. *I have probably been with more girls than anyone else in my school* and I'm only a sophomore. You'll probably think I'm full of ____ *but I'm not proud of that.* At all. *In fact I'm very ashamed of it. But I keep doing it, don't ask why.* I don't know. It probably has to do with insecurity. I don't brag about it, I don't even talk about it with my best friends because I think that's BS and very disrespectful. I am always honest with my partners and never deceive them into believing that our relationship has any real meaning or commitment involved. If that's not justification I don't know what is. I'm done rambling.

James

I honestly think that deep down inside James is a good guy, but no one's ever shown him the way out. He's ashamed of the way he acts but he feels powerless to change. No one has shown him what the end results of his actions will be: shame, lack of pride in himself, insecurity, guilt, dishonesty, disrespect for others, inability to commit, plus the incredible ability to justify everything he does. Until he sees that, he'll keep doing what he's doing, and keep on hurting. Hey ladies, would you dare to date or marry a guy like James?

Sexual "Freedom"?

So what does the sexually active person tend to bring into a permanent relationship? Fear and guilt! To see this for yourself stand back and look at the overall picture. At your school are the sexually active people the really healthy, happy people, or are they more likely to be the ones who always seem to have some traumatic thing happening to them? Ecstasy one day, tears and trauma the next?

A school administrator once told me how he met with half of the teachers in his high school and had them make a list of the kids

they felt were the most sexually active in their school. He then met with the second half of his staff and had them identify the most "messed-up" kids in the school. Neither group of teachers knew what the other half was doing. Eventually he took the two lists and compared them. Guess what? The lists were almost identical. *The messed-up kids were the most sexually active kids.* Now it may be anybody's guess WHY those two lists were the same, but let me throw out a suggestion. If you were dealing with the guilt and pain and fear I've just described, would YOU be able to concentrate on school? If your emotions were on a roller coaster, would you really care about geometry or history? Would you get messed up in the head? How could you not?

Hurt in one area of your life tends to affect other areas of your life. Kids from healthy families are far less likely to be sexually active than kids from divorced or unhealthy families. The better their grades are, the less sexually active they are likely to be. I'm not saying that just because you're from a split family or your grades aren't that good, your life's gonna be screwed up. Don't get me wrong. But the patterns people learn from their families tend to carry over into their relationships and often into their marriages. People who don't expect much from their future don't put much effort into the present. Or if they've never learned to look out for other people as much as they look out for themselves, they'll continue to act selfishly and bail out when the going gets tough.

Brad,

I know what you mean about screwing up your life by having sex at a young age. My girlfriend and I were sexually active and one day when I came home she told me she thought she was pregnant. I was scared senseless for a month. I kept telling her everything would be alright and don't worry if she was I (would help) take care of the problem (child). I didn't have a clue of what I was gonna do. I just prayed every night that she wasn't and that this was kind of a fluke. Well she finally got her period and we knew she wasn't pregnant. *I dumped her.* I just can't have the constant reminder of (a) mistake talking to me every day.

Call me selfish but I didn't love her and I'm a kid for god's sake so I did what I had to do.

Unsigned (Ninth grade)

One girl wrote me saying she had dated a boy for four years. When she was 14 and he was 15 they had sex, and *she said that when they were doing it she couldn't even look at him, she felt so gross.* After he had gone she took a shower, then a bath. She tried to work it out with the guy later, but *every time he would touch her, she felt gross and wanted him to leave her alone.* They broke up. Is sex supposed to be like that? NO! When you've saved sex for marriage there's nothing to feel guilty about! When this girl gets married, will she "feel gross" when she makes love with her husband? Will she wish he would leave her alone every time he touches her? It's very possible. If your first feelings about sex were guilt feelings, you can be emotionally trapped into feeling guilty about sex even after you are married. Is that a risk you want to take?

Another girl wrote to me saying, "Most of my friends tell me to stay a virgin. It gets really ugly if you don't." Look around your school and see if she isn't telling the truth. The kids who look like they're having the time of their life one weekend are the same ones falling apart the next. Why? The same girl answered, *"I guess when you have nothing you hold on to anything!"*

When you think about the person you will marry, do you look forward to your wedding night with an absolutely clear conscience or do you feel like this girl who said, *"I wish I could marry someone who waited, but I know no one like that would marry me."* Oh man . . . that hurts!!!! When I read that I wanted to cry.

The Honeymoon

I will never forget the first time I ever made love to my wife. Not only was it the first time with my wife, it was my first time with anyone . . . EVER! She was the first (and last) woman I ever made love to. When our wedding reception was over we drove down the California coast to a beautiful Victorian inn overlooking

Monterey Bay. It was a romantic old mansion, and our room was like something out of a fairy tale. Everyone will tell you that making love to the woman (or man) you love can be one of life's greatest physical pleasures, and they're right. But no one could have prepared me for what I experienced that night. I wish I could tell you more because it would help you understand, but I can't. That memory belongs to my wife and me—and no one else!

But there were some things I missed out on that night too. I didn't realize I had missed them until a few years later when I talked to other people about things going on in their lives and marriages. I couldn't even relate to their problems because I had never experienced them. My honeymoon (and every night since then) was free from the hurt, fear, and guilt that so many of those people felt. I can't tell you how thankful I am to the friends who encouraged me to wait until I was married, because that choice allowed me a freedom I could never explain to you. That night I was free to totally concentrate on how beautiful my wife was, to enjoy all the feelings, pleasure, and pure fun of being together for the very first time. And I can tell you that the pleasure has never dwindled from that day to this. I've been married for over 32 years and I'm telling you sex is better than it's ever been . . . EVER! So there. EAT YOUR HEART OUT! And trust me. That's what you're gonna want to feel after 32 years!

That's the way it's supposed to be. And it can be! So how come so many people are experiencing so much less? 'Cause they believed the lie that everybody's doin' it, and you're a loser if *you* don't. Don't *you* believe it!

One Last Letter

Years ago I read this story in a book by Charlie Shedd, *The Stork Is Dead.* It's a letter he received from a girl who married her high school boyfriend because she was pregnant. The things they did *before* they got married came back full circle to haunt her *after* they were married—things they both ran from and never dealt with until it was too late. Listen to her very concise description of

the hurt, fear, and guilt she felt. Her letter was entitled, "What It's Like to Be Married at Seventeen."

What It's Like to Be Married at Seventeen

Jimmy and I couldn't wait so now we are married. Big deal! Let me tell you what it is like to be married at 17. It is like living in this dump on the third floor up and your only window looks out on somebody else's third floor dump. It is like coming home at night so tired you feel like you're dead from standing all day at your checker's job. But you don't dare sit down because you might never get up again and there are so many things to do like cooking and washing and dusting and ironing. So you go through the motions and you hate your job and you ask yourself, "Why don't I quit?" and you already know why. It's because there are grocery bills and drug bills and rent bills and doctor bills, and Jimmy's crummy little check from the lumberyard won't cover them, that's why!

Then you try to play with the baby until Jimmy comes home. Only sometimes you don't feel like playing with her. But even if you do, you get this awful feeling that you are only doing it because you feel guilty. She is so beautiful, and you know it isn't fair to her to be in that old lady's nursery all day long. Then you wash diapers and mix formula and you hate it, and you wonder how long it will be till she can tell how you feel, and wouldn't it be awful if she could tell already?

Then Jimmy doesn't come home, and you know it's because he is out with the boys doing the things he didn't get to do because you had to get married. So, finally you go to bed and cry yourself to sleep telling yourself that it really is better when he doesn't come because sometimes he says the cruelest things. Then you ask yourself "Why does he hate me so?" And you know it is because he feels trapped, and he doesn't love you anymore, like he said he would.

Then he comes home and he wakes you up, and he starts saying all the nice things he said before you got married. But you know it is only because he wants something, and yet you want

to believe that maybe it is the old Jimmy again. So you give in, only when he gets what he wants, he turns away and you know he was only using you once more. So you try to sleep but you can't. This time, you cry silently because you don't want to admit that you care.

You lie there and think. You think about your parents and your brothers and the way they teased you. You think about your backyard and the swing and the tree house and all the things you had when you were little. You think about the good meals your mother cooked and how she tried to talk to you, but you were so sure she had forgotten what it was like to be in love.

Then you think about your girl friends and the fun they must be having at the prom. You think about the college you planned to go to, and you wonder who will get the scholarship they promised you. You wonder who you would have dated in college and who you might have married and what kind of a job would he have?

Suddenly you want to talk, so you reach over and touch Jimmy. But he is far away and he pushes you aside, so now you can cry yourself to sleep for real.

If you ever meet any girls like me who think they are just too smart to listen to anyone, I hope you'll tell them that this is what it is like to be married at 17![1]

---

[1] Charlie Shedd, *The Stork Is Dead* (Waco, Word Books, 1968), p. 61–62. Used by permission.

Chapter 14. Why Wait?
No Bad Reputation

In the Locker Room

In a guys' locker room there is always a bunch of guys standing around talking about sex. They are usually talking a lot bigger than reality, but anyway . . . finally it comes down to "who has and who hasn't." It was no different in my high school; sooner or later it always came around to me, which meant I was supposed to "fess up"! In the beginning, I would just say that no, I hadn't done "it" and then wait until the laughter subsided before I crawled out from under my locker. I was a virgin, but I usually tried not to make a big deal out of it. Yeah, I was still one of the guys all right, but I found out real fast that if I said much about the virginity thing, the non-virgins felt like I was preaching at them; that I was putting them down for not being virgins anymore. To them, people who were "pushing abstinence" were self-righteous geeks or "goody two shoes," and if you stayed a virgin you had to become one of "them." And who wants that? But the more I thought about that, the more ticked off I got. Why do I have to be the one apologizing for not playin' the "hit the b—— an' ditch" game (better known as "Wham, bam, thank you ma'am")? So I thought about it and figured out what I was going to do the next time some wise guy asked me about my sex life. I'd give him something he'd never forget. And I'd

use humor to do it. If he wouldn't drop it I was going to hammer him. I could hardly wait.

A few days later I got my chance when our local locker room idiot arrived. I knew it was only a matter of time before the subject of sex came up. (It's one of only two topics he talks about. The other is farting.) Sure enough, he turned to me and predictably said, "Hey Henning, have you done it yet?"

Now you have to wonder about this guy's mental capacity when he has to ask the same question on a semiweekly basis and still not remember the answer from the previous 2,000 times he's asked it. But sure enough he brings it up again and it gets the typical response from the group . . . they're all ears. But this time I was ready for them. The conversation went something like this:

Idiot: Hey Henning, have you done it yet?

Me: (Without looking up from what I am doing) Shoot, yeah.

Idiot: Ah, you haven't either. (See, I told you I knew what he was going to say.) You're such a liar! How many times?

Me: (Now looking up at the ceiling in contemplation) I believe it's eight hundred twenty-nine million, six hundred seventy-one thousand, two hundred fifty-four. No . . . no . . . wait . . . fifty-*FIVE*. I got your girlfriend last night!

Now usually that shuts most guys up just 'cause everyone's laughing so hard, even though I'm obviously joking. But not "The Idiot." This guy would always come back and say something like:

Idiot: You haven't had sex with a girl and you know it!

Now we take it to a new level . . .

Me: Actually you're right . . . (looking directly at him with a grin on my face) I haven't, but I got this girl I'm working on and she's gorgeous!

Let me ask you . . . what would every guy in the whole locker room want to know next? Of course . . . WHO IS SHE?

Me: I'm not telling you . . . you'll try to get her first, but when it happens I'll let you know.

Am I lying? No. Why? 'Cause I'm thinking about MY FUTURE WIFE!!!!!! I'm not gonna let these idiots tell me what I'm gonna do with my life! Why should I tell them anything?

At this point, if the guy keeps pushing me about the sex thing, now he's got me mad, and he deserves what's next.

Idiot: You don't have any girl. I'll bet you couldn't even find a girl who *wants* to do it with you.
Me: No, actually, there are lots of girls in this school that I could get to do it with me tonight, but I'm not going to —because then I would become just like you, and why would I want that? But I'll tell you something: In the next two hundred years you'll never become like me again. I'm a virgin *now* and I'm gonna be one until my honeymoon night! You got a problem with that?

Now some guys may even try to give you the old, "But you're not a man if you don't do it" thing, but if they did, my answer to them would be,

Me: Well, if that's what it takes to become a man, then last night my DOG became a man in my front yard and it was AWFUL!

And that's usually the end of the conversation, 'cause most of the guys are drowning from laughter.

Who Cares?

Brad,

Thanks for coming to talk to us about our sex life it was very interesting. I think everything you said was to a great value of mine, but really though having sex isn't a big deal as long as you use protection. I mean it's not like you can only have sex if you love the person. I had sex with this guy and I didn't even go with him, we just decided to do it! Nobody cares. Really all sex is something that I do for pleasure. Why would you just have sex with someone you love? Who really cares!!! Just because we're young still, and people think that at that age you're too young to do it because we don't know what we are doing, well that's wrong cause I know exactly what I was doing. I personally think it was one of the best things that has ever happened to me! Recently I had sex with my boyfriend we've been going out for 2 years we don't love each other, but we care about each other a lot. We have sex all the time, but it's for fun. We don't plan on breaking up any time soon.

Anna

Remember this letter from Chapter 10? Here it is again. Question: Will Anna stop at sex with just this one guy? No. Will there be lots of guys who want to get her into bed? Yeah! Will guys respect her for her attitude of "sexual freedom"? No. They'll want her sexually but they won't respect her. Remember . . .

**If a girl's easy to get to bed . . . she isn't worth keeping.
All guys know that.**

When Anna finally does decide (if she ever does) that she wants to settle down, get married, and raise a family, will those same guys be waiting in line to marry her? Get serious! Would any of those guys want to settle down in a loving, lifelong, committed marriage . . . with the girl known as "the town slut?" No. Or will the girl

in your school who has purposely saved herself for marriage be excited to marry the "player" of the school? Somehow I doubt it. Look at this guy's letter.

Mr. Henning

I would like to say that your presentation was good. It taught me a lot which could help me understand why me and my sister get into fights. I would like to give one more reason not to have sex, if you don't already know it. (This is for you girls) When females go out with a lot of people, and have sex with all of them, they get a bad reputation. Girls don't know this but once the word gets around we all want to do the same thing to her, and no one will take (her) serious. This reputation doesn't come and go, it stays with them for the rest of their life in that city. I also think you should teach this in the sixth, or seventh grade. Why? Well because that's when it starts.

Some people want you to believe that having sex doesn't hurt you or your reputation, but, in fact, it does.

What You See . . . Not What You Get

To illustrate this, let's say a guy meets "the new girl" in his school at a party. When he first sees her he is attracted to her and immediately starts to evaluate the possibilities. But watch how his mind changes the more he finds out about her reputation and background. In fact, play like you're the guy and answer yes, maybe, or no after each question.

1. Guy meets a good-looking girl at a dance
   Would you ask her out?   Y M N
2. She has a great personality
   Would you ask her out?   Y M N
3. She has dated A LOT of other guys
   Would you ask her out?   Y M N
4. She has a great figure
   Would you ask her out?   Y M N

5. She wears all padded underwear
   Would you ask her out?   Y M N
6. She is anorexic/bulimic
   Would you ask her out?   Y M N
7. She is a chain smoker
   Would you ask her out?   Y M N
8. She has had sex with over 25 other guys
   Would you ask her out?   Y M N
9. She has gotten pregnant twice, but got abortions
   Would you ask her out?   Y M N
10. She has a 3-month-old baby at home
    Would you ask her out?   Y M N
11. She has herpes
    Would you ask her out?   Y M N
12. She was known as the slut at her previous school
    Would you ask her out?   Y M N

Now be honest. Did you start changing your mind the more you found out about the girl? You know you did.

Do any of those things say she is a terrible person, that she has no value as a human being, or that she isn't worth knowing? No, not at all, but you could feel how your mind began to change the more you knew about her. Of course, if you're just a player lookin' for some action, you might consider asking her out. But if you're really looking to find the person you want to spend the rest of your life with, she wouldn't be your first choice. Or your second.

Virgins Can't Be Controlled

Here's the deal. Virgins (who are purposely choosing to be virgins) demand to be known *for who they are,* not what they do. What's cool is they don't get caught up in the win/lose cycle, and they can't be controlled. Why? Because they refuse to play the game. That way they can control the situation they are in, but they can't be controlled by anyone else. When I was in high school I had the reputation for being a virgin, but I also never got turned down when I asked for a date . . . ever! I just figured if I could

have a sense of humor about my virginity, I'd be OK, and once I did, it saved my life.

Who Will You Give the Power To?

When a guy or girl gives in to sexual pressure from friends they don't realize the power they are giving away. When you let your group of friends talk you into having sex before marriage, you may have just handed them the power to determine the direction the rest of your life will take. You may have allowed them to decide whether or not you are going to create another human being, whether or not you might live in poverty for the rest of your life because you're a single mom, or whether you get a sexually transmitted disease, have an abortion, or have a bad reputation. Because you didn't stand up to their pressure, you may have to live with hurt, fear, and guilt for the rest of you life, not to mention the effect you'll have on the people you're involved with. Some kids give the power away without a second thought! But before you do that, think about this. Will the people who pushed you into those bad decisions be there to help you when you need it most? I doubt it. They'll probably be thanking God it's you that has the problem and not them, and you can hardly blame them.

Sadder or Wiser?

Brad,

I really enjoyed your talk. What you said about everyone should wait for the person he/she is going to be with for the rest of their life, is true. But I didn't. I first had sex at age 13. I was at the end of the 7th grade. I had known him since 6th grade. We were going out for only a couple of weeks, when one day on a day we got an early dismissal, it happened. It wasn't even what I expected. It was boring, and non-caring. I thought it was gonna be so special. When I look back, it was the crowd I was hanging out with. All them were having sex and it seemed like I was the only virgin. Oh yeah, we broke up about a week after it happened. Some people don't think the crowd they are with

will influence them, but take it from me it definitely happens. I just wanted to see what it was like, that's all. I wasn't a slut before that, but after I was called that, and it still haunts me. My boyfriend now of 13 months jokes with me about doing it at 13 years old. It gets to me bad though. What saddens me the most is that when I have children, they might ask me when my first time was. I can't bear to tell them. I just want everyone to know that you should wait, sex isn't worth getting hurt over and you do get hurt, emotionally. Also, when you get in a relationship later on you have to tell your partner everyone you have been with. It's really hard to go through with. If I could go back in time I would in an instant and change so many things. I came to a point where I hated myself for it. I try and advise some of my friends now who are still virgins to wait, wait, wait! It's the smartest thing to do.

Unsigned

Dear Brad,

I thought you were a very good speaker. I also admire you for waiting to have sex until you were married. I too do not believe in pre-marital sex, but I didn't know why I didn't believe in it. I just thought it was wrong. I also thought that if I do wait it would be more special and people would respect me more. There's just a couple of problems. A lot of guys tease me about it and say they should just shoot me or gang rape me. They also say that it's gross or sick to stay a virgin. One of my best friends also said if I would just get "laid" I would loosen up and quit being such a BLEEP. But in her case she has a child and is only 16. People have little respect for her also. Well at least I have respect for myself and that's all that counts. Thanks for actually giving me a reason to stay a virgin.

Thanks

How to Change a Bad Reputation

If you already have a bad reputation at your school I don't need to tell you how hard that can be to live with. I'm sure you already know. The way you deal with it depends on whether or not the rumors are true. Most of the time, if someone is just spreading lies about you, enough people know your real character that they won't believe the rumors, and the lies will fizzle. But if you've made a series of dumb choices, you have some work to do. So let me show you the only way I know to deal with a bad reputation and start building a good one.

First of all, whatever you did to get the reputation in the first place has to stop. Admit you were wrong and make the decision to change. Make up your mind to never be involved in that activity again. Don't skirt your responsibility for the things that happened by focusing on the other people involved. "Well, they did it too." You can't change them; you can only change yourself.

If your reputation has been damaged by someone who just wants to hurt you, you can only deny the rumors and move on. Don't make things worse by getting into a big defensive deal and try to make them look bad. For example, if a guy lies and says that a girl had sex with him (and she didn't) all she can say is, "I don't know why he is saying that, but I can tell you it isn't true." And then walk away. If it did happen, don't deny it, but don't give details to anybody either. Rumors are almost never completely accurate, so you can say that what they heard isn't *totally* true. Keep things very vague, but don't lie. That will only bring down more trouble. That doesn't mean you should stand up in front of the whole school and admit you had sex, for instance, but if somebody comes up to you in the hall and asks about what happened, say something like this:

> It wouldn't be right for me to tell you everything that happened with (guy/girl) but I can tell you it wasn't exactly what you heard. I made some mistakes with them and I regret it now. Trust me, I'm not going to make that mistake ever again. I've learned my lesson.

OR

Look, I don't know where you heard all this, but please, I need your help to stop the rumors. I've made a terrible mistake. I don't want that kind of reputation. Please help me.

If a good friend asks you about what happened, before you answer them ask yourself these questions:

1. Is this person really trying to help, or are they just being nosy, trying to get the latest information?
2. Can you trust them or are they just part of the rumor mill? If you can't, say no more than what's in the example paragraph above.
3. Will they give you good advice, or are they in just as much (or more) trouble than you?
4. What is *their* reputation? If *their* reputation is bad, telling them what happened will only add to *your* already struggling reputation.
5. Talk only in private, not in the hallway or in a classroom, and, if at all possible, talk person to person, not on the phone. That way they can see your face, eyes, hands, and body language. They will know that you are telling them the truth about wanting to change and that you are sorry. And when it's face to face, you will know no one else is listening to your conversation in the background. Never put what happened into print! You never know where it might show up.
6. Keep the conversation short. Girls will sometimes get on the phone and talk for hours, and in this case it can only make things worse. The longer the conversation, the more information you will reveal.
7. Tell them you need them as a friend. Ask them to help you by keeping it quiet and asking other people to do the same.

8. After you've talked, go do something fun together. You will need the release, and it shows them you are still the kind of person they want to be with.

9. If you can, go to the person passing the rumors and ask to talk to them about "something" in private. Ask them for their help and to please help stop the rumors. Be polite, not demanding.

10. Even if they continue to pass rumors, do not do it back. It will only make you look more guilty.

11. Rumors have a way of dying out, even though reputations can last a lifetime. The only way to change a reputation is to CHANGE A REPUTATION. Don't hang out with the same kind of people that helped get you the reputation in the first place.

Whatever you do in life, make up your mind to never make the same mistake twice. Never! Now move on. No, don't TRY to move on . . . DO IT!

Chapter 15. Why Wait?
Don't Steal from Someone Else's Marriage

Brad,

I think it's very important that teens realize the differences between love and infatuation. Too often there are situations where teens believe they have found the one they love and they lose their virginity to them. The sad fact is usually soon after these people realize that they really aren't in love and they have to live with knowing that they lost something very precious to someone very unimportant and insignificant.

The biggest regret of my life is that I lost my virginity at age 15 to someone I thought I loved. My relationship with him became very abusive and extremely hard to deal with. My fiancé had also been involved in bad relationships but he has slept with more people than me. We both hate the fact that we couldn't share that first time with one another. Another issue that's hard to deal with is that he has a son from his last relationship and for the rest of our lives we have to deal with his ex-girlfriend being involved in his life. I wish more than anything I would have waited and so does he. I am so extremely happy with him.

Unsigned

Ever had someone steal something from you? Maybe as a kid you left your bike out overnight, or you left your favorite jacket in an unlocked locker at school and, sure enough, it's gone. Nothing makes me madder than someone stealing from me. One night, right before Mother's Day, someone stole a hanging flower basket right off my front porch! ("Look, Mom! See what I STOLE for you!!!") I've often wondered what I would do if I actually caught someone in the act, especially if I had a baseball bat in my hand.

There's lots of ways to steal from someone, and it's not always something as obvious as money or "stuff." In fact, money is probably the least valuable thing someone can take from you. For instance, have you ever had someone "steal your reputation" by passing lies about you? How did it make you feel? By lying they stole your friends, your reputation, your happiness, and maybe even part of your future. It's not fair, but they did it. That's stealing!

But have you ever thought that having sex with your boyfriend or girlfriend is stealing? Probably not, but it is. Think about it. How would you feel if you got married and found out someone else had had sex with your husband or wife? Would that be OK with you? NO! But right now someone, somewhere, could be doing that very thing to you. They could be stealing your future mate's virginity, and once their virginity or innocence is gone, it can NEVER be yours. How do you think that will affect your future happiness and enjoyment? Question is, are you the one doing the stealing?

Let me show you a diagram that will help you understand what I mean.

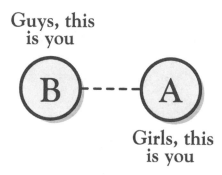

**Guys, this
is you**

**Girls, this
is you**

Guys, Circle A is your future wife . . . and girls . . . circle B is your future husband. This isn't the person who *promises* to marry you, this is the person who actually *does* it. Lots of people may promise to marry you but only one will, and you won't know who it actually is until your honeymoon night. I've seen lots of weddings cancelled at the last minute 'cause they figured out they weren't ready or that they were marrying the wrong person, so don't let yourself be fooled.

OK, so Circle A or Circle B is absolutely the person you will marry. No question about it. But let's say tonight, guys, you are going to date this other girl instead (Circle D). You're gonna *marry* Circle A but you're actually gonna *date* Circle D, above. And while you're out on your date, your future wife is out with another guy (Circle C).

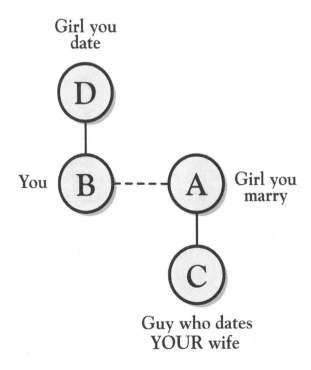

OK, guys, here's the question . . . Do you mind if this other guy (C) goes to bed with your wife tonight? In fact, let me put it this

way. Guys . . . do you mind if this guy does to your wife tonight what you're planning to do with your girlfriend tonight?

Hey girls . . . do you mind if that other girl (D) goes to bed tonight and shows your future husband a time he'll never forget? EVER?! Do you mind if she puts a little cool music on . . . slowly takes her clothes off and stretches out on your future husband's bed for him to view? Does that bother you at all? Do you care? YEAH, YOU DO!

Guys, that girl you're gonna date tonight—how far *can* you go with her on your date? Now that's a legitimate question! But there's an easy answer for it, and it goes like this. How far can that other guy (C) go with *your* wife tonight? Do you mind if he takes her clothes off and feels her all over? Do you mind if they have a little oral sex? I mean everyone is saying that oral sex isn't *really* sex . . . OK, so do you mind?

YOU'RE DARN RIGHT YOU MIND!!!!!!

And I totally agree with you. I wouldn't want anyone doing that with my wife either.

So the deal is guys, tonight, the girl you're dating . . . you treat her the same way you want the guy dating your wife tonight to treat *her*. And if you're not willin' to do that, you're gonna get what you deserve. Just remember, there's a guy out there somewhere that's going to marry the girl you're dating tonight and he's praying like crazy that you don't do something to her that they will both regret for the rest of their lives. And keep this in mind: the guy who will eventually date and marry the girl you're dating right now could be your best friend! You don't know.

Finish this sentence:

DO UNTO OTHERS_____.

That's right. "AS YOU WOULD HAVE THEM DO TO YOU."
You all know that's what we expect from others, so let's give them
the same thing first.

I once got a letter from a guy named Russ who said to me, "I
want my wife to be a virgin so I thought I would return the favor."
I wish I had Russ's last name, 'cause I'd print it right here in this
book so every girl who reads it could know who he is. Way to go,
Russ!

Chapter 16. Why Wait?
To Protect Society

A Fairy Tale

Once upon a time there was a place called Anytown. It was a quiet little town with parks, a library, a small shopping center, and several little churches. A railroad track ran right through the middle of town, dividing it into two distinct neighborhoods. All the really wealthy people lived on the north end of town. They had big houses, swimming pools, and a view of the mountains. Everyone else lived on the south side of the tracks. Anytown's two policemen had very little to do because there just wasn't that much trouble to deal with. Anytown was a great place to live.

One September, at the beginning of school, a new student came to town. Jen was in the eleventh grade and very pretty. She loved sports—especially volleyball and soccer—and she was smart, too. Jen had everything—everything but money. She lived in a trailer park south of the tracks in the worst part of town. Her dad had lost his job and had moved to Anytown to get back on his feet again. It was not easy, but Jen never let on. No one knew how tough things were because Jen didn't really feel poor and didn't act poor. Almost everyone liked her because she was . . . how should I say it? . . . she was sure of herself . . . somehow.

Mike always looked forward to the first day of school at Anytown High. It was time to check out the new girls and to see which of the old ones had become available over the summer. Mike was known as "The Stud," and he knew that every girl at school wanted to be with him. They wanted to go out with him—to capture his heart—to be the Only Girl for him. So he played the game. He had the greatest black Toyota 4x4 pickup and everyone knew whose it was 'cause no one else could afford a truck like that. His parents were rich, and everybody knew it. He knew he could buy anybody's friendship and did. He always had beer and pot for his friends and extra cash for anyone who was short of funds. Mike was the Wild One no one had tamed, and every girl in school longed for the chance to prove that she was the one who could do it. Nobody said "No" to Mike. That is, until Jen came to town.

She walked into class that day wearing jeans and a sweatshirt. Mike looked at her like she was a hot new car on the showroom floor—a new "trophy" to mount on his wall. He made his plans. She couldn't have known his reputation that early in the year, so it was going to be easy. His buddies all made their bets, and he made his move the next day when she passed him in the hall. "Hey, Jen! How'd you like me to drive you around town after school today? I just washed my truck and I need a beautiful passenger to help me show it off!" When she politely said, "No, thanks," he was stunned. No girl had ever turned him down! There had to be a reason. He followed her home that Friday and when he saw the trailer she lived in, he immediately understood the way to her heart (and body, he hoped). He would rescue her from all that misery with his money. He would be her security blanket. Several times over the next few weeks he asked Jen if he could take her out, but she kept refusing. He couldn't figure it out. He had tried everything. What was he supposed to do? She just wasn't impressed.

Mike got creative. He knew that every Tuesday night Jen walked home from volleyball practice and passed through the park on her way. He planted himself in the bushes at the entrance to the park, and just as she passed by he jumped out and grabbed her, wrestling her to the ground. She started to yell, but he covered her mouth and told her he wouldn't hurt her if she would just be quiet. She nodded and he let her up. She was really mad at first, but settled down when he started to

talk. *"I've tried to get your attention for weeks! All I want is to get to know you, and maybe go out or something. . . ."* *"I have no intention of going out with you,"* Jen interrupted. *"I've been watching you, too, and I don't like the things you do or the way you treat people. And I'd never go out with a guy who waits to ambush girls on their way home from school!"* She turned and sprinted home.

Instead of being turned off, Mike was intrigued. He couldn't get Jen out of his mind. He could have any other girl in his school at the snap of his fingers, but not Jen. She was different, and he liked that about her. He liked the challenge and he was determined to change her mind. He would not give up. One day as she was leaving school Mike asked if she would mind if he walked her home. She thought for a minute and finally said, *"OK."*

That walk was the beginning of a new relationship—a relationship that would change everything. Mike and Jen talked about school, classes they were in, sports, and movies they had seen. They chatted about what they would do that summer and plans they had for college. Finally Mike asked her the question that would change his life forever. *"I don't know how to put this, Jen, I'm going to sound like a jerk . . . but ever since I was a sophomore no girl has ever turned me down for a date or for anything else, for that matter. Then you came along and at first you'd barely talk to me, let alone go out with me. How come?"* Her reply cut him to the heart. *"I could never be close to a guy who does the things you do. I mean the parties, smoking, and the drugs. All your parties are stupid! Everyone gets drunk, has sex, and throws up! I'm a virgin, and I'm going to stay that way until I'm married! Why would I want to make love to someone and not remember anything the next day? I want so much more than that. And I won't even date a guy unless he feels the same way!"*

Mike couldn't believe his ears. Here was the kind of girl he had always wanted. He just never thought it was possible. All the girls he knew pressured him for sex as much or more than he had pushed them. He would never let her go! Jen was the girl for him, and he wouldn't let her reject him. But Jen stood firm. She said she would have nothing to do with him until he stopped doing all the other stuff.

Mike promised to reform. They began to see each other almost every day, and they talked on the phone every night. When Jen saw real changes in Mike's behavior she accepted his invitations to go out. Over the course of their senior year Mike's reputation totally changed. He became the very gentleman Jen had been looking for. When Homecoming came around no one ever doubted who the Homecoming King and Queen would be. Mike and Jen were the perfect couple. Everyone could see it.

Mike took Jen to meet his parents. They grew to love her too, and were ecstatic when Mike finally proposed. When they married a year later they moved into a beautiful home after Mike got a job in his father's business. A few years after that their first child, Julie, was born. Jen's life looked like a fairy tale. They really were living happily ever after!

Years passed. Mike became more and more successful and finally took over his father's business. They built the home of their dreams and became the envy of the whole town. The next decade brought growth and prosperity to Anytown. New businesses and homes sprouted up everywhere.

Julie grew up to be a pretty, athletic girl just like her mom. She got everything she ever wanted. Jen remembered what it had been like growing up in a trailer on the wrong side of town, so she made sure Julie had whatever she wanted. But she forgot that money could be a real trap, and Julie became very spoiled. In fact she became a lot like her dad had been in high school—wild, and out of control. Jen's fairy tale soon began to dissolve. She and Mike started to lose control of their daughter.

It all began when Julie met Gary, a transfer student from the big city. He lived all alone on the south side of town. No one knew for certain where his parents were, and he always seemed to be in trouble at school. In Gary's opinion, rules were made to be broken, and break them he did! He didn't care what anyone thought about him, and he ran with the other rebels of Anytown High. He used drugs and sold them; that's how he paid his way in life. He lived for sex. "Why deny what's natural?" he'd say. He was a free spirit looking for action, and that's what caught Julie's eye.

They first met at a party at another guy's house. His parents were gone for the weekend, so the party was an all-out, get-smashed kind of party. When Gary saw Julie come in the front door he thought she was beautiful and couldn't take his eyes off her. She liked the easy freedom he possessed and the way he took charge of everything. They hit it off right from the beginning. There was real chemistry. After a few beers and a dance or two, they decided to take a break from all the noise and go for a walk in the park. The moon was full and they both felt full of energy. They complained about life with all its rules and restrictions. Why were her parents so uptight about what she did? Why did they keep nagging her about the future and what she would do with her life? According to her teachers the world was due to melt away because of global warming anyway, so who knew if there even was a future? Why couldn't they live life NOW? What was everyone waiting for, when everything seems so unsure?

Gary asked Julie if she wanted to see where he lived. It was just over the tracks, a few blocks away, so they headed for his place. It wasn't much to look at—just an old shell of a trailer in the southeast part of town—but after a few more beers and a joint or two, none of that mattered. They had sex together. Julie had been physical with many guys before, but this was the first time she had gone all the way with a guy. It wasn't exactly what she had wanted her first time to be like, but she thought she loved Gary. Things could only get better. Over the next few months Julie snuck out of her bedroom almost every night. It seemed like she spent more time at Gary's house than she did at her own. Her parents never knew.

One July evening Julie's parents threw a huge party and invited people from all over the world: business associates, Hollywood stars, fashion models, political figures, and personal friends. Julie's mom bought her a beautiful formal gown to wear to this, her first real adult party. At first Julie thought it was going to be stupid and wasn't excited about the party at all, but that night she heard exotic guests talk of far-off places, of new things to do and be—exciting stories about parties and nightlife activities she couldn't even begin to imagine. It all sounded so fantastic, but was it really possible? Slowly it dawned on her that she could have it all. After all, she was "Mike and Jennifer's daughter." She couldn't believe she hadn't seen this before.

As Julie stood surveying the crowd, trying to make sense of these exciting new thoughts, she glanced toward the front door and felt her heart stop. Standing in the entryway was the most gorgeous man she had ever seen. She recognized him immediately because she had seen him many times in movies, and here he was in her home. Thoughts somersaulted in her head. "Wait until everyone at school hears about this! They will be soooo jealous! Tom—right here in my house!" She watched his every move. If only she could meet him! Before she had finished the thought, a close family friend led Tom through the crowd and introduced him to Julie. She stood speechless. She still hadn't taken a breath. He was actually talking to her like she was an important person! She was mesmerized. He asked if she would like to go outside and talk for a while, and she gladly agreed. They walked down the long driveway, out the gated entrance, and across the street into the City Park. She was almost delirious. At the fountain in the middle of the park, he turned, looked into her eyes, and said, "You are the biggest surprise of this evening! I never expected to meet such a beautiful girl in Anytown. I've known you less than an hour, and already I feel I could share anything with you! I can't talk with my girlfriend this way, and we've lived together for two years. She doesn't understand me as well as you do, and she's just plain hard to live with. I think it's just about over between us." He said many more flattering things to Julie, and she took in every word.

Tom suddenly changed the subject and told Julie she should come to Hollywood sometime and visit him—that he would love to show her around. He told her he knew a modeling agent who might be able to get her in the door at Seventeen or YM magazine. "You're obviously beautiful enough," he chuckled. Then he looked into her eyes, took her hands one more time, touched his forehead to hers and gently kissed her. As they walked back to the party, he slipped his extra hotel key into her hand. "Come over later tonight, after everyone is gone."

If anyone had asked Julie about Gary the next morning, she would have wondered who they were talking about. Her night with Tom had made her forget anyone else she had ever been with. She felt like she was really "in love" for the first time in her life. She refused Gary's phone calls. She avoided him when she saw him in town that next week. How could she ever have settled for a guy like Gary, when she was

worthy of a man like Tom? In spite of her parents' protests she went to Hollywood and moved in with the man of her dreams. She never thought of Gary again.

Gary couldn't believe he'd been dumped. Even though Julie didn't call him the whole week after the party, Gary figured she was just upset over some dumb thing. The next week he began to hear rumors all over town about her and Tom being together, but he refused to believe them. Julie wasn't impressed by all that glitz! She'd always told him that money didn't matter and that he was a "star" to her. Surely she would call! But she never did. When she moved to California, Gary blew up. "Man . . . What's her problem? Why'd she do this to me? I don't deserve this! That's the last time I'll ever trust a woman—they're all the same! They use you, then screw you!" He had actually been planning to ask her to move in with him. He thought it was love . . . and now this. Screw it! He would dump all of them from now on. He would never let this happen to him again.

Deeply hurt, he began to drink more and do more drugs. It helped to ease the pain. He used as many girls as he could. Somehow it helped to even the score. He even got one girl pregnant. "She deserved it. She was a slut anyway." The other guys he ran with began to act the same way. In less than one year Anytown had totally changed. It was now unsafe to walk the streets of Anytown at night. Drugs were readily available; the parties were endless. It was rumored that one guy OD'd at a party and died the next day. Gangs began to take over and Anytown wasn't a nice place to live anymore.

Meanwhile, down in Hollywood, Julie had been dumped for a Seventeen *model because Tom had become bored with her. He had started to say mean things about her figure, and that she would never make it in modeling if she didn't lose weight. She was devastated. She started on pills and almost quit eating altogether, but nothing seemed to help. In no time she became obsessed with her weight and became bulimic. She felt horrible most of the time and lost her job because she was so sick. She even wondered if she might be pregnant. She didn't know, and didn't want to find out. She wished she could go home, but she was too embarrassed to try to go back. Her life had not turned out at all the way she had expected it to. Too depressed to do anything*

else, she just stayed in her apartment and got drunk. No one cared. Her mom and dad had given up. She was totally alone in what had become a very lonely world.

THE END

MORAL OF THE STORY:
IF THERE ARE NO FAIR MAIDENS
THERE WILL BE NO PRINCE CHARMINGS.
NO PRINCE CHARMINGS, NO MAGIC KINGDOM.

(Dear) Brad Henning,

I missed your talk on the second day but I heard your speech in 9th grade. Basically I think you're a pretty funny guy and have some good things to say, but I think you are wrecking us guy's chances of getting some good sex with girls by telling them to wait until marriage. I'm sure when you were in high school you wanted to score as much as possible but now you have changed your view because you have settled down. I don't think there is anything wrong with having sex with your girlfriend in high school even if you're not planning on marrying her. I think sex is a natural instinct and if two people are ready to do it, I think they should. I know you'll probably use this letter as an example to show girls what pigs men are but this is the way I feel and there's nothing wrong with it.

Senior Guy

Senior Guy, your wish is my command! In fact, I decided to put your whole letter in this book for *everyone* to see. And no, not ALL men are pigs . . . just some!

Dear Brad,

You know quite a bit about sex. You probably get it on a lot. You are right about all that stuff. I totally agree. (But) I don't think it is bad to have sex when you're not married because all it is fun

and games, nothing more. I think sex kicks booty and I will try to get it whenever I have a chance. Keep up the good work. You should think about teaching at high school.

Sincerely,
Ted (another pig!)

As Long as It Doesn't Hurt Anybody . . .

Everybody's heard the line, "Hey, as long as it isn't hurting anybody, why not?" That's obviously Ted's philosophy. Well, OK. I guess we've all tried using that line a time or two in one way or another. I know I did when I was a kid. (It never worked, but I tried it.) But when it comes to sex, is that philosophy gonna fly? Can we say, "As long as it isn't hurting anybody, it's OK?" No, 'cause it IS hurting somebody. In fact, it's hurting a lot of somebodies. It's hurting our whole society.

What? How can having sex hurt our whole society? Well, first off, let me tell you what I mean by "society." If you think about it, society is really just a bunch of people who interact and live together in some sort of structured community: your boyfriend, girlfriend, brothers and sisters, mom and dad, neighbors, everyone. Each person is born into a family, and that family lives in a neighborhood full of other families. Put all the neighborhoods together—they form a town. Put all the towns together—they form a state. Put all the states together and you've got a nation full of people united together to work as one. So really, "society" is just a lot of "somebodies" like you and me, who somehow interact and affect each other.

But come back to the question. How can messing around with your girlfriend or boyfriend destroy society? Here's how.

Everything You Do Affects Others

Literally everything you do affects others for better or for worse: your attitude, your habits, your behavior—everything. Not only are your actions affecting other people, so is the life you are

modeling to everyone who watches you. Your actions are showing your community what you value most. Ted, in the last letter, shows by his actions that he values sex more than he values people, and he'll try to get it whenever he can, regardless of what it does to anyone else. Will his actions affect only him? No, 'cause not only is he hurting each girl he takes advantage of, he's also sending a message to the kid down the street who is watching and thinking, "Man, if he can do it, so can I!" And, sure enough, that kid will do it too. The first guy modeled it for the second guy, and the second guy will model it for the next guy. Each one, in his own way, has changed society, and it will never be the same again. Want a real live illustration? Just the other day I found out there had been a sexual attack on a girl in a school in my town! Some guy pulled a girl into the guys' restroom, and while his friend pinned her arms behind her back, he grabbed and slapped her breasts. Did that affect anyone else? Sure. Now there's a whole group of guys doing the same thing. "If he can do it, so can I!"

"I think sex kicks booty and I will try to get it whenever I have a chance." I was just thinking, I wonder if Ted, the guy who wrote that, has a younger brother? What's Ted teaching him? I also wonder if Ted has a sister. Does he mind if other guys are taking advantage of her the same way he's taking advantage of other girls?

But there's a bigger problem here. Who's to say what's right or wrong when it comes to sex and dating? Is it just my opinion against someone else's?

Absolutes

When people say there are no absolutes (what's right for you may not be what's right for me) they ultimately mean everybody should be able to do whatever the heck they want to do, when, where, and how they want to do it. But that produces chaos!!! Would that work in sports? In a family? At work? Most people who believe there are no absolutes (by the way, are you *absolutely* sure there are no absolutes?) are the first ones to yell "That's not fair!" when someone *else* wants to do something that hurts *them*

or gets in *their* way of having a good time. But as soon as that person says to you, "That's not FAIR!" they have just admitted that there is some idea of "fair" (right and wrong) that you both know about, and they think *you* just crossed the line. Aaaaaahhh . . . so there ARE absolutes!

These "absolutes," or rules, or whatever you choose to call them, aren't just some code that someone made up to keep people from having fun, they are rules based on values designed to protect everyone involved, values that work best for people who want to live together effectively with a minimum of conflict. Every culture has them and it's amazing just how much all cultures and societies are alike.

Cultures Have Rules

When it comes to families and sexuality, a culture must have rules or things will start falling apart very quickly. When someone says, "There's nothing wrong with sex outside of marriage," or "What's right for you may not be what's right for me," they've just described chaos!

Every generation has a value system when it comes to sex. Next time you're with your grandparents (or anyone you know who's over 65) ask them what it was like to "date" back when they were teenagers. Ask them what people thought about a girl who got pregnant when she wasn't married. Ask them how many divorced families they knew. Have them tell you how people felt about their families and their children. Then ask your parents what things were like when they were in high school. Same questions: dating, pregnancy, divorce, etc. Now that you've got a pretty good picture of what life was like 25 to 50 years ago, look at the values that most kids have today. Then ask yourself, Is my generation more, or less, sexually active than the generation before me? Do we have more or fewer out-of-wedlock pregnancies? More abortions or fewer abortions? More cases of sexually transmitted disease, or fewer? Are rape and sexual abuse increasing or decreasing? Is my generation becoming more sexually satisfied, or less? How long does the

average marriage last now, compared to 50 years ago? Then ask yourself, are we better off now? I don't think we are. Something's wrong. Our society is being destroyed. What happens between a guy and a girl *sexually* will affect the families they eventually create and the relationships within those families. Those families don't just *affect* society, they ARE society! That's why what YOU do, or don't do, sexually is so important.

What Happens When Sex and the Ultimate Dreams Collide?

Back in Chapter 3, I described a guy's ultimate dream. (Remember, not every guy is like this but most are.) Let me refresh your memory.

Many girls

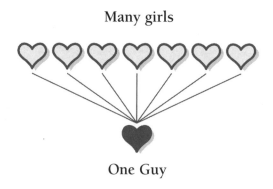

One Guy

"Access to many women, rejected by none."

So here you've got a guy who's producing millions of sperm every day, feeling like he wants to share all his "wealth" with the world. His body is built to want to "go forth and multiply!" It's not that the guy doesn't want one girlfriend or that he doesn't want to be married someday, it's just that the thought of settling down with *one woman* (which is what any girl worth having would make him do) gets more than a little scary. When he's with a particular girl he can't just get up and go do whatever he wants anymore. He has to think about her and the relationship between the two of them.

It bothers him that there might be guys out there having more fun than he is, doing all the things he thinks he's missing out on by settling down so soon. Or worse, he's wondering if he might have found someone better than the girl he got, if he'd just stuck it out a little longer. If you think only in biological terms, his body just wants to have sex with as many available women as possible. He values his freedom. Listen to these guys.

> Brad,
>
> I have thought about what you said. No, honestly!! It was very good advice you gave about not having sex. But I'm not going to follow it. Sorry. I had a lot of fun.
>
> Guy Student

> Brad,
>
> Your speech was alright. Better than most but it needed more on sex. I don't think that you stopped anyone from having sex because everyone thinks sex is great, also it feels GOOD. I just put on two condoms and take my chance. I plan to smack-skins till I die. Keep trying and keep failing. Oh yeah, thanks for getting me out of class for three periods. That was cool.
>
> Derek

Cosmopolitan interviewed a guy who admitted,

> Hey, it took evolution more than 100 million years to come up with the penis. It takes some of us almost as long to realize that it's a lousy navigational aid. [1]

Will his realization change his behavior? Are you kidding? He's actually admitting that it's a crazy way to live, but he's gonna live

---

[1] David Jacobson, "Why Do Men Want To See Other Women?", *Cosmopolitan*, October 1997, p. 58.

that way anyway! Unfortunately, he's going to run right smack into women's ultimate dream.

One girl

One guy

"One man who understands, respects, and takes care of me for life."

A woman's biology forces her to be very careful about who she gets involved with sexually. Before about 1960 (around the time The Pill became available) sex often meant a baby, and a woman wanted to be darn sure that the father of that baby would be around to take care of her. Before welfare stepped in she had only herself or her family to look to if the guy that got her pregnant disappeared. So back then, before a girl said yes to sex with a guy, she would make sure that he said "I do" to her, to her family, and therefore to society. Marriage was the only place she could safely be sexually active, because by marrying her, the guy was promising to stick around and take care of her and any family that would come. It was a fulfillment of her desire to be safe and have a place to raise her children.

The Two Worlds Come Together

Let me bring these two worlds together. What would happen if both men and women expected to get their ultimate dream from each other, all at the same time?

If girls always said "YES" to every guy's ultimate dream, why would any guy *ever* settle down with just one woman, buy a nice house, have a bunch of kids, and support them for the rest of his life? If he can get women to give him what he wants now . . . for free, why would he want to settle down and pay through the nose for life? Why would he sacrifice his freedom for that? His philosophy would be, "Why marry? Let's just mess around." Of course some guys can *talk* marriage with the best of them, but when it comes right down to it, marriage scares guys to death. (How common is it to see articles in women's magazines that say, "Why Men Fear Commitment?")

But if girls keep saying "yes" to guys' ultimate dream (sex without marriage), they will never get THEIR dream (a secure life for themselves and their children). It's his dream, or hers—one or the other, but not both. These dreams are on a collision course. The two dreams can *never* live together successfully under one roof. One of them has to change. In other words, you can't be "uncommittedly" (his) committed (hers). There is no such thing. If he got his wish, his way of life would be a threat to hers. If she gives him sex, she risks having a baby with no secure place to raise it. Even with all the support available to single moms today, it is a fact that she will most likely live in poverty the rest of her life, and her kids will not do nearly as well in life as kids from intact families. So long, ultimate dream! Welcome to the 21st century.

So let me ask you the question again. Is your generation more, or less, sexually active than the generation before you? Are you having more out-of-wedlock pregnancies or fewer? More or fewer abortions? More cases of sexually transmitted diseases or fewer? Are rape and sexual abuse increasing or decreasing? Is your generation more, or less, sexually satisfied? Are they more, or less, emotionally healthy? The answers are becoming more obvious.

Look at the following letter from Tina. She describes exactly the kind of relationship I'm talking about.

Brad,

I really appreciate the time you spent teaching us. The session you gave was overwhelming. Not only could I partially relate, the stuff you taught was so intriguing. I have been involved in a sexual relationship. But the problem was that once we began to have sex our relationship went down hill. It was like a roller coaster. If I said "NO" things were OK but when I said "YES" they were bad. Being up and down setting my feelings and emotions wild. Trying to do anything I could to make him happy as he possibly could be but he did nothing to make me happy. Don't get me wrong the sex was good but on the other hand, the worst thing that could possibly have happened to our relationship. Six months later when our relationship ended I was heartbroken and the two things that hurt most was that I knew he didn't love me like I loved him and that our relationship ended because of sex. Now I refuse to involve sex in relationships and things seem to go a lot better. Thank you for the vast knowledge you taught me.

Thanks,
Tina

The Family, Society, and the Ultimate Dreams

All of society, if it's going to last, has to have its foundation based in the family. Destroy the family structure and all of society collapses. A woman's ultimate dream (one man for life) supports that family foundation. A man's dream (many women) does not. He must not get his dream, and society, if it is to stay alive and healthy, *must help him NOT get it.*

Conditional Relationships

Uncommitted sexuality results in conditional relationships. "If you do this for me, I'll do that for you. If you don't make me happy—I'm outta here!" There's nothing to hold the relationship

together. It becomes a relationship full of begging, bribing, and threatening, and it doesn't work. That's exactly what happens to a lot of couples who live together, but never marry. They are never *forced* to work out their differences. In the back of their minds they always have that one option: "If I don't get what I want or it gets too difficult . . . I'll LEAVE. I didn't make any promises." But anthropologist Margaret Mead made it clear when she said,

> No known society has ever invented a form of marriage strong enough to stick that did not contain the "till-death-do-us-part" assumption.[2]

A married couple has chosen to leave themselves no options. They have promised to love each other "until death do us part," and they *have* to work it out. They may not feel like it, but they are committed to do it anyway.

The War Between His Body and His Morality

The biggest war in all of society is fought every day between every guy's body and his morality. His body must not win. The family and society must win.

> Although women are physiologically capable of greater orgasmic pleasure than men—and thus may avidly seek intercourse—they are also much better able to abstain from sex without psychological strain. In the United States the much greater mental health of single women than single men may be explained in part by this female strength. But greater control and discretion—more informed and deliberate sexual powers—are displayed by women in all societies known to anthropology. Indeed, this intelligent and controlled female sexuality is what makes human communities possible.[3]

---

[2] Margaret Mead, *Male and Female: A Study of the Sexes in a Changing World* (New York: William Morrow Company, 1949).

[3] From *Men and Marriage* by George Guilder © 1986, 1992 used by permission of the licenser, Pelican Publisher Company, Inc., p. 12.

In marriage, a guy's sexuality goes from being turned on by *anything* (pre-marriage) to being committed to a *person,* to a family (his own kids), and to a stable society. Sex isn't only for fun and pleasure . . . it becomes vastly more important. It's the force that drives him to his wife because of his commitment to her. It's the biggest stabilizing force known to mankind. That's why marriage is far more than "just a piece of paper."

Guys Are Almost Expected to Cheat

We act like we don't have much of a problem with all this sex-out-of-marriage stuff. Guys are almost *expected* to cheat and play around. (If you don't believe that, watch MTV sometime.) A couple of years ago the President of the United States was taken to court because of his sexual misconduct. What's most revealing is that over 50 percent of American people felt like it really wasn't that big a deal. But let me tell you, if a man like the President can cheat on his wife and then lie his way through it with just a wink and a nod, then he could cheat on anyone, including you (all society)! Can he say, "Hey, it's not hurting anybody else, so what's the big deal?" Would his wife and daughter agree? Cheating becomes a way of life. Those actions take on a life of their own and begin forming patterns displayed for all to see, want, and copy. That's why, since President Clinton's "confession," oral sex has become the number one sexual activity of American teenagers.[4] "He did it, so why can't I?"

Sidestepping Responsibility

So how are we choosing to handle all this Sex-in-America stuff? Simple. Instead of teaching people to be responsible for their behavior, we sidestep the issue by handing the responsibility off to someone else. We just pass the buck. When a girl gets pregnant, for instance, there's no real problem. If dad doesn't step up to the plate and become responsible, mom just applies for financial sup-

---

[4] "Is Oral Sex Really Sex?" *www.healthscout.com/cgi-bin/WebObjects?Af.woa/11,* January 15, 2001.

port, and Uncle Sam comes running. The babies are taken care of; the girl gets an apartment, food stamps, and medical coupons. So who needs the baby's daddy? We just wipe him out of the equation, and Uncle Sam takes his place (funded by you, the taxpayer). People in the inner city call a girl's 18th birthday "Independence Day" 'cause now she can have a baby and get welfare for life. No job, no responsibility, and no husband. Doesn't get better than that! Chaos!

> Twenty-five percent of teen mothers will receive *public assistance* by the time they reach their early 20s.[5]

> Nearly 60 percent of adolescents giving birth for the first time have their delivery fees covered by *public funds,* usually Medicaid.[6]

> Teenage mothers are not only more likely than other young women to have grown up in a single-parent household, they are also more likely to end their own marriage in divorce.[7]

> According to a study done by the Robin Hood Foundation, a New York City charity, taxpayers will spend in the vicinity of $7 billion this year to deal with social problems resulting from recent births to girls under the age of 18.[8]

Depriving Men

But what we don't seem to recognize is when the father is removed, the stability of the family, and of society, has just been undermined. It's just a matter of time before it *all* crumbles. Society says, "If the guy doesn't want to be responsible, no problem! We'll just help *her* out by eliminating *him*." The problem is that

---

[5] *Sex and America's Teenagers* (New York: The Alan Guttmacher Institute, 1994), p. 58.
[6] *Ibid.,* p. 59.
[7] *Ibid.,* p. 60.
[8] Steven A. Holmes, "'96 Cost of Teen Pregnancy Is Put at $7 Billion," *New York Times,* June 13, 1996.

our "solutions" all backfire because they are teaching him to be even *more* irresponsible. We also deprive him of his two most fundamental needs: *the need to give and receive love, and the need to be needed.* What's scary is he probably has no idea what either one of those two needs is. After all, he doesn't *feel* empty. Quite the opposite. He feels free! (Empty . . . but free.)

That emptiness may be the reason men are four times more likely to commit suicide than women, and why men are four times more likely than women to suffer heart disease before age 50. They are running on "Empty." Men are more likely to be homeless and alcoholic. Men are lonely, and "loneliness," says Dr. Warren Farrell in his book, *The Myth of Male Power,* "is a strong predictor of heart disease."[9] That's why I'm not surprised to find that men not only have the highest incidence of heart disease, but of diseases of all kinds. "Men die earlier than women from all 15 of the leading causes of death."[10] Unloved and unneeded. But get this. Bachelors are 22 times more likely to be committed for mental disease than married men, and 10 times more likely to be put in hospitals for chronic diseases. Single men have three times the mortality rate of single women from all causes. They produce more violence and crime, and suffer from more mental illness, mild neuroses, depression, and addictions. They are far more prone to institutionalization, to poverty, to unemployment, to nightmares, and to suicide. So when our "solutions" make it easy for him to be irresponsible, he becomes even *more* of what he already is . . . IRRESPONSIBLE . . . and more unhealthy, which he takes out on all of society!!

What About the Children?

Years ago, Dan Quayle, former Vice President of the United States, tried to express the strong case for traditional families by saying that the two-parent family was much more stable, and far healthier, than the one-parent family. He got hammered for it. It wasn't the politically correct thing to say. A lot of people felt he

---

[9] Dr. Warren Farrell, *The Myth of Male Power* (New York: Berkley Books, 1993), p. 186.
[10] *Ibid.,* p. 181.

was putting down single parents who were trying hard to raise their kids as well as two married parents could. But Quayle was simply stating facts. Now, years later, study results show he was right.

> Research shows that many children from disrupted families have a *harder time achieving intimacy in a relationship, forming a stable marriage, or even holding a steady job.*[11] (emphasis mine)

A harder time achieving intimacy? Forming a stable marriage? Holding a steady job? Just because kids are from families that are "disrupted"? Yes! Psychologist Urie Bronfenbrenner of Cornell University says that kids raised in single-parent families are . . .

> . . . at greater risk for experiencing a variety of behavioral and educational problems, including extremes of hyperactivity and withdrawal, lack of attentiveness in the classroom, difficulty in deferring gratification, impaired academic achievement, school misbehavior, absenteeism, dropping out, involvement in socially alienated peer groups, and especially the so-called "teenage syndrome" of behaviors that tend to hang together—smoking, drinking, early and frequent sexual experience, and, in the more extreme cases, drugs, suicide, vandalism, violence and criminal acts.[12]

So not only does premarital sex change you and the person you're with, it also alters the future of the children that accidentally come from your relationship. You may have seen that firsthand. You may be a product of that kind of situation. Of course that doesn't automatically mean you are somehow messed up 'cause your parents were, but the patterns are there, and it's not easy to break out of them. Is that something you want to willingly pass on to *your* children? The potential is very real.

---

[11] Barbara Dafoe Whitehead, "Dan Quayle Was Right," *Atlantic Monthly,* April 1993, p. 47.

[12] Urie Bronfenbrenner, "Discovering What Families Can Do," in Blankenhorn, Bayme, and Elshtain, eds., *Rebuilding the Nest: A New Commitment to the American Family* (Milwaukee, Wis.: Family Service America, 1990), p. 34.

Each year over 1 million teenagers get pregnant. In fact, one-quarter of all young women have been pregnant by the time they turn 18, and by age 21 half have had a pregnancy.[13] To give you an idea of just how many girls that is per year, picture this: If every unmarried pregnant teenage girl held hands with all the other pregnant girls, the line they formed would be 568 miles long. That's the distance you'd cover if you started at the Canadian border, drove through Washington, then Oregon, and stopped somewhere near Yreka, California. And that's just how many get pregnant in ONE year!!!! A little over 30 percent of those pregnancies end in abortions and around 20 percent end in miscarriage. That means approximately 50 percent of the girls give birth to their babies.[14] Once a girl gets pregnant out of wedlock, *every* decision she has to make is difficult. There is no easy way out. She and her baby (and her family, and the father, and the father's family) will be affected by her decisions for the rest of their lives.

Marriage Is the Salvation of Men!

But there is a positive solution to all of this, and we know from history that it works. The solution is marriage.

Marriage, like nothing else, offers a man his greatest potential. The *absence* of commitment to marriage can kill him. Guys aren't messed up just 'cause they're GUYS. It's just that guys are rarely held accountable for their actions, or told, No! "No, you can't do that. No, I will not sleep with you!" When guys are left to do or be whatever they want, with no restrictions or accountability to society, they become physically and mentally unhealthy. Society's ability to secure the greatest good for all mankind hangs on its ability to hold men responsible for their sexual behavior. And *that* hangs on women's willingness and ability to say, "No, not until marriage." And I don't mean just when there's a *promise* to marry, I mean actually getting married. It's marriage (not the promise of marriage) that's the life-changer.

---

[13] *Sex and America's Teenagers* (New York: The Alan Guttmacher Institute, 1994), p. 43.
[14] *Ibid.*, p. 44.

For instance, did you know that young adults who are *married* change poor habits and behaviors much easier than their single peers do?

> Young . . . adults . . . decreased their drug and alcohol use when they got engaged, married and had children. . . . Conversely, those who stayed single were a high proportion of drug and alcohol users. "If you feel a responsibility to and for another person, then you are more apt to control your own behavior and play a role in controlling the partner's behavior." . . . Couples who lived together but were not engaged or married showed no such drop in drug use. . . . When people divorce, their drug use increases again—only to decline once again if they remarry.[15]

Marriage brings stability. Sex doesn't, living together doesn't . . . but marriage does!

Conclusion: Putting It All Together

I started this chapter by telling you a story, and then I asked the question, "What does messing around with my girlfriend/boyfriend have to do with destroying the whole country?" Now here's the answer. Kids today are having sex with each other but are less committed to one another. Guys are sexually undisciplined and seem to be out of control. Girls feel used and alone when left to deal with sexual consequences on their own. Men are learning to use deception to "get what they want," so women are learning to never trust men. Neither are feeling loved. Both are physically and emotionally getting "beat up." They are getting pregnant, catching diseases, and having abortions. If a girl gets pregnant and keeps her baby, she probably has no means of support, because the father has usually abandoned her. Because she finds herself too busy with the new infant, she loses her freedom. She will most likely live in poverty for the rest of her life, existing as best she can on welfare, which you, the taxpayer, will pay.

---

[15] *The News Tribune*, Feb. 3, 1997, citing Jerald Bachman, study, 1976–1994, Univ. of Michigan Institute for Social Research.

Her new "husband," Uncle Sam, takes the place of her way-ward boyfriend by providing the support that HE should have provided. Since the boyfriend is no longer needed financially, he'll never recognize his true relational value to his family. He has been made optional. Because he never marries, he lives his life externally, striving for success, sometimes at a breakneck pace, but becomes less healthy, more sexually addicted, and more uncivilized. Because of the cost of his out-of-control behavior, taxes go up even more, putting pressure on *every other man* to be financially successful.

When children are produced, they will most likely grow up to become troubled kids themselves, showing far more behavioral and educational problems than kids from intact families. They will tend to hang together, do drugs and drink together, and tend toward more violent behavior. They will be more sexually active, which will lead to even *more* girls getting pregnant. They will become like their parents. The cycle is complete.

So there you have it. That's the "price" of being sexually ac-tive outside of marriage. If you tell me having sex with a person outside of marriage isn't hurting anyone, you aren't being honest. It hurts everyone!

So I guess the question comes down to this: What would you *really* have to lose by waiting for marriage? When you think about it, not much. I'm not saying give up sex forever. I'm just saying postpone it. Wait until the time is right . . . and that means waiting until marriage. And marriage, by definition, is "a total commitment of the total person for total life."

One last thing. At the beginning of this chapter, I showed you a couple of letters I had received from a couple of guys. Now I want you to reread them. When you do you'll be amazed at how shallow they sound in light of what you have just finished reading.

(Dear) Brad Henning,

I missed your talk on the second day but I heard your speech in 9th grade. Basically I think you're a pretty funny guy and have some good things to say, but I think you are wrecking us guys'

chances of getting some good sex with girls by telling them to wait until marriage. I'm sure when you were in high school you wanted to score as much as possible but now you have changed your view because you have settled down. I don't think there is anything wrong with having sex with your girlfriend in high school even if you're not planning on marrying her. I think sex is a natural instinct and if two people are ready to do it, I think they should. I know you'll probably use this letter as an example to show girls what pigs men are but this is the way I feel and there's nothing wrong with it.

Senior Guy

Dear Brad,

You know quite a bit about sex. You probably get it on a lot. You are right about all that stuff. I totally agree. (But) I don't think it is bad to have sex when you're not married because all it is fun and games, nothing more. I think sex kicks booty and I will try to get it whenever I have a chance. Keep up the good work. You should think about teaching at high school.

Sincerely,
Ted

Brad,

I have thought about what you said. No, honestly!! It was very good advice you gave about not having sex. But I'm not going to follow it. Sorry. I had a lot of fun.

Guy Student

Section Four
GIRLS ONLY; GUYS ONLY

Chapter 17. For Girls Only

What Motivates Men?

What motivates men? Ever wonder? Actually, it's really pretty simple. Let me show you. A while back I stayed with some friends for several days, and their daughter *graciously* gave me her room (actually, her parents booted her out!). The girl was a cheerleader, so there were pompoms on the floor, trophies on the desk, and pictures of her cheer squad next to the mirror. Pictures from last year's prom hung on the wall with a single wilted rose tied with a ribbon. All this was displayed as an inventory of her high school years. Pretteeeey amazing, I'd say! Actually it was quite educational.

I couldn't help comparing her room to most guys' rooms I've seen. But let's not go there!

What really caught my eye was a poster of two soccer players that was hanging on the wall. It showed them taking a break, trying to catch their breath. One guy was lying on the ground, obviously injured and in pain. The poster read:

> No pain, no gain
> No gain, no goals
> No goals, no scouts
> No scouts, no college
> No college, no cheerleaders
> No cheerleaders?
> Get up, man! Get up!

But wait! This poster was on a *cheerleader's* wall, not a guy's wall! Why? Because this girl knew something about guys and what motivates them. And what would that be? (OK, this is a major point here. Much of your life as a woman will depend on whether you understand this or not.) Here it is.

Nothing, and I mean NOTHING, can motivate a guy like a woman can!

The Most Powerful People on Earth

The weaker sex is the stronger sex because of the weakness of the stronger sex for the weaker sex.[1]

The most powerful people on earth are young women! Over and over again, young women have proven that they have the power to get men of all ages to do just about anything they want them

[1] Vern McLeallan, *The Complete Book of Practical Proverbs & Wacky Wit* (Wheaton, Illinois: Tyndale House Publishing, Inc., 1996), p. 241.

to do. Believe it or not, if a guy thinks he can have the girl of his dreams, he will even give up his wild life, commit to marriage, and support the children he brings into the world. In the process his life is tamed—*and it probably needs taming desperately!*

Women play an enormously powerful role in men's lives. If women were willing to work together, they could use that power to transform all of society for the better, because the natural desire of a man for a woman is the most powerful motivational force known to mankind. Whatever a girl *demands* of a guy . . . THAT'S WHAT WILL HAPPEN . . . *if* he wants to keep her. She has the power to affect *everything* he does—but there's a problem with that. With power comes responsibility, and every woman has to decide if she's going to motivate men for good, or let them get away with what is ultimately bad. If she doesn't understand that she is the "fair maiden" (object of his desire), she will not motivate her man for good. If she doesn't restrict her sexual attentions, her power is diminished. The only way she can safely promise sex to her man is to demand that he commit himself permanently to her in marriage.

Men *can* change, and *will* change, when women realize a man is motivated by the woman he desires (especially if she seems just out of his reach). That motivation is primarily sexual in nature, and that's not a bad thing at all. In fact, it's a very good thing. A man's sexual nature drives him to a woman, and that passion goes very deep. He knows he will never be able to satisfy his longing and find sexual fulfillment if he can't prove to a woman that he can fulfill *her* needs. The problem is that many times he doesn't even know what her needs *are,* let alone how to fulfill them. And just what are her basic needs? Love and security, by way of commitment. He can't possibly fulfill her needs and at the same time live a wild and sensuous life, going from body to body. She isn't going to buy that for one minute. So if he's going to get the girl he really wants, he's going to have to settle down, and she has to demand that he does.

Most women have no concept of the raw power of sex in a guy's life. A guy may be uncontrollably drawn to many girls (sex), but he longs to find his mate—the one girl who will be the fulfillment of his dreams. The other thing women don't realize is that he's also *scared to death!* "What if she gets too close and she finds out I'm an idiot? What if I don't measure up?" He agonizes, wondering if he will ever be able to satisfy her and all her needs. To him, they seem like a bottomless pit. His body craves hers and his imagination is going wild! Deep down he wonders if she will be what he wants. Will he ever be sexually satisfied?

Girls Set the Patterns

So here's the deal: Like it or not, ladies, YOU are the one in control, and YOU are the one who needs to set the pattern. Whatever you, as women, allow to happen in your relationships with men determines the future of our society. It's women who need to control the pattern, not men. Problem is, a lot of you girls have found out that if you don't say "yes" to "Prince Charming" you'll lose him. (And he won't stay very charming.) On the other hand, if you do say "yes," he'll just get what he wants and leave anyway. Because of that it doesn't seem like you are the one with all the power, but you are. No wonder women ask, "Will guys ever grow up?" The answer is no! No, they won't. Not under those circumstances, they won't. Why? Because you're letting *them* set the pattern for dating, and that pattern is teaching them some very selfish habits for the future. It's the *pattern* that has to change. The *pattern* is the problem.

Why Should He Change?

If a woman doesn't demand maturity from her man, generally he won't change. Why should he? He's having too much fun. Unfortunately, much of his fun is at the expense of women. So while he may be getting older, he's not growing up. But wait a minute! Am I saying women are responsible for men's behavior? Somebody asked that same question of Dr. Laura Schlessinger, family thera-

pist and radio talk show host. The interview was done by *Modern Maturity* magazine. Her response?

> Dr. Laura: That's right. Men would not do half of what they do if women didn't let them.
>
> Interviewer: But why isn't it men's responsibility to not do bad things in the first place?
>
> Dr. Laura: That a man is going to do bad things is a fact. That you keep a man who does bad things in your life is your fault.[2]

Please hear me out here. If I was talking to a bunch of guys right now instead of you girls, I'd be in their faces telling them to grow up and start treating girls right. I'd tell them it's *guys'* responsibility to get *their* act together and quit acting like a bunch of goofballs. Darn right! But I know full well that it's still *girls* who ultimately will change them. Girls are the *motivation* for that change.

Now don't misunderstand me. Men don't want to be *told* what to do or what not to do. "You're not my mother!" *Telling* them to be good is one thing, *motivating* them to be good is quite another. The first will alienate him; the second will win him. Guys want a reason to change, a reason to settle down, and the only "reason" that works is a woman.

Once Upon a Time . . .

Think about the fairy tale at the beginning of the last chapter. Tom, the movie star, will never grow up. Why? Because every girl that comes within range of him is in total awe. No girl will ever tell him to get lost if he treats her badly, 'cause she knows he would leave her. Gary, the drug dealer, won't grow up either. Why? None of the girls coming into Gary's life will ever demand the change in him that is so desperately needed. Girls always give in to his desires. At first it seems like both these guys are getting

---

[2] Dr. Laura Schlessinger interview, *Modern Maturity Home*, Sep/Oct 1999.

their fantasy, but at the end of the story it ultimately destroys them and the girls (and the community, for that matter). Mike, on the other hand, was forced to grow up because Jennifer *stood up to him*. Deep down, his *real* desire was to have a woman in his life who could see through all the blather—and love him anyway. She loved him by calling his bluff: "Change, or I'm gone!" And the *community* prospered.

. . . The Best There Ever Was

No man wants to be Just Any Guy. That's why I said earlier that if a girl is easy, no guy wants to keep her; if she's easy, any guy can get her, and that makes him just *any guy*. Girls, why do you think guys practice skateboarding for hours, trying to master the latest moves? Why do they spend whole afternoons making free throws, or endlessly practicing runs on the guitar? Every man wants to be The Best . . . at something! Now a guy knows he probably won't be the best pitcher, or quarterback, or skateboarder there ever was, but he at least wants ONE WOMAN to think he's the best SHE ever saw, and he wants to know that she's proud to give herself totally to him.

I don't know how many guys I've heard say, "I fell in love with, and married, the first girl that wouldn't let me get away with anything. She called my bluff—she knew what I was, but she loved me anyway." It was a woman who made the difference. She set the pattern and wouldn't let him take it over. In return, the guy loved and respected her so much that he was willing to settle down, get married, raise a family, and support that family for the rest of his life. Why? Because he won a girl's heart—the girl no one else could win. She rejected every other man, but she said "yes" to him. It cost him everything, but he knows she was worth the price.

Have you ever seen what happens when a girl refuses to date a guy unless he is willing to totally change his bad behavior or habits? Oh yeah! It's funny, *and it works*. She's the *judge, the jury, and the selection committee; she has the power to accept or reject any guy's advances and requests. She sets the standard, telling him what he has*

to do to finally be chosen.[3] To be otherwise makes her unworthy. If she hadn't demanded changes, would he have been worth waiting for? Not on your life! Listen to these girls:

Dear Mr. Henning,

My boyfriend used to drink, do drugs, and be in a gang before he met me. I told him before we went out, to be with me, that all has to stop. And it did. And now our relationship is better than ever. I hope you know what a good influence you have been on me. And keep giving your message 'cause you're good at what you do.

> Sincerely,
> Antoinette

Brad,

All the stuff you said was surprisingly correct. Guys play games, like the one I'm involved with. He one day acts like he likes me then other times seems he doesn't want to talk to me. But because of your speech I realized that I was smothering him. So now I act like I don't care if he calls back, and he does.

> A Girl

Now at first, it might look like this last girl was playing a game, *acting* as if she didn't care if the guy called her. But I don't think she was. Do you see what happened here? At first she was always at his "beck and call," letting him call the shots—teaching him to be selfish, but later she backed off, showing him that she wouldn't let herself be manipulated. Afraid he might be losing her, he freaked out, and now he treats her right. She thought she was smothering him, and maybe she was, but what was really going on was that he didn't respect her because she wasn't demanding anything of him.

---

[3] From *Men and Marriage* by George Guilder © 1986, 1992 used by permission of the licenser, Pelican Publisher Company, Inc., p. 12.

Men and Marriage, by George Gilder, is one of the top 10 books I've ever read. He does a great job explaining what I mean.

> In a world where women do not say no, the man is never forced to settle down and make serious choices. His sex drive—the most powerful compulsion in his life—is never used to make him part of civilization as the supporter of a family. If a woman does not force him to make a long-term commitment—to marry—in general, he doesn't. It is maternity that requires commitment. His sex drive only demands conquest, driving him from body to body in an unsettling hunt for variety and excitement in which much of the thrill is in the chase itself. The man still needs to be tamed. His problem is that many young women think they have better things to do than socialize single men.[4]

What Will Men Get in Return

When a girl is sexually unavailable before marriage, the man has to focus on her as a whole person, not just on her body and looks. In that process he learns to love and be loved. He learns how to win her heart. He learns self-discipline and responsibility, gets a job, and becomes productive. Before he actually commits himself in marriage he will have to understand her, listen to her, communicate with her, and not take her for granted. He has to discover that it's not his "right" to act on his impulses, and that sex is not the ultimate value. Instead of spending his whole life standing back and admiring his many options from afar ("Look at all those girls, man!"), he begins to grow up and become close with one person. Learning to be focused on a relationship brings purpose to the rest of his life, including his career and his children. *If a guy can discipline his body (by waiting) then he can control every other aspect of his life.* And what girl in her right mind would want to marry a guy who can't control himself?

---

[4] From *Men and Marriage* by George Guilder © 1986, 1992 used by permission of the licenser, Pelican Publisher Company, Inc., p. 12.

You've Got the Power—Use It!

Ladies, do you believe enough in your future marriage (and your friends' future marriages) to stand up for what's right sexually? What would you have to lose? Some guys at your school would probably rebel for a while and date girls from *other* schools, but the guys from *those* schools wouldn't put up with that for very long. Besides, seeing the girls at their own school, day after day, and wishing they could be with *them* would get old, real quick. If the girls stood up for what they really wanted from the guys, the guys would change. They wouldn't have a choice. Remember, "Men would not do half of what they do if women didn't let them"—and, "If you keep a man who does bad things in your life, it's your fault!"

I saw this work firsthand at a high school in eastern Washington. After my assembly was over, a guy wrote me a note saying he thought what I said about sexual abstinence before marriage was right, but he didn't care. He was going to "screw every girl he could get a hold of." He wrote his note on a 3x5 card but didn't have the guts to give it to me personally, so he handed it to a girl to give to me. I asked the girl if she knew who he was (he didn't sign it), and she told me his name. So I wrote his name at the bottom of his note, gave it back to the girl and said, "Pass this card to every girl in school." She did! I don't think that guy could beg, borrow, or steal a date for the rest of that year. Do you think he's gonna get his act together? If he ever wants to get another date in *that* school, he will! If he doesn't change he'll have to move to another school, 'cause "he ain't gettin' any girls from OUR school!"

The Big Picture

At this point you are probably thinking, "Hey, I just want a boyfriend. I don't care about all this stuff. I just want to know how I can get a guy to like me!" But listen . . . it goes much, much deeper than that.

If guys don't control themselves and learn to treat people (women and each other) in a civil way, they will carry that same behavior into their marriages. Healthy marriages and families make the whole civilization healthy. Creating healthy families takes a lot of planning, sacrifice, dedication, and hard work. That hard work starts now, with the guy you are presently dating. People who are allowed to live selfishly and treat others badly now, will carry that same behavior and attitude into their marriages and families. Selfish guys will always produce selfish families. Selfish families will always produce selfish societies. And selfishness will never produce long term happiness. EVER!!! So if you still say that all you want is a boyfriend 'cause everyone else has one, you may be acting just as selfishly as the guys are!

If You Don't Understand This, You're Not Ready to Date!

Every time you date a guy he learns something: he learns what works, what doesn't work, what he can or cannot do. Each new girl he dates gives him more information that he can use in the future. If he gets hurt or looks stupid with one girl, he remembers to never do *that* again. If he gets sex from one girl, he remembers what it took to get it, and he'll repeat the same process with the next girl. If you allow him to be selfish, he will learn to be more self-centered. If his bad behavior pays off for him . . . *"ALL RIGHT!"* He's learned a system, and as long as that system works he'll stick with it. The next girl he dates will get the same treatment.

Think about it this way. If some guy is treating *you* like trash, guess what? Some *other* girl somewhere *taught* him to do that. How? By letting him get away with it! He didn't start out his dating career being selfish. He learned it. He learned it from every girl he ever dated.

But what would happen to a guy if the girls he dated *didn't* let him get away with anything? He would begin to realize, "Hey, I could get dumped if I keep this up! Not only that, everyone will *know* I got dumped." At this point he'd know he had a problem, and he would have only one of three choices:

1. Change his behavior and keep the girl.
2. Stay the same and get dumped. (But everyone will *know* he got dumped, and that's painful.)
3. Stay the same and *dump the girl first.* (But that only works once or twice, 'cause all the other girls in school will figure out what he's doing and will pass the word. Then nobody would date him.)

So girls, if he doesn't change his behavior, let HIM feel the pain. LEAVE HIM! In the process he'll learn a great lesson: "IF YOU TREAT A GIRL BADLY SHE WILL LEAVE YOU, AND THAT HURTS!" And guess who taught it to him? YOU DID! Believe me, every girl in his future, and especially his future wife, will thank you.

I'll say it one more time . . .
**If you don't understand what I just explained,
you're NOT ready to date!**

When You Say "No," Mean What You Say!

Everyone knows you can't "just say no!" Well, wait . . . yes, you can, and you need to say no, but along with the verbal "NO" come the actions that support that "NO"! Your actions must be as believable as your words. If they aren't, you will be misunderstood and possibly be taken advantage of. At least some guys will try. So if your lips are saying "no," but what they are doing says "yes," that's not fair—and it's extremely confusing to the guy. If you say "no," but your clothes are saying "yes," or if your "no" is always being said in the back seat of his car, you can expect him to misunderstand what you're trying to say.

It really ticks me off to see these movies where the girl is saying, "No! Stop! Stop!" while she's ripping his clothes off and he's tearing hers off, and they're breathing hard and mashing lips. (Which *has* to hurt!) They might get away with that kind of stuff in the movies, but in real life a guy might go to jail for not stopping, and

he can't figure out why it's his fault! "Yeah, she was *saying* 'no,' but she took all her clothes off and . . ." From a guy's point of view, sex "can be a crime, a misunderstanding, or buyer's remorse."[5] The problem is that he can't tell which one it is until it's too late. The deed is done. The next morning, when she really thinks about what happened the night before, she can change her mind and call it rape and there's nothing he can do about it. He's in big trouble. Ladies, that's power! It's also not fair, and it's not right.

How Far *Can* You Go?

Girls, it will save you a lot of trouble if, right now, you will decide just how far you will go, and then stick to it. Make up your mind that when you say "No," you mean it—that "No!" doesn't mean "try again in a few minutes." Decide right now that the way you *look* and *act* will also say "No." That doesn't mean you're some kind of prude and you can't ever wear a bathing suit in front of a guy, or something. But what it does mean is that you can't wear a thong bikini and expect guys to understand you want to be a virgin on your honeymoon night. You might just as well scream, "Take me! Take me!" and then throw cold water in his face when he tries.

Now even though you may understand the "no" concept, you also need to know what's okay and how far you *can* go with a guy who's not your husband. If you need more explanation, go back and read Chapter 15 again. But the general rule is: If a girl is dating your future husband tonight, how far is okay for her to go with him? What's OK for them is OK for you. Deal? Do you mind if they hold hands? Kiss? French kiss? Hug? Touch over clothes? Touch *under* clothes? Take clothes off? Bump and grind a little? Do you care if they have intercourse? Oral sex? If what they're doing tonight would make you mad or disappointed in your future husband, then you can't do it with your boyfriend tonight, either. That's only fair.

---

[5] Dr. Warren Farrell, *Why Men Are the Way They Are* (New York: Berkley Books, 1986), p. 312.

But as you are evaluating how far is too far, ask yourself: Is what we are going to do tonight training this guy to be a better husband in the future, or is it teaching him to be selfish and out of control, getting whatever he wants, when he wants it?

QUESTION: Do you hope and pray your future husband is choosing to be good and is waiting for you tonight? Do you hope the girl he's with is helping him to wait?

THEN TREAT YOUR BOYFRIEND TONIGHT THE WAY YOU WANT THAT GIRL TO TREAT YOUR FUTURE HUSBAND TONIGHT.

If You Want the Knight on a White Horse, Be a Princess WORTH FIGHTING FOR!

We've talked about motivating a man to win the "fair maiden," but so far we haven't asked what kind of person *she* is. Is she just some "ditz" who wants all the goodies her knight can bring home? What man is going to give up his life for *that* kind of girl? No, she must be strong, intelligent, beautiful in his eyes, and one who encourages him to be the best he can be. She's a woman who understands that there are battles to be fought in life, and she supports her man in the fight. He wants an equal partner, a woman who will fight alongside him—only *together* can they win! To motivate her man, she must first hold herself to a high standard. Then, and only then, can she demand and expect the same from him. She becomes the force that encourages him to succeed. Nothing else will. For him the battle is the search for a meaningful life, a life worth living (his Holy Grail) and it's a fight to the death.

Again, the hard part for the girl is that the average guy might not have any clue or understand any of what I just said. "Holy Grail . . . what?" At this point in his life he may only want a girl with big boobs. He may have no idea that there's even a battle goin' on, let alone that he's in it. But trust me, ladies . . . it's comin'!

What Kind of Guy Do You Want?

Girls need to be aware that there are two kinds of guys. There are good guys and there are some not-so-good guys. Seems obvious. Problem is, they can actually look very much the same from a distance, but they are *very* different in reality.

Not-So-Good Guys (AKA Bad Guys)

Not-so-good guys are users. They take what they want with little concern for anyone but themselves. They live for sex, money, and power. You don't dare get in their way, 'cause if you do you'll get run over. Competition IS their game; the "bottom line" is the ultimate value. If the numbers don't add up in their favor, they get out. They apply the same logic to relationships and women. Control is the key. They use everything to their own advantage. They enjoy selling their product because their "product" is themselves, and they're good salesmen. Selling themselves has become an art. It's their business—their focus. And any woman who "buys" becomes both the consumer and the consumed.

Good Guys

Then there's the good guys. Good guys love life more than power, money, or sex, and yet they know those things can be important and enjoyable in their rightful place. They value "the challenge" of life, not just the product or "bottom line." People and relationships are important to them. When life gets tough, it's their relationships they depend on most. These guys are honest, kind, trustworthy, and fun, but they know how to be tough when they need to be. Those qualities may make them seem boring at first—somehow less "powerful" than the not-so-good guys—but the good guys are in relationships for the long haul. These are the guys you want to find.

A lot of the time girls *say* they want "good guys," but then they *act* as if they really want "not-so-good guys." Look at the posters girls have on their bedroom walls and you'll see what I mean. You'll only see pictures of the most successful men out there: musicians, movie stars, and athletes. They may be sexy, too, but that's second-

ary. Girls are being fooled by the "image" of success. You don't believe that? Look at the way most of those "poster guys" live their lives and how they treat their women. See if they tend to be the good guys or the not-so-good guys.

It's All in How You Define Success

Consciously or unconsciously, girls look for a guy who shows potential, especially in the area of leadership. He may be the quarterback on the football team, or he may lead the debate team. He may be the loudest, goofiest guy in class, the lead singer in a rock band, the best skateboarder in school, or even the drug-dealing leader of a gang. No matter what "field" he's in, he always shows potential: the ability to take action, to lead. He's someone who demands attention and gets what he wants, which implies that he has the ability to lead and take care of you! Now he might be a total jerk, but if he's the *best* jerk, many girls will date him just because he's strong. Often his favorite line is, "I don't care!" and he looks like he means it, *but don't you believe it. He cares immensely.* Girls interpret the "I don't care" to mean, "I know exactly what I want and I know where I'm going. If you don't like it, tough!" He acts tough and looks tough. He stands up to people and does what he wants. To everyone else he may look like a total loser but to you he has "potential." Underneath it all, what *really* appeals to you is his potential to be successful at taking charge, at taking care of you. A woman married to a gangster knows what her husband does for a living, but she married him anyway. Why? Because he is a powerful, successful man! BUT . . . that power to take care of you won't go very far if his *character* lands him in federal prison!

Success Illusion

Men and women both struggle with "success illusions." As an experiment, ladies, call up one of your girlfriends and tell her something like "This morning I met this guy at Starbucks and he was driving a brand- new Beemer convertible . . . he works for Microsoft . . . this summer he's traveling in Europe . . . blah, blah,

blah." Your girlfriend would be excited and discuss him with you for hours. That kind of guy is every girl's dream. Now call a different girlfriend and tell her, "I met this guy at Happy Donuts and he was driving a '72 VW bus . . . OK, he's out of work, but he's looking for a job. . . ." Would your girlfriend be excited for you? No way. Remember, the posters most girls have on their walls are pictures of the richest, most successful, famous men, not pictures of unemployed auto mechanics.

What do guys have on their walls? They choose pictures of beautiful, semi-clothed women, with no thought for those women's abilities, successes, or potential, outside of how they look. *Playboy's* Miss June is only beautiful; not particularly successful or talented (but she has big boobs). The only potential she shows is her potential in bed! She doesn't even have a real name, 'cause that would be too personal, and guys looking at Miss June don't want a person, they want a "thing." That's why they call her a "Playmate," not a "mate."

Who Wants to Marry a Millionaire? Why???

A while back there was a show on TV called "Who Wants to Marry a Multi-Millionaire?" Over 100 men, all millionaires, were interviewed for the opportunity of a lifetime: one of them was to be picked to go on live TV, broadcast to millions of people, and watch as 50 money-hungry potential brides were paraded in front of him. His job was to pick one of them and marry her . . . all on live TV! Remember, none of the women would know who he was, and they would not be allowed to see him until the very end of the show. *Thousands* of women applied to be on the show, all willing to marry a guy they knew nothing about, just because he had money. Okaaay. . . .

First the interviews, then the bathing suits. After an hour or more (and a million commercials), the guy narrowed the group down from 50 to 10, then from 10 to five. In the final minutes of the show, when the five finalists were nervously standing on the set dressed in their bridal gowns, Mystery Millionaire Man came out from his off-camera hideout and chose "the love of his life."

He got down on one knee, put a three-carat diamond ring (worth $38,000) on her finger, and married her! Right on the spot! Remember: none of the women had ever seen him, and knew *nothing* about him! Did they want to get on that show for love? No way! Did he? No. He did it for sex. The women were all beautiful. The one he picked for his wife later posed for *Playboy* magazine. He knew what he wanted. He had the pick of the litter!

But the story didn't end on TV. They went on their "honeymoon" cruise all right, but when they came back she wanted their "marriage" annulled. It didn't last a week. (Surprise, surprise!) And *why* did she want it annulled? It turned out he didn't have as much money as he said he had. The media portrayed *him* as the jerk and her as the disappointed princess: that *he* didn't measure up to *her* standard. And just what *was* her standard? Two things: First he had to be successful (money), and *then* he had to be loving. He was neither. (Just how loving do you think a guy can be if he picks out his wife in less than an hour on national television?) Loving or not . . . she dumped him.

Her criteria for marriage: Money, and lots of it!
His criteria for marriage: Beauty and sex!

Did either of their value systems work in the long run? No!

Poor Guys with Lots of Money

The guys with lots of money get the gorgeous girls, and *guys know it*. What's sad is that neither the girl nor the guy really wins in the end. The magazines we read make us *think* they have the "Good Life," but in reality they don't. A rich guy never knows if he is loved for who he is or for what his money can buy. (Girls with fantastic figures struggle with the same thing.) What if he finds out she was only interested in *his money* and not *him*? A lot of guys are afraid to find out. He couldn't live with himself if it was just money she wanted. Some guys will get her to sign a prenuptial agreement, marry her, and then never slow down long enough to find out *why* she married him. If it was for the wrong reason, the pain would be too much. Instead he chooses to work harder, play

harder, and drink harder—whatever it takes to keep from thinking much about his life. The fear of failure and rejection is literally killing thousands of men every year.

Just like women don't like being judged solely on their "sex potential," men don't like being judged only by their "earning potential." Have you ever really thought what it must be like for men in our culture? If you think it's hard to be an average girl in a supermodel world, think what it must be like to be an average guy in a "*Fortune* 500" world.

Look at women's magazines and see how they portray a woman's wedding as "the most important day of her life." Is love at the center of it? Of course not. The ring is. A DeBeers ad entices with,

> You'll turn it in the light without even thinking. Stop in the middle of a sentence just to look at it. The days will go by. And the years. But every time you glance down, you'll smile and remember how *you* became *we*.

> Long after the wedding dress is in the attic, the diamond will still be on your finger. *So make sure it's the one you really want.*

The Diamond Engagement Ring
How else could two months' salary last forever?[6]

When I saw the ring in the magazine ad I called a local jewelry store and asked what a one to one-and-a-half-carat diamond ring (like the one in the ad) would cost. The woman said an average-quality diamond in an average setting would *start* at somewhere in the neighborhood of $8,000. THAT EQUALS TWO MONTHS' SALARY????!!!! When I stopped and worked it out, this guy would have to be making $80,000 or more per year (before taxes) to give her "the one she really wants." And *that* ring is at the *lower* end of the spectrum! How many young men getting married right out of college could afford to give their fiancée a ring like that? Very few! So who are the girls looking for and dreaming about? The guy with

---

[6] *Cosmopolitan*, August 1996, p. 105

the $80,000-a-year job. How does that make the typical guy feel? "Inadequate" doesn't even begin to describe it.

By the way, are those ads in men's magazines? Of course not! They're in women's magazines. Why? Because *she's* the one who picks out the ring and motivates *him* to get it for her. How does she do that? By using her sexual beauty. She is the one in control. THAT'S POWER!

Looks and Sex Appeal: Get Any Man You Want!

A woman's beauty—sex appeal—is a powerful thing, and most women know it . . . or figure it out. The media have known it for years. They know they can sell almost anything if they can tap into that power. For instance, on the cover of the April 1998 *Cosmopolitan* magazine, right next to a very sensual picture of model Liz Hurley, there is an article entitled "Get Any Man You Want!" How do you suppose you'll do that? Look at the cover of the magazine (or any *Cosmopolitan* magazine for that matter) . . . *THAT'S* how! Sex and beauty! A very *capable* woman could bench-press 300 pounds, handle an Uzi, and be President of the United States, but if she doesn't take care of the way she looks and the way she carries herself she will have no power with men. But the power that comes with beauty is a dangerous thing both to her and to him.

The Trap Is Set . . .

A young, attractive woman wearing a low-cut outfit like the one Liz Hurley was wearing draws a lot of male attention, but because of that attention she makes a fatal mistake. She begins to think that when she finally wants to settle down and get married, she will have her pick of any guy she wants, because right now it looks like they all want her. Do women really believe that? Here's an article from *Cosmopolitan* called "Stay Single."

Finally, think of the abundance of the opposite sex as man insurance: Just knowing there are plenty of them on tap lets you stop worrying about nabbing one now and focus on other aspects of your life. It's the perfect time to advance your career, go back to school, travel, start writing that screenplay, or do whatever you've been putting off. And guess what? All that self-improvement will make you even more attractive to the zillions of guys just waiting for you to come along.[7]

No it won't! It will scare them to death! So does she settle down right away? Heck, no! She's having too much fun with all that attention. She decides to play the field, bide her time, and use her beauty to get what she wants. But the guys she's dating aren't about to settle down, either. They're having just as much fun as she is. Neither one is pressing for marriage, 'cause, "Hey . . . this is the 21st century!" Or, "We're just living together . . . *for now.*"

So, instead of getting serious about a particular guy and getting married, this young woman decides to have her own career and play the field for a while. So it's off to school for a few years, then into the work force to make her mark in the world. Nothing particularly wrong with that. But too many times her thought is, "I'll have a career for a few years and *then* I'll settle down with a husband and family. So we'll just live together . . . for now."

But time has a way of playing tricks on a woman who thinks that way, because her time for marrying the "good men," as she calls them, is limited. She doesn't realize that the older she gets the less "power" she can maintain through her beauty. While she's young she can easily seduce men with her body. It's like they're drunk. Look what men throughout all history have risked or given up just for a one-night frolic with the woman of their dreams. It's amazing! But do those men tend to settle down with those same women? No!

Many women think they can, at their convenience, get any man they want by seducing him and then marrying him. But what a woman like that doesn't understand is that her time is running

---

[7] Stay Single, *Cosmopolitan*, July, 2002, p. 106.

out. When she grows older and the competition broadens to include the new "crop" of young, available women entering the market, she'll see too late that the men she could have seduced or married five or ten years ago are now looking elsewhere. The successful men, who are now so attractive to her as potential husbands, may now be trading in their 30-year-old girlfriends for girls a whole lot younger and sexier. On top of that, she didn't see that she was teaching her lovers to be as selfish and uncommitted as she was. She chose to live by the way most men (or a lot of them at least) pattern their lives.

As time passes, men gain *more* power (success) while she slowly *loses* hers (beauty). The woman who "loves to control men" through sex and beauty will find out too late that her sex appeal at age 30 or 40 isn't the same as it was at 20. She won't be able to compete. Now she's on her own: no family, no husband to love and grow old with, and maybe no money. She may have children from a previous fling, but she has no one to help her raise them. If she's not careful she'll become desperate, and desperate women don't have all that much sex appeal to successful men. That's why there are 50 percent more divorced or separated women between the ages of 35 and 65 than there are men. Men remarry at three times the rate women do. But they're starting their second marriages with women 10 years younger.[8] At that point in time it's men who are in control.

Catching Him and Keeping Him

There's another side to the trap. Women who think they can use sex to get a guy (and they can) don't understand that sex won't keep him, and keeping him is the hard part. Remember: *Whatever you use to get a guy, that's what you'll have to use to keep him.* If you use sex to get him, you'll have to use sex (and a continuously great body) to keep him. Just because you marry a guy doesn't mean his character is going to change. The character he had coming *into* the marriage is exactly the character he is going to have throughout the

---

[8] Dr. Warren Farrell, *Why Men Are the Way They Are* (New York: Berkley Books, 1986), p. 18.

marriage. If he was sexually undisciplined before you got married, he will be undisciplined afterwards too. Your behavior never taught him to focus his sexuality in marriage alone. His focus is sex—for sex's sake—any time, anywhere he finds it. He doesn't want you; he wants sex! You'll keep him for a while, but as you get older and the "bait" starts to fade in comparison with the "new crop," he'll go after the new crop, leaving you in the dust.

Why So Many Women Are Angry

"NON SEQUITUR" © 1998 Wiley Miller. Distributed by UNIVERSAL PRESS SYNDICATE Reprinted with permission. All rights reserved.

Can you see why so many women are angry at men? On the one hand they are tired of baby-sitting men, putting up with their immaturity. On the other hand they're angry at being used and then tossed aside for "a newer model." But women need to avoid the mistake of lowering themselves to the same level as those kinds of men.

Women make the mistake of thinking they can somehow get back at men by becoming just as wild, uncommitted, and sexually out of control as they are. "If men can do it, so can I!" Look at women's magazines and see just how desperate women have become, and how their game plan isn't working.

To give you some examples, here is a list of all the featured articles from the cover of just one women's magazine.

1. Sex Survey: Your Chance to Speak Out!
2. Multiple Glorious Orgasms—Your Guide to Sexual Satisfaction
3. Men's Revealing Sexual Dreams—What You Can Learn from Them
4. If He Had the Chance, Would Your Man Cheat?
5. How to Seduce a Man—Your Guide to Flirting
6. Living Passionately!—Turn Your Ho-Hum Life into a Splendid Journey
7. Sex with a New Man—What You Must Know [9]

Is all this sexual stuff going to solve the problem with men? No! The longer a woman stays in this "wild mode," the more difficult it will be for her to find a suitable man who will still want her when she decides to settle down. The results of her wild years will be devastating, but by the time she realizes it, it will be too late to turn back.

Desperate Women Do Desperate Things

Women who think they have the right to live life any way they choose, have sex whenever they want it, and be as uncommitted as men are, have believed a lie, and they will live out the rest of their lives in deep regret. Most men, believe it or not, still want to marry a virgin—a *feminine* virgin.

As a woman's biological clock goes off and her desires for a husband and family go unfulfilled, she becomes even more desperate, angry, and unlovable: the very thing most men *don't* want. The more desperate she becomes, the lower her standards get. The lower her standards, the lower the quality of the men that she attracts, and the more hurt and bitter she becomes. At that point she figures, "If that's the way you want it . . . OK! Two can play at this game!" And since "all's fair in love and war" . . . then war it is! She'll take them on one at a time! She thinks she can battle men on their own turf. Big mistake!

---

[9] *Complete Woman,* December 1994

To Be Like a Man . . . Play by Men's Rules!

Now if you want to fight guys on their own turf, OK. Fine. It's your choice. But you won't like the outcome, believe me. Men think, "OK! You want to be on the same level with us guys? Then *play by our rules.* Don't come into *our world* and try to play by *your rules!* After all, we aren't trying to change everything in *your* world. Our rules say the fittest survive. Can you take it? When the going gets tough, the tough get going! So when things get tough, don't do the 'cry thing.' In our world, crybabies get laughed at. If you get laughed at, you can't suddenly switch to ladies' rules and yell, 'Chauvinist!!!' and expect us to come running to save you. You can't *choose* which 'guy rules' you want to live by. It's ALL or nothing!"

Men will say, "You want non-relational sex like your magazines say you do? Fine! But don't get all bent out of shape when the guy you were with on Saturday doesn't call you on Monday. Don't get crabby when you get pregnant and he dumps you. In *our* world you don't ask for help . . . from anybody. (That's why we don't stop and ask directions.) You're pregnant? Deal with it! Either go all the way with the guys' rules, or don't go at all." What a horrible way to have to live!

The more women try to remove themselves from traditional female roles, the farther they get from the very thing they really want. If you women *say* you want to be treated as equals with men, fine, but look at the way so many men treat each other. Is that what you *really* want? Is it really better in a man's world where life is a never-ending competition? A world of *things*? No, it's not.

Women and Casual Sex

When a woman tries to be as casual about sex as so many men seem to be (which isn't good at all), saying things like "You don't have to love me, let's just have sex," many men will take advantage of her. But when that same woman finally wants to find a guy and settle down, she realizes she doesn't know any guys she would *want* to settle down with. And none of the guys she knows will want her, either, or take her seriously. Why? 'Cause no man wants to marry "one of the guys." He wants to marry a *woman*. At that

point she can't just change her mind about being like a guy and living by guys' rules, and suddenly want to be a good wife and mother (women's rules). No one will let her. You can't change horses midstream.

When you girls try to live like guys, without the femaleness, without the modesty, guys won't respect you. They will use you, eat you up, and spit you out. They will only take advantage of your weakness 'cause that's what they do with each other. Watch what happens to the weak guys at school and see if it's not true. A guy's world spits out the weak and makes way for the strong. That's how men survive in the dog-eat-dog world of business, sports, and politics. I'm not saying that a guy's way of living is right, or better than a woman's. Not at all. What I am saying is, *that's the way it is in a guys' world* and women can't expect it to change.

Looks, or Personality? (What Guys Really Want Deep Down)

Cosmopolitan ran an article that actually got it right about guys (but it's probably the *only* thing they got right). In this one article called "What Men Really Go For", they wanted to find out once and for all, "Do men prize looks over personality?" Here's what they found.

> "Men will always slobber over a gorgeous babe . . ." but is that what really wins in the long run? So, to put the issue to the test, *Cosmo* sent an attractive woman out on the road two different times. The first time she was dressed in khakis, a button-down shirt, light makeup, and a carefree hairdo. She didn't show her attractiveness and actually looked a little "unkempt." She purposely acted flirty and quite friendly. But the second night she dressed up with beautiful hair, flawless makeup, a "flattering outfit" that made her look stunning . . . but she acted like a total "bitch." The night she played the flirty, friendly girl she received four hellos, two offers to buy her a drink, a compliment on her smile, a wink, a cigarette from a professional hockey player, and an invite to sit with a Frenchman. But on the "bitchy-but-beautiful" night she sat at a bar totally alone and didn't "get hit on" once all night. One

guy actually came up to her and said something like, "Man, it can't be that bad, can it?" When she ignored him he just walked away saying, "Jeez, who stole your Prozac?" She said, "That was the only conversation I had all night."[10]

Beautiful, yes. Attractive to guys? . . . Absolutely! But nobody wanted her badly enough to take the challenge.

There will always be better-looking people than you. So what?!! Why get all bent out of shape and jealous? Most girls have been in the situation where the guy they are with sees a gorgeous girl enter the room and falls all over himself, staring. But if the first girl is smart, remains confident, and can admit openly, "Boy she's a looker, isn't she?" . . . THAT girl has won her man forever. When a guy is out with you and looks at a beautiful woman, it's not that he wants her more than he wants you, or that he wants to dump you to get her. Not at all, but he isn't blind either! If he continues to stare at her (which would be very rude) you may need to subtly help him take his attention off her and direct it to something else. It works the other way around too. A girl may see a good-looking guy (she's not blind either) and momentarily admire him from afar, but still want her own man. Comedian Tim Allen put it this way:

> Men look at women the way men look at cars. Everyone looks at Ferraris. Now and then we like a pickup truck, and we all end up with a station wagon: the best of both worlds. . . . What's interesting is that we often find the right kind of woman immediately and then, because of a taste for the Ferrari and the pickup truck, avoid the station wagon for as long as we can hold out.[11]

All guys have different opinions about looks. One guy thinks a girl is gorgeous and the other guy thinks she's just average. You girls do the same thing over guys, and you know you do. The point is, not everyone will be physically attracted to you, or you to them, so don't worry about it. It's a waste of time. I can tell you

---

[10] "What Men Really Go For", *Cosmopolitan*, August, 1990.
[11] Tim Allen, *Don't Stand Too Close to a Naked Man* (New York: Hyperion, 1994), 66.

this, though, it's the smile and the clear eyes that make a guy fall all over himself for a girl. Look at the movie stars. It's their smiles that men respond to. The pouting model inside a *Seventeen* magazine may look sexy, but it's the smiles of the stars that show up on the front covers of magazines. Julia Roberts is a good actress, but there are lots of good actresses out there. When you close your eyes and imagine what she looks like, what comes to your mind? That's right. Her smile! How about Sandra Bullock? Same thing.

PERSONALITY (smile) WINS OVER BEAUTY AND BODY EVERY TIME! Julia Roberts and Sandra Bullock don't have all that fantastic a figure (sorry Julia and Sandra) but they sure get the attention of the guys.

Beauty Isn't All It's Cracked Up to Be!

It seems like every girl's dream is to someday be a stunningly beautiful woman with a great figure; the envy of all the rest of womankind. But have you ever really thought what it would be like to be that beautiful? Remember the article "She's So Pretty It Makes Me Sick!" from *Sassy?*

> Many beautiful women never get a chance to test themselves beyond their looks, and they live in fear of losing their looks . . . Plus, being beautiful can be lonely. Beautiful women find it difficult to have female friends due to the jealousy factor. And a lot of men don't approach them because they're afraid of rejection. They feel safer approaching more average-looking women.[12]

A long time ago a bunch of guys were asked, "What do guys want in a girl when it comes to looks?" I'll always remember their response 'cause it shocked me when I heard it, but I also agreed with them. They all said basically the same thing: "She doesn't have to be all that gorgeous, but we want her to do the best with what she has." It's true! Yeah, guys will always be blown away by the "babes," but again, so what? Why give in to all the pressure to

---

[12] Alison, "She's So Pretty It Makes Me Sick!", *Sassy,* 60.

have to be gorgeous? Being a beautiful girl isn't all it's cracked up to be. That same *Sassy* article described a girl who, since the age of 16, has been battling bulimia. She said, "I feel a constant pressure to be thin, to always look perfect. It's like I have this impossibly high standard I have to maintain at all times." Who wants to live like that all her life?

Hollywood is full of women who live in constant fear of losing the one asset they have: their looks. Did you know that before every big "event" in Hollywood there is a "rush" on the plastic surgeons' offices as women get their last minute "makeovers"? Can you imagine the kind of life that creates that kind of paranoia about the way you look? You may get stares from people, but the life you have to live *between the stares* is hardly worth living.

Women Confuse Men

(Luann 2/11/99)

LUANN reprinted by permission of United Feature Syndicate, Inc.

Guys don't understand what girls want or how girls live their lives 'cause everything is so different from the way guys live their lives. You girls need to know that much of a guy's life is the life of GUESSING AND LOOKING STUPID! Most guys don't feel safe in relationships because they're always having to guess about things. Guess what she wants for her birthday! Guess what size she wears! Guess what she *really* is thinking. . . . Guess if her "no" is really a "yes" in disguise, if she wants to be kissed, what she would like to do on their next date (knowing all along that he's "just supposed to know.")

So he takes her out and spends a lot of money on her, and wonders all night if she is really enjoying herself. If a girl accepts a guy's invitation to go out, he doesn't know if she said yes because she really wanted to go or if she was just bored and didn't have anything else to do. Maybe she said yes 'cause she's trying to get even with her ex-boyfriend by going out with a different guy. Or the very worst: maybe she just didn't know how to say no without hurting the guy's feelings. Or . . . (hope, hope) she really *did* want to go out! But he doesn't know which one it is! All night long he feels that any move he makes might be wrong, and that means looking stupid.

Why Guys Like Sports

That's why guys like sports so much! Sports have concrete ideas and set principles that never change in the middle of the game. You always know where you stand. You know the rules and you know what the score is. You may even *lose,* but you know *why* you lost!

In the "game" of relationships with girls, there aren't any clear-cut rules like there are in sports, so how's a guy supposed to know how to "play"? You don't get awarded points, so you don't know if you're winning or losing. Or sometimes there *is* a point system and you get points for . . . for . . . I don't even know what for! For example: a guy goes to work all day, comes home to his wife and thinks, "Hmmmm, I made 50 points for working all day." "No," she says, "That's only one point." Oookaaaaay. . . . The next day he brings her one red rose. "Way to go!" she says, and gives him another point. He's thinkin': "Work all day, get one point. Buy her one rose, get one point. Hellooooo!!! What kinda game you runnin' on me?"

Sometimes a relationship makes a guy feel like there's two different players who are supposed to be on the same team, but they each have different goals: like playing basketball and suddenly being told that the goal is to get a touchdown! To make matters worse, lots of guys are confused as to whether women are their teammates or their opponents! On top of that, the rules don't seem

to be the same for guys as they are for girls. Look at what a guy sent me from the Internet:

If a guy works too hard, he never has any time for her.
If he doesn't work enough, he's a good-for-nothing bum.

If she has a boring, repetitive job with low pay, it's exploitation.
If he has a boring, repetitive job with low pay, he should get off his butt and find something better.

If he gets a promotion ahead of her, it's favoritism.
If she gets a job ahead of him, it's equal opportunity.

If you mention how nice she looks, it's sexual harassment.
If you keep quiet, it's male indifference.

If he cries, he's a wimp.
If he doesn't, he's insensitive.

If he makes a decision without consulting her, he's a chauvinist pig.
If she makes a decision without consulting him, she's a liberated woman.

If he asks her to do something she doesn't enjoy, that's domination.
If she asks him, he's doing her a favor.

If he tries to keep in shape, he's vain.
If he doesn't, he's a slob.

If he buys her flowers, he's after something.
If he doesn't, he's not thoughtful.

If he talks dirty to a woman, that's sexual harassment.
If a woman talks dirty to him, that's $3.99 per minute.

No wonder guys have a tough time in relationships with girls!

Competition between Guys and Girls

I know there's a real push in our culture for women to have equality on every level with guys, but women don't realize what that "equality" is doing to guys. Any man trying to outdo a woman in a business venture or a sport, or just trying to win an argument in a relationship, knows he's on dangerous ground. For the guy, none of the rules *he* lives by seem to apply, so he feels like women don't play fair. It's like they cheat! Girls just shrug it off and say guys just have too big an ego problem. But that's not it. Look at this example and see how confusing it all is for a guy.

The Wrestling Team

I met a guy once that told me a story about when he was on the high school wrestling team. He was a fairly popular guy, worked hard, and was a good wrestler. There weren't too many guys in the league who stood a chance against him. But he met his match one day when he found himself scheduled to wrestle the ultimate challenger . . . a girl! Now this girl thought she had the right to wrestle, just like a guy does, and that just because she was a girl it shouldn't mean that she couldn't compete with guys. "After all," she said, "I have a right! I'm a girl!" That seemed logical, at least to her.

Now it wasn't that this guy didn't think he could beat her at wrestling, it was the "rules" surrounding the match that he knew he couldn't win. See, the deal is, wrestling is a sport that requires . . . how do I say . . . close contact: grabbing under the crotch to flip the guy over, or around-the-chest holds to slam your opponent to the mat. I mean, it's pretty personal stuff out there. But this is a girl! How's he supposed to do *that* with a girl? Here's what he faced:

1. If he refuses to wrestle . . . He's a chicken!
2. If he beats her . . . He's a jerk!
3. If he loses to her . . . He's a wimp!
4. If he grabs her in the wrong place . . . He's a pervert!
5. If he talks mean to her . . . He's harassing her!

Lose, lose, lose!!!!!! But not in *her* mind. She had "a right" and "no guy is gonna keep me from wrestling just 'cause he's got a fragile ego!'"

The poor guy didn't have a chance. He also had no choice. He decided what he would do. When the match began, he simply grabbed the girl, slammed her to the mat and pinned her in a matter of a few short seconds. As she lay on the mat, stunned, he crouched over her and, pointing his finger in her face, he said, "Don't do this! This isn't fair to you, or to us guys!" When he walked off, sure enough, half of the crowd was booing, the other half cheering. Did she have the right? Maybe. Was it worth it? Probably not. What did it do to the guy? It destroyed him. He was telling me this about 10 years after it happened and he *still* felt bad. He couldn't win. *It wasn't the guy who didn't understand the girl; it was the girl who didn't understand the guy.*

Watch What You Wear

Your clothes are your billboard. They can define you in a moment —for better or worse.[13]

A few months ago I was asked to fly out of state just to meet with some girls in a small middle school. The way they were dressing was causing such a problem in their school that the principal was willing to spend the money to have me come and talk to them. In the nine years that I've been traveling and giving this talk, girls' clothes have gone from being occasionally questionable to being routinely obscene. (I sound like your dad, huh?) So before I close this chapter I want to get in a little advice.

What you wear reflects who you are and what you want. If you say you want a guy to treat you with respect and then you

---

[13] J. D. Heiman and Lynn Harris, *Singled Out Guide to Dating* (New York: MTV Books/PocketBooks/Melcher Media, 1996), p. 17.

wear a low-cut dress to the prom, what's he supposed to think? "Guys take everything you do now as an indication of something you might do later. . . ."[14] A low-cut dress *now* means even lower (or off) *later.*

Guys are very visual. VERY! Never forget that. A guy is turned on by what he *sees* more than any other thing. And it's not so much what you AREN'T wearing that's the big deal, it's what you ARE wearing that's the big deal. Girls posing for *Playboy* are almost always wearing *some* clothes, maybe not much, but they have *something* on. *Playboy* knows that a guy gets more excited by the *idea* of taking off what the girl has on than he does by the picture of a naked girl. Victoria's Secret has made a business out of that fact. A very successful business!

The Golden Globe awards were on TV the other night and I watched in amazement how the women dressed. It was ridiculous! At one point I called my wife in to see this one actress (I won't mention her name) 'cause she was wearing a dress that looked like it had been shredded across the front by a lion! The straps (?) kept falling down, and it was obvious she wasn't wearing anything underneath. Every guy watching was hoping she'd make *just the wrong move. . . .*

Think about "crop tops." There isn't a guy alive who hasn't at some time in his life hoped some girl wearing a crop top would bend over so he could get a good look. I remember riding a ferryboat to Seattle once, when a woman wearing a crop top came walking down the stairs while my family and I were eating lunch on the deck below. I looked up and, without even trying, I could see "everything." She didn't care. I've never forgotten it. (Typical guy, I guess.)

The more skin the guy sees, the more he thinks he'd like to feel it. His body is programmed that way. The magazines and movie industries know it. Look through any teen magazine and check out how the clothes or bathing suits emphasize the chest, belly button, or stomach of their models. Most of the articles

---

[14] J. D. Heiman and Lynn Harris, *Singled Out Guide to Dating* (New York: MTV Books/PocketBooks/Melcher Media, 1996), p. 35.

in the magazines focus on sex. They push the limits to get guys addicted to sexual images, 'cause they know the guys will come back wanting more. The more out of control the guys become, the more business for the magazines and their advertisers 'cause they know teens will spend about $172 billion in retail shopping per year.[15] Like drug dealers, they're using you and the guys' addiction to make money. What they don't tell you is the end result of that addiction.

I have a *CosmoGirl* magazine on my desk that has Jessica Biel on the cover.[16] She looks gorgeous. The pose: chest out, butt up, belly button showing. She's wearing this white, tight tank top with tight, low cut jeans, and of course she's got this incredible smile and long dark hair. You need to understand that this is a very *carefully* crafted cover. You know why? 'Cause they want you to believe this is how you get a guy. (That's what will make you want to buy their magazine.) When the average girl looks at the cover of this magazine she immediately wants to look and be like Jessica. Who wouldn't? (And what guy wouldn't like to date her?)

But if you were to look at the *back cover of the same magazine* you'd see what reality looks like. The front cover shows what they want you to get hooked on, but the back cover is how life really is. The girl on the back cover is hanging up the phone, obviously having just ended her relationship with her boyfriend 'cause she's got big tears streaming down her cheeks. But dang, if she doesn't look good in her Calvin Klein jeans! Which, by the way, you can barely see in the picture.

Now why would Calvin Klein put such a downer ad like that on the back cover? Simple: "We'll get 'em hooked on looking like the front cover 'cause guys will love it." Calvin Klein knows full well that guys who date those girls won't choose them because they're such wonderful people. They'll date them 'cause they're so dang sexy. Will a guy be able to stick around after he gets what he wanted from the cover girl? Heck no! If he sticks around too

---

[15] Tacoma News Tribune, *Teenage Consumers Spending More*, Knight Ridder Tribune, March 26, 2002.
[16] *CosmoGirl*, October/November, 1999.

long the cover girl will find out just what kind of guy he is—a user—and she'll dump him! If she does that, EVERYONE will know she dumped him. He can't take that chance cause that would make him a LOSER! So what does he do? He dumps her first.

When girls are taken advantage of and then get dumped, they get depressed. (Back over of magazine.) When girls get depressed, what do they do?

THEY GO SHOPPING!!!!!!

And Calvin Klein knows it! So he hooks girls into looking like the front cover, gets them to buy his stuff, and then when their lives crash he'll sell them the stuff on the back cover to make them feel good again. The whole time he knows that girls will never question what's really happening. And because they never question it he knows he's safe and he can even fool them into believing he "REALLY CARES."

Moral of Calvin Klein's Story

Sex is how you get a guy (cover) but it won't keep him (back cover). So even when life sucks, just remember, at least you can always *look* good. Buy our stuff. We care!

No, they don't!!! They just keep offering new products, hoping you'll believe the lie that the right combination of "stuff" will bring you the guy who will make you happy. If the right guy doesn't come along, they hope you'll try another combination of "stuff." But let me ask you something. If you really did what the magazines say, would you really get what you want? Maybe you've tried. How's it going?

So What *Should* You Wear?

Rule of thumb: Try to wear clothes that will draw a man's eyes first to your face, and only later to your body. I know that's not

always easy, but that's the goal. Remember the definition of Love? "Choosing the highest good for the other person." Flaunting your body in front of your boyfriend (or teachers, or any other guys) is not choosing the highest good for them. So love them by choosing carefully what you wear. Remember, it's not just your boyfriend who gets turned on, *it's every man who sees you, regardless of his age.*

Principles to Live and Date By

I want to end by giving you a list of principles that summarizes most of what I've said in this chapter and the rest of this book. I first thought of doing this after I read a book called *The Rules*. Boy, oh boy, did *that* book get hammered!!!! All the feminists went berserk, saying the two authors weren't being true to what feminism is all about, and that it was manipulative. Personally I thought the book had *some* good stuff in it, although I obviously didn't agree with everything. So I'm going to give you what I'll call *Principles to Live and Love By*, kinda my own rules. (Betcha I get hammered too.)

But first let me say that girls *must* become what they were intended to be . . . REAL WOMEN: individuals who know who they are, and what they value in life—people who aren't swayed by popular opinions or fads (or feminists). When this happens, they will become THE MOST POWERFUL FORCE FOR GOOD ON THE FACE OF THE EARTH . . . PEOPLE WHO HAVE THE POTENTIAL TO CHANGE ALL OF SOCIETY . . . INCLUDING MEN!

1. **Don't wait for a man to make you happy.**

   Concentrate on being the best you can be. Find out what you're capable of. Learn to be confident in yourself, and choose to be happy. Build a well-rounded life: learn to play a sport, develop hobbies, read, travel, and know what you believe in. Incidentally, that's the kind of woman a guy would want. Live your life in a way that says to him, "Even

if you don't ask me out my life will be happy and success-ful. Besides, there may be other men besides you that I'm interested in." Desperate women with little self-confidence aren't all that attractive to eligible men. Whether you ever get married or not, this outlook will serve you well.

2. **Women are the most powerful people on the face of the earth . . . so act like it!**

   You *already* have the potential to change the world (men included), so don't try to get power by becoming like men. A man is motivated by the woman he desires. Become the best woman you can be. Look for role models who actually live the kind of life you really want. Talk to them, learn from them, imitate them.

3. **Your sexuality is your gift to your future husband. Don't give it to someone else.**

   Sex before marriage undermines all the other principles and creates selfish, uncommitted men. Decide right now that your words and actions will all say NO to sex before marriage. Women *do* have the power to help tame men by withholding sex until they're married. If you don't use that power, and your man gets what he wants sexually *before* marriage, you will never get what you need and want *after* marriage. Send a clear message to the guys you date. If your lips are *saying* "no" but what they are *doing* says "yes," you're not being fair, and it's extremely confusing to the guy. If sex is all a guy wants, he's not worth having; it's usually the girl, not the guy, who's taking all the risks when it comes to sex. Remember: your future husband is going to devote the rest of his life to your welfare and happiness. Doesn't he deserve a wife who saved herself for him alone? (And he needs to do the same for you.)

4. **You control the dating pattern, not him.**

   Whatever you demand . . . that's what will happen. Period!
   Take control of the pattern, not just the date.

   Generally, a man won't settle down and become responsibly
   committed if he doesn't have to. Pain is a good teacher. A
   guy needs to learn that if he treats a woman badly or selfishly, he'll lose her.

5. **He wants to win your heart, so let him. Don't keep pursuing him.**

   The greatest reward for any man is to win *the heart of the
   woman he loves*. He doesn't want it handed to him. He
   needs to learn that if he doesn't have the guts to ask her
   out, he'll never get the girl of his dreams. He has to learn
   to be courageous. That's part of growing up. It also makes
   him feel good about himself. Never take that process away
   from him. Let him be the good guy—the hero. That way
   he'll know he is worthy when he wins your heart. Men feel
   their best when they have to work hard to win you.

6. **Don't give your heart away too soon.**

   It should take time for a guy to *earn* your trust. Slow down.
   Don't tell him everything you're thinking and don't automatically believe everything he says. Learn to keep your
   emotions and feelings to yourself at first. Always leave him
   wanting more, whether it's a phone conversation, a date, or
   a kiss. Let him experience what it means to long for someone. If the intrigue is over, he will get bored and move on.
   Guys want girls who have a little "mystery" about them,
   especially when it comes to sex. Lose the mystery and you'll
   lose him.

7. **Whatever you use to get a man, that's what you'll have to use to keep him.**

   Getting a man is the easy part. Keeping him is the problem. If you use sex to get him, you'll have to use sex to keep him. While your body is definitely a part of the equation, always win a guy by your personality and character. If you're blessed with beauty, be careful how you use it, and remember, it doesn't last forever. The older a woman gets, the less "power" she can maintain through her beauty, so the power had better come from somewhere else.

8. **Do the best with what you have physically, but don't rely on it.**

   A girl doesn't have to be all that gorgeous, but guys want her to do the best with what she has. Men like to date and marry feminine women. They do not like to date and marry women who are trying to act like men. Watch the way you dress, the jokes you tell, the way you talk, and the way you act. Be different from "the guys."

9. **You can tell a man, "I love you," if your actions have already proved what your words will declare.**

   "I love you" is a verbal painting (description) of actions already taken. Be extremely careful how soon you say those words in the relationship. You may love many men in your lifetime, but you will marry only one. When you actually say those words, the dynamics of the relationship will immediately change. Always *treat* a guy as if you loved him, but don't *say* the words too soon.

10. **Look for a successful, competent guy.**

    If a guy is doing nothing with his life, he shouldn't be able to get you, either. If you refuse to date him until he becomes

productive, the process will help teach him not to be lazy. Never try to "rescue" a man or you'll have to "mother" him the rest of your life! Appreciation for a man's success is one of the fastest ways to his heart.

11. **Date guys close to your own age.**

   If you date a guy younger than you, you will tend to look desperate, and it rarely works. But dating older guys can also be a serious mistake. Freshman girls, for example, tend to be flattered when junior or senior guys ask them out, but those guys are usually far more experienced, and they know how to get what they want. When you're in high school, date guys who are close to your age. Dating a guy who is 19 or older, when you are a freshman or sophomore, is dangerous. You would absolutely have to know his background and have a deep trust in his character before you could ever go out with him.

12. **Never date a guy just 'cause he's the only one asking you out.**

   It's not fair for a guy to spend time and money on a girl who isn't really all that interested in him. If you do that, you will be teaching him that "girls are just out to take advantage of guys." Your reputation will also go down the tube.

13. **Guys want to date and marry intelligent girls (but they're also scared of them).**

   Most guys are scared to death of looking stupid in front of a girl, so *just be careful.* Someone asked a bunch of college guys how smart a girl would have to be if they were going to date her. Virtually all the guys said she would have to be at least "average" in intelligence. But when asked how intelligent would she have to be if they were going to try to take

her to bed, the guys all said she would have to be "below average." So being smart helps keep the bad guys away!

A lot of girls think being smart automatically means you're doomed when it comes to having a boyfriend. Don't believe it. Do you know any smart married women? Yeah? OK then, if love and marriage can happen to them, it can happen to you. Never give up, and never lower your standards. Try to be patient. Flaunting your brainpower will never win him, but sitting on your brains won't either. Use your smarts to help him know you were smart enough to want HIM.

14. **What a guy shares with you in private, stays private. Be trustworthy, or he'll never be vulnerable with you again.**

When a guy shares something with you that he knows you may not like, or you may not agree with, he's being "vulnerable." For your relationship to work, a guy must be free to say what he's thinking and struggling with, whether you agree with him or not. The unbreakable rule is this: Whatever he shares with you will stay private. When he's vulnerable with you he knows he may look weak, and that scares him. But that's what it *means* to be vulnerable. When guys finally open up, girls quite naturally want to share the great news with their other friends 'cause it's such a big deal. The problem with that is they each tell it to their other friends and, before you can blink, the whole school knows! If that happens the guy learns he can't trust any girl from now on. From that point forward he's on guard as to what he can, or can't, say to the one girl he's supposed to be close to. That means no one will ever really understand or know him.

There are two notable exceptions to this, however. The first is that some guys are "sex discussers." "Oh, I don't want to *DO* anything, I just want to be vulnerable and *discuss it a*

little." But the end result is the same. He really *does* want to do it. Watch out. Being vulnerable doesn't mean focusing on sex. The second exception is that if he was to tell you he was contemplating suicide or something as drastic as that, that is not the time to keep quiet. Tell him you are going to go for help and that you want him to go with you. Don't do it behind his back unless he refuses.

15. **Don't ever put up with a guy who tries to control you. EVER!**

Don't make the mistake of trying to fix this kind of guy. Move on. Let someone else do the counseling. Healthy relationships are not about fixing each other.

If a guy tries to force you into having sex with him, turn him in to the authorities. If he's doing that to you, then he's done it to others before you, and he'll do it to the next girl as well. Stop him. If he is demanding sex and you don't think anything else will get him to stop, one way out is to tell him you'll do it—but only with a brand-new condom from the store and not one of his. When you get to the store, call your dad AND THE COPS, and don't leave the store till they come.

16. **Dump the Magazines**

I know—if you dump your magazines, how will you know what to wear? How will you know what's cool? How will you know how to get a guy? Maybe it's time to learn to think for yourself! Most teen magazines are giving you a false picture of the world and how it works. The more you fill your mind with that stuff, the harder it will be for you to see the truth.

One last thing. Girls often ask, what are the biggest turn-offs for guys? Okay, if you really want to know . . .

Girls who giggle (Guys think you're laughing at *them*.)
Girls who never stop talking
Girls who need every hair in place
Girls who constantly wonder how they look
Girls who are too thin, and look like they're gonna break
Girls who can't play or ever get dirty
Girls who act dumb
Girls who cry all the time
Girls who have lost their mystery
Girls who never smile
Girls who always need attention
Girls who are boy-crazy
Girls without a mind of their own
Girls who can't be spontaneous
Girls who won't play sports
Girls who brag about their grades
Girls who "screech" when they see their friends
Girls who are only into "chick flicks"
Girls who only say "yes" or give in to everything
Girls who "tell all"
Girls who only talk about themselves
Girls who make guys have to "guess" at everything
Girls who have to spend every minute with their girlfriends
Girls who can't take a joke
Girls who make everything seem like it's the guy's fault
Girls who ask us questions they don't really want an answer to
Girls who smoke
Girls who wear a lot of makeup
Girls who take things too seriously

Girls . . . the next chapter is to the guys but I want you to read it anyway. It will help you figure them out a little more. Have fun.

Chapter 18. For Guys Only

I was up at the hardware store just last night trying to find something I needed, and I was getting nowhere. Frustrated, I decided to leave. As I headed down the aisle toward the front of the store I saw a guy talking on a cell phone, and he had the look of a deer caught in the headlights. His jaw dropped wide open and he pointed at me. "You!" he yelled. "You changed my life!!!" Just then a buddy of his rounded the corner, did a double take, and said, "Hey, hey, you're that guy . . . you changed my life!"

It turned out that several years ago Mike and Tim heard my two-hour assembly. Later they had gone to a deal I do just for guys—an evening where I teach them how to do creative dates, etc.—and it changed their lives. We talked for almost half an hour in that aisle. They told me story after story of things they had done for their girlfriends and what their responses had been. They were both currently in their first year of college (they heard the talk in ninth grade) and they admitted that in the years since the assembly they had had several chances to take advantage of girls sexually, but had decided not to because of what I had said. They were having a ball and loving the responses they were getting from the girls they were dating. Because of the talk they had heard, they had decided to wait to have sex only *after* they had gotten married. But as they

were telling me all this, they started cracking up laughing, 'cause they also said that on their wedding night they were **gonna** *make up for lost time! YES!!!!!*

Those two guys had learned a couple of secrets that, unfortunately, most guys never learn, and they were loving the results. So in this chapter we're gonna go after some of that stuff. Does it work? Oh, yeah!

Dear Mr. Henning

My name is Gary and I live in _____. You did a seminar at my school about a year ago, on creative dating and whatnot. I would just like to thank you for all of your help and ideas. I used to be a guy who never had a date for the dances and such, and now I am sought after. I cannot thank you enough for your ideas and your help.

At my school a couple weeks went by and everybody forgot about all the tips you gave us, except me. I was thinking about asking a girl to homecoming in a creative manner. The only thing was, she was the head cheerleader, all-around best looking girl in school. I knew it was a long shot but it is better to shoot high and miss than shoot too low and hit.

She had a zero period math class this year. I asked the teacher if I could interrupt his class for a few minutes and he said it would be fine. My family had two cell phones, so I took one, and I duct-taped the other one under the girl's desk. I waited around in the hall until the middle of the lecture and I called the cell phone under the desk from my cell phone. It rang for what seemed like forever, then the girl picked up and I asked her. She said "yes." Never have I been so excited . . .

. . . Then we went to a real nice dinner. I parked my car but I didn't take it out of "Drive" knowing that it wouldn't start. We had dinner and got back into the car. "Oh, God, this is so embarrassing. My car won't start, let me get into the trunk and get some jumper cables." I got back in the trunk and I pulled out one rose, two wine glasses, a candle, and a bottle of sparkling

cider. Words cannot describe the look on her face. Then I let her keep the glass so she will always remember the night we had together . . .

. . . I would just like to thank you one last time for all your help. I have gone from "That guy who never has a date" to "The guy everyone hopes to get asked by, in some creative way."

Thank you

But First . . .

All right, we're "just guys" here, so let's talk "guy" stuff. And, of course, what topic could be more near and dear to us guy's hearts (and other body parts) than the issue of . . . sex? (!)

Huh. GUYS AND SEX . . . I don't know . . . it's like those words somehow just go together, don't they? Anyway guys, I gotta ask you, How honest d'ya wanna be here? Let's put it all on the table for just a few minutes . . . *SHALL WE?*

Guys and Sex

GUYS LOVE SEX! (As if you didn't know that.) I know it's scary to actually see that in print, but it's true. No matter what kind of weird, kinky, sexual thing you can imagine, you can just bet some guy somewhere has done it. I realize not all guys feel the same sexual intensity, but for the most part an awful lot of us guys tend to be on the brink of being out of control a lot of the time. If someone left a *Playboy* magazine on the coffee table and everyone except you left the room, would you peek? Do you catch yourself looking through magazines to find the gorgeous girls in the low-cut dresses or underwear ads? Or do you rent videos that you know have nudity in them and, when no one else is with you, stop, rewind the video, and watch it again . . . IN SLOW MOTION? Do you know where to find all the sexy books in the library, or the local bookstore? Have you ever tried to peek down some girl's dress? Have you ever gone to the beach just to watch girls strutting around in their bikinis? Well, welcome to being a guy!

The Problem

Us guys were designed to respond to what we see, especially when it comes to females. God made us that way. I'm glad. I like it! When we see a girl with an unbelievable figure in a bikini, we can't help but react physically. For some reason our brains immediately seem to go dead, but other parts go, "Hey . . . life is good!"

The purpose of sex is pleasure. (All right!!!!) *And making babies.* (Dang!) Now why would such a pleasurable thing and making babies go together? It kinda seems like a dirty trick is being played on us, but actually there's a reason for it. Think about it. (Now as I say this, it's gonna make us guys look pathetic, but someone has to say it.) Guys, would you be willing to marry a girl, *purposely* have children, and then spend the rest of your life working your butt off to support your wife and raise those kids, *knowing in advance that there would be NO sexual pleasure in it AT ALL?* Be honest. Would a guy *ever* want to settle down and make a baby? Would he want to stick around after the baby was born if he knew he wouldn't (as some guys would say) "get any?" Most guys wouldn't and you know it. Not a chance! What's the upside to *that*?

So the next question is: What would happen to the population of the world if there was no pleasure in sex and guys refused to do it? We'd die out within one generation. If sex didn't feel good and you got a baby every time you *did* do it, *no one would do it!!!!* It would be over!

Sex was designed to bring two people together for pleasure, and then . . . SUCKER YOU INTO PROCREATION! (I'm sorta joking here.) Yeah, some joke, but there's truth to that. Take pleasure or procreation out of the equation and all of creation falls apart. Raising a baby requires someone to be committed and responsible, and it makes sense that if you were the one to make the kid, then you should be the one to take care of it.

But if we could have sex and *not* make a baby (pleasure but no procreation), why would we have to be committed to just one particular girl? "Heck, we're just having fun here!" But once the fun's over, you would just move on to something (or someone) more fun. So a lot of guys think, "Why screw up the fun with all

this commitment stuff? There's so many girls out there who are willing to give you what you want—why bother with the ones who just want you to 'commit' and permanently remove you from the dating pool?" Problem is, if us guys really lived like that, we would never grow up and be responsible. EVER!

Sex Forces Us to Change

I heard a marriage counselor tell the story of an immature, self-centered guy who, on his honeymoon night, got the education of a lifetime in just one little confrontation with his new wife. The wedding was over and the newlyweds were alone in their hotel room. The groom decided it was time to let his new bride know just who was going to run this family. He took off his pants and threw them at her. "Put those on!" he said. The shocked bride replied, "I can't wear your pants!" "That's right," he said, "and don't ever forget it! I will always be the one to wear the pants in this family!" The bride then took off her panties and threw them at him and said, "Try these on!" Looking very shocked, he said, "I can't get into your panties!" She replied, "And you never will if you don't change your attitude!"

Over the centuries sex has forced a lot of us guys into decisions we really didn't want to make. If guys want the pleasure (and we do) then we have to take the responsibility that comes with it. What that means is sex forces us guys into changing the way we live by forcing us to be more responsible for our decisions. If we deny the responsibility that sexuality brings, the whole family structure collapses, and if it collapses, so does the whole of society.

A woman's body is a powerful thing. That's why pretty much all us guys are "girl watchers." *Guys' bodies are designed in such a way that they are drawn to a woman's body.* So when we see a woman's body we get all excited and turned on!! YES, WE DO! When a guy sees a gorgeous girl his mind starts going wild. The more he looks, the more turned on he gets. All those feelings are natural and right, but they need to be kept in control. The amazing thing is most guys can't think of one good reason why they *should* control it, and that's where it gets scary!

The Problem

The problem all starts when we begin thinking that if sex is natural and right (and it is), then it ought to be natural and right *any time we want it.* In fact we think: If a little bit of sex is natural and right, then *a whole lot of sex ought to be REALLY natural and right!* If one girl is good, then two girls ought to be better. And if two is great, then a whole *bunch* of girls ought to be fantastic! We think if sex is good, then *any* sex is good. And if sex is natural, why are we denying ourselves? It's *natural,* for crying out loud!

But if there's no control or limits on who, when, or where, what starts out as a natural sexual impulse can end in child molestation, pedophilia (sex with children), exhibitionism (showing yourself), voyeurism (peeping Tom), sadomasochism (whips-and-chains), sex with animals, or rape. A guy never starts out as a child molester and then becomes a nice guy. He starts out *innocent,* and then deteriorates if he doesn't stay in control of himself. Being out of control leads to some incredibly dangerous things. One of the most dangerous of those things is, believe it or not, pornography.

Pornography

If you think about it, pornography, at the bare minimum (and I do mean bare), is just pictures of women (seldom is it men) with their clothes off. When you put it that way it just doesn't seem like that big a deal. Who cares? So what's the problem? The problem is when a guy looks through a *Playboy*-type magazine for an hour or two and then looks at his girlfriend or wife, he starts feeling like he got gypped—like there's gotta be women out there who look like the babes in the magazines. All the guy knows is that his girlfriend/wife doesn't look like THAT! And whoever the guys are who have those kinds of girls, "they sure gotta be having a lot more fun than I am." I mean, SOMEONE is messing around with those girls in the magazines. Right? Yeah, well . . . there are some problems with that kind of thinking.

The Illusion

The problem with *Playboy* is that what you see isn't exactly what you get. We all hope and pray it is. We just don't want to admit it. A number of years back the editor of *Playboy*, Gary Cole, said in an interview that they take somewhere between 6,000 and 22,000 pictures for just ONE centerfold spread, and even then they still have to do airbrushing.[1] The models are posed in the most beautiful homes, with the most beautiful furnishings, while taking off the most beautiful clothes. Everybody knows they have makeup on and they're looking their best, but they *still* have to airbrush them. Everything is a setup. Movie actresses have "stunt bottoms" (and other "stunt" body parts) who will stand in for the star to make her look "better than life" on the screen, but it makes us believe she *really* has the perfect everything—that there *really is* someone who "has it all." But Hollywood makeup artists and costume designers will tell you they've never met an actress who liked her body. There was *always* something they hated about their physical appearance. So in real life no woman can possibly live up to the pornographic standard of perfection.

Reality

What happens, then, is when we meet and marry the woman of our dreams and discover she needs a little "airbrushing" herself, we feel gypped. The more exposure a guy has had to the perfect airbrushed girls (fake) (pornography), the more gypped he is going to feel with a real woman. Nothing he does with a real woman seems to satisfy him as much as *Playboy* promised it would.

The More Pornography, the Less Love

The more sexual stuff we view, the less "in love" we tend to be with our mates. Someone actually did a study that showed that the more pornography men were given, the less satisfied they were with their wives. What that could also mean is the more sexual

---

[1] Dr. Warren Farrell, *Why Men Are the Way They Are* (New York: Berkley Books, 1986), p. 74.

experience us guys have before marriage, the less satisfied we are going to tend to be in our marriages. The more false images we have built up in our minds, the less our mates could ever match up, *or keep up*. We will have built this impossible standard of what a woman should look like, act like, and be like, AND STAY LIKE, but there is no woman who could ever live up to it. Not even the movie stars. Believe me, on your honeymoon night, there won't be any stunt bottoms in bed with you.

So us guys start feeling gypped. OK, but think what women must feel. Women feel imperfect, rejected, and used, facing endless competition with the figments of men's imaginations. Even if her body and looks seem perfect at first, no woman's body stays that way forever. If you get hooked on the "Perfect Imaginary Body" and expect your wife's body to look like that and stay like that forever, you'd better think again. It won't—and neither will yours! (Look at your mom and dad.) If you demand perfection of her and she can't live up to it later, will you dump her? If you're thinking yes . . . does she know that?

A Harem of Imaginary Brides

Pornography starts a process in the imagination that is very difficult to live with because it makes us guys turn inward toward ourselves, not outward towards relationships with *real people*. The end result is dangerous and long-lasting. C. S. Lewis wrote,

> . . . this harem [imaginary playmates], once admitted, works against his ever getting out and really uniting with a real woman. For the harem is always accessible, always subservient, calls for no sacrifices or adjustments, and can be endowed with erotic and psychological attractions which no real woman can rival. Among those shadowy brides he is always adored, always the perfect love, no demand is made on his unselfishness, no mortification ever imposed on his vanity. In the end, they become merely the medium through which he increasingly adores himself.[2]

---

[2] C. S. Lewis to Mr. Masson, March 6, 1956, Wade Collection, Wheaton College, Wheaton, Ill., Cited in Payne, *Broken Image*, p. 91–92.

In other words, a guy looking at a picture of a naked woman thinks he's in love because of what he feels. Why? 'Cause she always treats him right, always adores him, and asks nothing of him. They never fight and he can enjoy her any time he wants. But it's only for what HE gets out of it; she never makes demands, never talks back, doesn't get mad, and never says, "NO! I've got a headache!" She's always ready and available. He can change pictures any time he wants and she won't even get ticked off. Best of all, he doesn't even have to call the next night and have a long conversation with her. If he forgets her birthday, heck! What does she care? She doesn't mind. She doesn't care if he belches or farts, and he doesn't have to spend a lot of money on her to get what he wants. He *never* has to make changes for her. He is free at last. It's pleasure with no commitments or expectations. The tragedy is that *he never grows up!* He never learns to be unselfish, never learns to communicate, and never learns to give or receive love. He thinks he's got heaven, when he's actually in hell.

Laurie Hall is a woman whose husband got totally hooked on pornography. In her book, *An Affair of the Mind*, she writes,

> . . . the porn viewer designs the (*imaginary*) woman's sexual response to suit himself. Because he allows no feedback, he believes the lie he has created. When a man believes a lie about a woman's sexual response, he will also be grossly out of touch with other parts of her nature.[3]

The *Playboy* Fantasy

Let me give you a perfect example of being out of touch. Look at Hugh Hefner and his *Playboy* fantasy. Most guys would give anything to have what they *think* he has, but look deeper and you'll see he's really got nothing.

A recent headline read,

Hefner, 7 Girlfriends, Set to Celebrate His 75th Birthday.[4]

---

[3] Laurie Hall, *An Affair of the Mind* (Wheaton, Ill.: Tyndale House, 1996), p. 110.
[4] Kelly Carter, "Hefner, 7 Girlfriends Set to Celebrate His 75th Birthday," *Tacoma News Tribune*, April 8, 2001.

That's right . . . seven! The article explains that all seven girl-friends are going to celebrate his birthday . . . together . . . all wearing lingerie, just for him. He describes it as "a typical relationship, times seven." Oh how cute! The girls range from age 19 to 28, and they describe "Hef" as "an amazing friend, so loving, warm and caring." Hefner humbly responds to these comments by saying, "I don't think there's any exploitation going on. It obviously benefits all concerned, or everybody wouldn't be here and so happy." Really? You might want to ask Hef's estranged wife (who lives next door with the couple's two sons) how she feels about that. But it seems that for Hefner the "imaginary harem" is real enough. Right? Look again.

Hefner . . . as Just an Average Guy

Let's say Hugh Hefner wasn't a famous multimillionaire who lives in a huge mansion somewhere. In fact, let's say he's just an average guy like you or me, living in a little apartment down the street. He owns an '87 pickup with a gun rack in the window, and works at an 8-to-5 job that doesn't pay all that much. One night, on his 28th birthday, he gets a couple six-packs of beer and tries to talk seven girls from the local high school into coming over to his house to celebrate his birthday with a little hot tubbing. Of course, he doesn't tell them that his estranged wife, who lives next door with their two little boys, will make a visit sometime during the evening's festivities. QUESTION: By the end of the night, do you really think there's gonna be seven half-naked high school girls in a hot tub with him, saying things like "He's an amazing friend, so loving, warm and caring?" Is this ever going to happen? ONLY IF HE PAYS THEM TO!!!! And that's exactly what the real Hugh Hefner does!!!! Guess what that makes the girls? That makes them prostitutes! Does Hefner have a *real* relationship with those girls? No. No more than the guy with the beer and his hot tub. If Hefner is capable of such great relationships, why is his wife living in the house next door while he's in the hot tub with seven babes? All Hefner has is money and lots of girls available for hire. And hired

girls will tell you anything you want to hear, especially if they get a mansion to go with it!

Personally, I don't believe Hefner knows what a real relationship looks like. Pornography won't allow him to. Does the naked girl in the centerfold really want a deep relationship with the kind of guys that buy *that* kind of magazine? Is *that* what she's been dreaming about all her life? Hefner has been fooled into believing he is really loved by his "harem," but they are only servants at his beck and call. Take away his money and his mansion and make him an average 75-year-old guy, and those girls will disappear as fast as they came. Hefner's girls are "always accessible, but always subservient," and *they could never make demands on him.* He wouldn't allow it. If they ever did they'd have to look for new housing, just like his estranged wife next door had to do. That's why the "harem" keeps changing from month to month and year to year. He adores them only for what he can get, and they adore him for what *they* can get. He uses women merely as toys to "increasingly adore himself," which apparently is what he has learned to do best.

Who Wants . . . Rejection?

Lots of us guys start to retreat into the imaginary world of porn, away from real relationships with girls, because we are scared to death to be rejected by the real thing. Pornography keeps us at a safe distance. We never have to interact in real give-and-take relationships. We never have to learn to share, communicate, apologize, or argue fairly. We never have to learn to be unselfish. Unfortunately, we begin to believe the real world is made only for us and our pleasure—that the real world can be perfect like the imaginary world in the magazines. But it's not. Far from it. The girl in the centerfold is a real person, but who thinks about that? Her *body* sells, not the person inside. Marilyn Monroe once said, "Hollywood is the only place that will pay you ten thousand dollars for a kiss, but won't give you fifty cents for your soul." And her tragic death proved it.

Effects of Pornography

So what are the real results of pornography? A guy named Dr. Victor B. Cline wrote a booklet called, "Pornography's Effects on Adults & Children,"[5] and in it he describes a four-stage pattern common to nearly all of his clients. It was especially true for guys who got involved in pornography early in their lives. I guess the question is: Could this be happening to you? Look and see.

Stage 1. Addiction

It all starts rather innocently. A guy starts looking at pornography here and there, maybe at someone's house, then he buys a magazine or two of his own, or maybe he sorta checks out the Internet. He thinks what he's doing is normal, and rationalizes it by saying, "Hey, all guys do it." Within a short time he's pretty much hooked. He can never seem to get enough. He always wants more. The drive becomes so strong that he thinks about it all the time. Mental pictures play in his mind whenever he's awake, and he fantasizes about them every minute of the day. Masturbation becomes a main part of his mental game. It becomes his way of release. Once addicted, he is powerless to stop. Shame, divorce, or loss of family can't motivate him to give it up. He couldn't break the habit on his own even if he wanted to. The addiction has begun to rule his life.

Stage 2. Escalation

Over time the guy needs more explicit, wilder sexual images—kinky things that will give him a higher high. If he is married he will push his addiction onto his wife with ever more erotic or violent sex. But because of his mental addiction, he often *prefers* pornography and masturbation to actual sexual intercourse. Of course this will destroy the relationship he has and whatever love there is left in it. Intimate sexual relations with his partner have now been replaced with fantasy. Dr. Cline states, "I have had a

---

[5] Dr. V. B. Cline, *Pornography's Effects on Adults and Children* (New York: Morality in Media), pp. 3–5. Used by permission.

number of couple-clients where the wife tearfully reported that her husband preferred to masturbate to pornography than to make love to her."[6] There was less hassle; he was better at pleasing himself and obviously more available than his wife was.

Stage 3. Desensitization

What used to be "unbelievable" sexual excitement is now "no big deal." The new stuff he starts looking at may be illegal and repulsive—*way* over the line. He keeps giving himself permission with his continual rationalization: "Everybody does it!

Stage 4. Acting Out Sexually

Now he begins to act out what he sees in the pornography, including "compulsive promiscuity, exhibitionism, group sex, voyeurism, frequenting massage parlors, having sex with minor children, rape, and inflicting pain on themselves or a partner during sex."[7] But it's never enough. He always wants more and nothing will stop him.

His sexuality never develops in a normal way. Relationships have no meaning, only sexual fantasies do. All sex becomes meaningless; he thinks only about what he can get. Eventually he dumps his wife or girlfriend for lack of desire for her. Their sexual relationship has lost its "kick." His habitual behavior now lacks any form of discipline. He is out of control. Consequences have little effect. His addiction is everything.

Are You Addicted to Sex?

Sexaholics Anonymous (sorta like Alcoholics Anonymous but it's for people with sexual addictions instead) published this sexual addiction test. Obviously it's aimed more at married men, but it will still give you an idea of where you stand. See how you do, and BE HONEST!

---

[6] Dr. V. B. Cline, *Pornography's Effects on Adults and Children* (New York: Morality in Media), p. 4.

[7] *Ibid.*, p. 4.

Twenty Questions (Answer Y or N)

__1. Have you ever thought you needed help for your sexual thinking or behavior?

__2. That you'd be better off if you didn't keep "giving in"?

__3. That sex or stimuli are controlling you?

__4. Have you ever tried to stop or limit doing what you felt was wrong in your sexual behavior?

__5. Do you resort to sex to escape, relieve anxiety, or because you can't cope?

__6. Do you feel guilt, remorse, or depression afterward?

__7. Has your pursuit of sex become more compulsive?

__8. Does it interfere with relations with your spouse?

__9. Do you have to resort to images or memories during sex?

__10. Does an irresistible impulse arise when the other party makes the overtures or sex is offered?

__11. Do you keep going from one relationship or lover to another?

__12. Do you feel the "right relationship" would help you stop lusting, masturbating, or being so promiscuous?

__13. Do you have a destructive need—a desperate sexual or emotional need for someone?

__14. Does pursuit of sex make you careless for yourself or the welfare of your family or others?

__15. Has your effectiveness or concentration decreased as sex has become more compulsive?

__16. Do you lose time from work for it?

__17. Do you turn to a lower environment when pursuing sex?

__18. Do you want to get away from the sex partner as soon as possible after the act?

__19. Although your spouse is sexually compatible, do you still masturbate or have sex with others?

__20. Have you ever been arrested for a sex-related offense?

Solution

Let me say here that your life is yours to live. I mean, you have to decide what you're going to do with it, but each decision you make today will affect your life tomorrow, sometimes drastically, for better or worse.

If you are struggling with pornography, now is the time to start dealing with it. Make the decision to change the way you live. It won't be easy, but it will absolutely be worth it. You *will* need help. If you're addicted, you've probably tried to quit before. How'd you do? So like I said, regardless of which stage you're in, you are going to need someone who understands your struggle—someone who knows how to help and will be there with you. If you can, find a group like a Sexaholics Anonymous (call 1-615-331-6230) or look them up on the internet at www.saico@sa.org. Or, you may want to find a professional counselor, or maybe see someone in a church who's trained to deal with problems like yours. Look in the phone book and start calling around.

So, Sexually, Where *Are* You Right Now?

Let's talk about where you are right now. A virgin? Nonvirgin? Still trying to decide? Horny as heck? Yeah, well, that's probably a given. Look, here's the problem. You know as well as I do that if a guy's looking for sex, he can find it. But let me give you a little insight here.

I've never met a guy who *purposely chose to wait for sex until marriage* and wished he *hadn't* waited, but I've met thousands of guys, or at least read their letters, who have told me they didn't wait and now wish they had. Just yesterday, as I was leaving a school, two junior guys stopped me in the parking lot to tell me the mess both of them were in, and to ask me what to do. One guy thought his girlfriend was pregnant; the other guy had sex with his girlfriend a few days before and totally regretted it. He had been curious about sex, but now he wished he had waited. What would *you* have said to them?

What I said to them, and what I'm telling you now is: Make up your mind. If you're no longer a virgin, OK. That's reality.

You can't undo that. But don't keep going in that direction! If you were about to walk over a cliff, the most appropriate, aggressive decision you could make would be to turn around and go in exactly the opposite direction, RIGHT NOW! It's the same thing with sex. If you're no longer a virgin, all right. You can't change that. But don't continue walking toward the cliff, either! The smartest, most appropriate decision you could make would be to turn around and go back the way you came. In other words . . . STOP! Don't hurt yourself, or your future wife (or someone else's wife) any more. Turn your life around, start heading in the right direction and never make the same mistake again. Trust me, man, you'll never regret it!

If you're still a virgin, good for you, but be careful. If it was only for lack of opportunity, then you've never really been put to the test. And if you aren't careful . . .

Let me tell ya, *if you will make a conscious decision that, from now on, you're going to wait until you're married, life becomes much, much easier.* Why? Think about it! There's no more condom worries, disease worries, pregnancy worries, or abortion worries. No more plotting and planning about how, when and where. No more "Will she? Won't she?" worries. So many decisions will never have to be made. How cool is that? No one can control you. Instead of thinking about getting sex all day long, you could spend your time thinking about how to love the girl you say you really love. I'm telling you, girls are looking for guys like that.

Rules to Live By

Like I said, though, it's your life and you've got to live it. So have at it! But, if you don't mind, let me give you what I call my "Ten Suggestion for Guys"—suggestions I think will really help you. I thought of calling them the "Ten Commandments," but that sounded a little too . . . what? . . . heavy, and besides, it's already been taken, and there's only nine. So *suggestions* it is. These aren't just something I pulled out of the air, either. They have been tried and found to work. See what you think.

1. **To be "morally good" is good for you, so live that way!**

    Morals are ideas that make for good health and a good life.
    Go against them and you get hurt. It doesn't take much to
    look around and see how much pain is out there just because
    people have decided to do whatever the heck they wanted
    to do, thinking they would have so much more fun ignor-
    ing what's morally right. In the long run it destroys them.
    Watch their lives and you'll see it happen right before your
    eyes—and the results are scary. Live a moral life!

2. **Get a sense of humor about your sexuality.**

    You are a sexual being and that's a great thing. Learn to love
    and even laugh about that part of yourself. It's not something
    to be down about at all. There will be a time in your future
    that sex (doing it) will become a big part of your life. It's
    worth waiting for. "Yeah, I'm waitin' till I get married but
    then I'm gonna make up for lost time!!!!!" Don't destroy
    your future sex life by doing something stupid now.

3. **Decide now that you are going to wait for sex only in
    marriage . . .**

    . . . so that when you do get married you will have the
    best, most uninhibited, fantastic sex you can. Anything that
    has the potential to destroy that is "out" for you. If a girl
    is pushing you for sex, say no. Why? *Because you love her.*
    Tell her you want the best for her and her future as well as
    for your own. You may *want* to have sex with her, but you
    know it's not the best for her life or for yours.

4. **Do not let sexual feelings rule your life.**

    What you feel about sex is just that . . . feelings. Feelings
    just are, and they change . . . often! If you're feeling horny,

get up, leave the house (or wherever you are), and go do something active. You can't do two things at the same time. Sexual feelings are not wrong, but sexual behavior sure can be. (Always remember, you can go to jail for poor sexual behavior.) By the way, don't blame everything on hormones either. Hormones may drive you sexually; they may also drive you to make a jump shot or mow the lawn, but they never MAKE you do anything!

5. **You be the one to set the sexual limits in your relationships.**

That shouldn't be her job, it's yours. Stand up for what's right. Every time! The girls you date will love and respect you for it and they'll pass the word to the other girls at school that you're safe to date. Again, it's not that you don't want to do it, it's that you know there's something better in the future and you don't want to wreck it for them or you.

6. **Decide what kind of girl you really want, then concentrate on becoming the kind of guy that THAT kind of girl would want.**

You can't change her. Don't even try. What you *can* do is concentrate on *being the kind of guy she would want to change for.* You still have to be honest as to who you really are and what kind of life you want to live. For instance, she may like the kind of music you hate. Don't lie and tell her you love it or something. Just learn to appreciate her kind of music but still love your own. She may love to read and you might love to play sports. Fine, but it won't hurt you to sit down every once in awhile and read something you know she really likes. It will help you understand how she thinks and what's important to her, and it will make you a better person in the long run.

7. **Live a life of reality, not a life of secret fantasy.**

   Give up all pornography of any kind. Don't give it away to some other guy either, 'cause it will mess him up. Porn will only hurt you, your girlfriend, and your future wife, so quit looking at it. For you to compare your girlfriend to what you see in *Playboy* is totally unfair. How would you feel if your girlfriend held up a *Forbes* magazine and said, "Why can't you be a successful millionaire like this guy 'cause that's what I really want!" It would make you want to crawl under a rock. That's how girls feel when you try to compare them to the magazines and videos, so get rid of them.

8. **Watch where you spend your time with girls.**

   Stay out of bedrooms, back seats, and movie theaters that are showing movies with nudity in them. Probably 90 percent of all nudity in the movies is women. When you are with a girl and some naked girl appears on the screen, who are you really visualizing as being naked? Your date, and she knows it! Same thing happens when you are in her bedroom. You see her bed and what do you immediately think about? Not sleeping!

9. **The sooner you decide to live rightly, the sooner your life can change for the better, so get on with it! Decide today! The disciplined life is the only life worth living.**

Dating: If You Don't Know This, You Aren't Ready!

Every time you go out with a girl you are building both *your* reputation and *hers*. Hopefully by now you understand the "network" girls have. One screw-up by you, and every girl in the whole world seems to know it. On the other hand, one *good* move by you (treating her right) and every girl will know that too! Every girl you have ever dated is *right now* spreading the word that you

were either a good guy or a bad guy. If you destroyed a girl and broke her heart in the process, do you think no one noticed? You think all the other girls at school weren't watching, listening, talking? Do you think the girls you'd *really* like to date in the future weren't paying attention? On the other hand, if you treated a girl great, even if the relationship ended, all those other girls will see that dating you was one of the *best things that ever happened in that girl's life!* They are building your reputation and you haven't even dated them! But the only way this works is *if you treat every single one of them right!* If you mess up with one girl, OK, it happens. But go fix it. Apologize. If you hurt a girl and never make it right, that hurt will never go away. She may never get over it, and your reputation will be shot not only with her, but with all the other girls who saw it happen. It's kinda like if you did it to ONE, you did it to ALL of them. So humble yourself and go make it right. (I heard that! "This sucks!")

By the way, do girls know how to get even with guys who screw up? Ohhhhh, yeah!!! How? There are all kinds of ways, but the real payback comes when the girls all get together and trash the guy's reputation. How? I heard of some girls who decided to get back at a "Jerk" guy by having sex with him, then when he bragged about it, told everybody the great orgasms were all faked and he was no good. The guy thought he was putting notches on his belt, but it turns out he was putting a noose around his neck instead.

If guys talk trash about girls to the other guys, in the end it's the guys who get trashed. When girls don't trust guys they won't take a chance going out with them. They'll choose someone else to date. So, in the end, the guy loses, too. Most guys who get turned down for dates get turned down because girls don't trust them. So guys, wise up! Quit worrying about what the other *guys* at your school think. You don't want to date THEM, you want to date the GIRLS!

It Just Makes Sense

Let me go back to something for a minute. If you think about it, a moral life makes a lot of sense. Most people think a moral life tends to make a dull life. But it doesn't. A moral life almost

always brings you the most advantages. Why? Because if you treat people right, you tend to get what you really want from them. No, that's not being selfish, it's being smart. That doesn't mean you're *guaranteed* to get what you want, but most of the time it will bring you the most success. People *want* to hang out with someone who treats them right. Take advantage of a person once and they will stay as far away as possible from you, and if you were to live your whole life that way, you'd get nothing in return.

If this still sounds selfish to you, think about it this way. Have you ever driven the speed limit because you thought you might get a ticket if you didn't? Is that being selfish? No. Have you ever wanted to scream at your teacher or your parents, but you decided not to because you knew it could definitely hurt your future? Yes! So you treated them right 'cause it was *to your advantage* to treat them right. Now I still think people need to do what's right *just because it's right*, whether they get anything out of it or not, but you gotta know doing right is also *practical*. The person who said, "Do unto others as you would have them do unto you," was *very* smart. It helps both the other person and it helps you. It just makes sense.

When you treat a girl the way she should be treated, she will be reading between the lines, wondering why you are treating her so nicely. "Is it me you love or is it something you think you're gonna get from me that you really want?" *THAT'S* why you do what's right, 'cause when you do it long enough and consistently enough it just screams the fact that you have the kind of character that any girl would want in a guy. She knows she can trust you. And since she's probably had too many guys try to take advantage of her, when she finally finds a guy like you, who loves her—REALLY loves her—she'll tell every girl in school about you. YOU'VE GOT IT MADE!

The Key

So the key is to live your life in such a way that even if someone says something bad about you or starts a rumor, people will totally crack up laughing 'cause they know it couldn't be true.

When you're wondering if what you're about to do with a girl is right, ask yourself, "What will people think of me (and her) because of what I'm doing? (Because they *will* find out!) Will all the other girls say good things about me, or will they think I'm a jerk?" Remember, even when you break up with a girl, the way you do it will determine if your reputation is getting better or worse. Be very careful.

Decision Time

So now it's decision time. You can run, but you can't hide. I want to know right now . . . FROM NOW ON, HOW ARE YOU GOING TO TREAT THE GIRLS YOU MEET AND DATE? You have two choices:

> Live life on the wild side, take what you can from as many girls as you can, and take your chances when it comes time to get married—

> OR

> Treat *all* girls right and watch your reputation grow into something that will work for you the rest of your life. It means you will have to stay away from the "action" now, but later you will be more likely to marry the girl of your dreams. (And then you can make up for lost time!)

CHOOSE!

No More Excuses . . . Ask Her Out!

OK. No more excuses. Now you actually have to DO it. You have to actually meet a girl and ask her out. Sounds pretty easy on paper, but you and I know it's not! Huh? So where do you start? You start with making a good first impression; *then* you deal with what to say.

Your Appearance Says it All

I spoke at a college a couple of years ago and afterward met a guy with 17 face piercings. OK, if you like getting pierced, fine, but this guy had gone crazy. He had studs all over his face: eyebrows, ears, lip, tongue, nose (on both sides). The one on his eyebrow was infected. What was funny was he couldn't figure out why he couldn't get a date. Good grief! I'll tell you why! The guy looked ridiculous! If a girl tried to kiss him she'd get a nose ring in her eye! But what it really comes down to is this. If a girl ever wants to get married in the future, she most likely will want to date guys who have potential for success; the guys that have the financial potential that will bring her security. Knowing that (and as mean as this may sound), a guy with 17 piercings isn't gonna look all that potentially successful, therefore he is less desirable. Can you imagine a company wanting to hire him as a sales rep? Hmmmm? Now was the guy still a good guy? Yeah. We talked for a long time. He was a great guy! But finally he realized he was going to have to make some changes, or not date.

And tattoos . . . 10 years from now is your wife, Amy, going to be all that excited about you having a tattoo on your arm that says "Jennifer Forever"? Three guesses. . . .

Or you guys that are into chew. . . . (no comment)

So ask yourself . . . What kind of a girl do you really want? (Looks, character, personality, habits, beliefs, goals?) Now stand in front of the mirror and honestly evaluate whether or not what you see (and smell) is the kind of person who has any chance at all of getting the kind of girl you've just described.

Yes or No?

Are you the kind of guy that a girl will look at and say, "I could spend the rest of my life with a guy like him!"? ("All except for that 'Jennifer Forever' thing") Or will she see the pierced eyebrow, nose, lip, tongue, ear . . . and say . . . "I don't think so!"?

There's an old saying in sports that goes, "If you're winning, stick with your game plan. If you're not winning, change it." The same thing goes for girls and relationships. If you're winning, great. If you're not, don't be stupid. Change the way you're going at it or you'll keep getting the same results. Some guys take the philosophical approach: "But a girl should like me for what I am." Fine . . . **AND GOOD LUCK!** If you are having success dating the kinds of girls you really want, Great! Keep doing what you're doing. But if not . . .

I once knew a guy who always looked like he'd just stepped out of an auto mechanic's shop. Now I have great respect for mechanics—but most of the ones I know take showers! He didn't. He never shaved, his hands were always black with grease, and his clothes were always a mess. His car looked very much like he did. There were old oil cans and car parts in the back seat, candy wrappers and empty Coke cans on the front seat. In the glove compartment was a half-eaten McDonald's burger from Lord-knows-when. You couldn't quite see out of the front window 'cause, well, I'm not sure *what* was on there. Surprise, surprise . . . no girls wanted to date him, but he couldn't understand why. For years I worked with him, trying to get him to clean up his act. Finally, one day, I got so fed up with him that I took him out to his car, dragging a big wastebasket behind me. I made him clean out his car then and there, but the next time I saw him it was as bad as before. This went on for years. Finally a very desperate girl came along and, after they dated for awhile, she married him. Several years later she left him for another man. Gee . . . who would have guessed it?

No, I'm not saying everyone has to go for the preppy look or something, but what I *am* saying is how you look (clean clothes, hair looking good, face washed, ears and nose clean, car vacuumed, etc.) determines the kind of girl who will go out with you (and *keep* going out with you), so take a reeeeealllly good look.

Asking Her Out

This is where most guys panic. I know the fear you feel about asking a girl out, and believe me, it's natural to feel that way. I

remember taking 45 minutes, wandering around in a Hallmark shop, trying to get up the courage to go to the clothing shop next door to ask this girl out. When she said "yes," I about fainted. Most guys feel that way the first time they ask a girl out 'cause they're afraid of the rejection.

OK, so can a guy ask a girl out without risking the rejection thing? No, not totally, but you *can* reduce the risk by following the steps I'm about to give you. If you don't remember anything else, remember this: if you can make her feel safe (It's the *security* thing, remember?) and she knows she's going to have fun, chances are she'll say yes.

Going Out, or *"Going Out?"*

First of all, it's one thing to offhandedly say to a girl, "Hey, what are ya doin'? You want to go get a Coke or somethin'?" but it's a totally different thing to ask her out on an official "DATE." One says,

> No big deal. I can find something else to do if you can't go, but it would be fun to be with you. Just thought I'd ask.

The other is asking for some sort of commitment:

> I'm asking if you are interested enough in me to spend some time alone together. If you are, it may have the potential to become something much more in the future. So what do you think?

The first is easy for the girl to say yes, or no, to. The second has to be weighed. For the guy, though, either scenario can lead to the same thing . . . time with the girl . . . and ultimately a possible girlfriend. So before you talk to the girl, think which kind of date you are offering to her. Either kind is OK, but eventually you'll have to ask her on an official date.

If you decide to ask her out on an "official" date, here's the way to do it. Believe it or not, there are *fifteen* steps, and don't think you can skip any one of these steps, either. They are all important. Here we go.

How to Ask a Girl Out

Step 1. Look nice, smell nice, and act nice when it comes time to ask her out. Remember, she is evaluating you *right now,* as you are talking to her. Do you look and act like the kind of person she would have a good time with? Do you look like you're excited to go out with her, or does it look like it was a toss-up between her or reruns of "Baywatch?" Do you smell like a locker room? Clothes clean?

Step 2. Never ask her out over the phone if you can do it face to face. Why? 'Cause you want her to look you right in the eyeballs. Girls can tell a lot about a guy by looking him in the eye. Remember the old saying, "The eyes are the window to the soul." It's true. By looking you in the eye she can tell if you're safe to go out with, so you want her to see your eyes. The cool thing for the guy is it's harder to turn a guy down when she's standing right in front of him. (Yesssssss!!!)

Step 3. Don't ask her out in front of her friends. If her girlfriends are listening to you ask her out, they may start giggling and stuff, and she may turn you down even if she actually wanted to go out with you. Peer pressure from her friends can get you a "NO" as quick as bad breath can.

Step 4. Tell her *where* you want to take her, before you ask her if she will go. Most guys start by saying something like "Hey, whatcha doin' Friday?" The problem with that is she has no idea what you have in mind and is too afraid or embarrassed to ask, so she may say she's "busy" 'cause she doesn't know what else to say. Remember, she's as nervous as you are at this point. If she doesn't know where you are planning to take her she may not feel safe in saying yes, especially if she doesn't know you very well. She might really want to go where you are planning to take her, but if you don't tell her where that is, she might turn you down before she knows what she's gonna miss. Keep

in mind that she is evaluating not only you, but also what you're going to be doing together. Both are important.

Step 5. **Tell her when the date would be.**

Step 6. **Tell her when you would be picking her up and when she would be getting home.**

Step 7. **Tell her if there will be anyone else with you on the date.** A girl might really want to go out with *you*, but hate the couple you were thinking about doubling with. Don't ever show up with someone she wasn't expecting to be with.

Step 8. **Tell her how you plan to get to where you are going.** Are you driving, or is someone else? She may trust you but not trust some other person to drive. If your parents are driving she may not feel comfortable with them. She needs to know so she can decide.

Step 9. *NOW you ask her if she would like to go!!!*

Step 10. **If she says yes, be enthusiastic and excited.** Try not to look too stunned. (That's a dead giveaway.) If she says no to you, see Step 15.

Step 11. **Tell her what you will be wearing.** If you show up in a T-shirt and shorts and she is wearing a nice dress . . . dang! You screwed up! She will begin to wonder what *else* you didn't tell her. (It's the security thing again.)

Step 12. **If her parents don't know you well, ask her if it would help for you to talk with one of them.** Most girls will immediately say no, but you will make her feel safe if you are willing to meet her dad and mom. It's also one of the reasons you never honk from the curb and expect her to come running out. If a guy came to pick up *my daughter,* but he was afraid to come to the door and risk meeting me, then I, as her dad, would think he had something to hide. If he tried that, my daughter would stay in the house and he could sit at the curb all night for all I'd care!

Step 13. **Call the night before the date to confirm details.** This is the REAL way to get a girl's phone number by the way. After you've asked her out, but before you let her go, tell her you'll call her the night before your date to give her

any details you may have missed. At that point, ask her for her phone number. Always have a piece of paper and pencil ready to write it down. You'll look like an idiot if you ask her for her number and then have to ask her for a piece of paper and a pencil! Be prepared. (Don't write it on your hand, either!) Make sure you call her when you say you will. If you say you'll call her and then don't, she knows she can't trust you. If she can't trust you with the little things, she can't trust you with the bigger things either.

Step 14. Call her after the date is over. By the following Monday (or at least within a couple of days after the date), send her a note, a flower, or call her (or all of the above) just to tell her how much you appreciated and enjoyed the time together. When it comes to dating, one of the hardest things for any girl is wondering how the guy really felt about her, and if he will ever ask her out again. Even if you didn't have all that great a time, you can at least communicate the fact that you *appreciated* the time you had together. It's called "being gracious," but remember, don't lie.

Step 15. If the girl says, "No," when you finally ask her out (step 9) NEVER ASK WHY!!!! What you *can* say is, "Are you sure? It's going to be a great time!" If she still says no, you say, "Hey, no problem. Maybe I'll catch you some other time." THEN YOU IMMEDIATELY WALK AWAY!!! The longer you stick around after asking her, the weirder it gets. If you ever ask her out a second time, she will remember how weird it felt the first time you asked, and chances are she'll say no again. By the way, she may have said no for a good reason. She may have had a previous date and *wished* she could get out of it to go with you, but she knows she can't. She may have to work or baby-sit, or maybe she's on restriction. Then again, I know some girls who will say no the first time just to see how the guy

will handle it. Or there's the possibility that she really may not want to go out with you and she just doesn't want to hurt you. The point is, it's her right to say no, so don't ask why. Later on, if you ask her again and she says no again, if she really wants to go out with you *she'll let you know.* But if she doesn't, go on to another girl. Don't bug her. Leave her alone or she will tell all the other girls in school that you're a pest, and then no one will want to go out with you.

First Dates Are Very Important

The first date is always the hardest one because there are so many things to think about (and so many things that can go wrong!). So many, in fact, that it's mind-boggling and can scare you to death. So think through as much as you can *before you go out* the first time so you can focus your attention on *her* and not have to worry about what could go wrong.

Start by trying to make the first date a "safe" date. In other words, set yourself up for as few risks as possible. If you're the kind of guy who tends to have struggles talking with a girl (you haven't learned to be a good communicator yet), choose to go to a place that's close by. Having to "fill" several hours alone in the car while you drive would kill you! Always make the first couple of dates shorter rather than longer, time-wise. You always want to leave a girl wanting *more* time with you, not *less*. You don't want her to be thinking, "Is this date EVER gonna end?"

If being dressed up stresses you out, then do something casual. If you feel uncomfortable you'll come across like you wish you were someplace other than with her.

Something like a spaghetti dinner would not be a good first date. It might be too messy for her and you may come across like a slob. Never take her to a movie with any kind of nudity or sexual situations . . . EVER! It's obvious why. All in all, try to keep that first date uncomplicated.

What to Talk about on a Date (Especially a First Date)

Ever been on a date and the conversation went dead? What on earth do you do? I remember dating this girl once and I don't think she said five words the whole night. It really ticked me off. Man, she sat hugging her car door all night like I was going to rape her or something! She wouldn't talk, and if I did ask her something—anything—she would mumble something and then just sit there. It turned out she had just broken up with her boyfriend and really missed him. Sure, she had a problem, but I realized I was the one caught unprepared. I didn't know *what* the fat to do.

So what *do* you do if that happens, and how do you make it never happen again? The answer is . . . THINK AHEAD! Prepare some things ahead of time that you can talk about, and then when the conversation goes dead you're ready. This may seem a little too mechanical for you, but hey . . . whatever works! The more you do this the more natural it will become. But for now . . .

Six Conversation Starters

Here are six conversation starters that will not only help you be a good communicator but will also give you good information for future dates with the same girl. I don't remember where I first heard these—all I know is . . . they work! All six topics happen to start with the letter F. (And no, it's not the one you're thinking.) Look, if you think my six are stupid, fine. Come up with your own. But the issue is to think things through ahead of time so that if your date goes "dead" on you, you're prepared. I know some guys who have actually typed these six topics out on their computers, shrunk them down, laminated them, and kept them in their wallets for emergencies! One guy told me he was on a date, eating at some restaurant, when his mind went totally blank and he couldn't think of anything to talk about. So he told his girlfriend he had to go to the bathroom. In the bathroom he took out his wallet, glanced over the six things I'm about to give you, put them back in his wallet, and went back to the table, where he struck up a conversation that

lasted for hours. Trust me here. It's pretty easy, but you'll have to practice it a little.

Your assignment is to take each one of the six topics I'm about to give you and come up with two or three questions for each topic. Think them over so that they're easy to bring up, in a way that sounds pretty natural for you. Try them on some friends without telling them what you're doing, just to see how they work.

OK, so here they are. I'll give you a couple of examples for each one, just to show you what I would do if it were me. Oh, I almost forgot. Make sure you keep a journal with the girl's responses to these questions (after you get home and you're alone) 'cause you're going to want to remember what she says. Learn to be a good listener and "student" of the girl you're dating. She'll love you for it, and it's good practice for when you get married.

1. Fun

    a.   Tell me about yourself. What do you like to do for fun?

    b.   Do you play any sports? (By the way, if she says that she doesn't like sports all that much, but she agreed to go to the baseball game with you, that says she really, *really* wanted to go out with you. Right? That's good information!)

2. Food

    a.   What's the best restaurant you've ever eaten at? Why? (Remember what she says 'cause it'll tell you what to look for when you want to take her out to eat.)

    b.   What's the *worst* restaurant you've ever eaten at? (By the way, if she says it's the place you're on your way to . . . that's good information!)

    c.   Tell her your favorites, and why.

3. Friends

a.   If the girl you've asked out is from another school, ask her if she knows a friend of yours from that school. If she says something like "Yeah, I know her/him and they're such jerks," it might not be the best conversation, but it will tell you a lot about the kind of friends she has and whether or not you'll want to go out with her again.

b.   Ask her who you saw her with last week. Be careful if it's another girl, 'cause it might look like you are interested in the other girl and not her.

4. Family

a.   Ask her if she has any brothers or sisters. Usually the girl will tell you how she feels about them, and that will let you see what her attitude is like and how she treats people she has a problem with. If she treats the people closest to her like they are all such a bother, guess how she'll treat you when you have your first argument?!

b.   Does she have a brother? How old is he and how much does he weigh? (That's *REALLY* good information!!!!!)

c.   After meeting her parents for the first time, ask her about them and how she gets along with them. You might start by telling her a little about your relationship with your parents and how you get along. That will naturally lead into her parents and what they are like. If you were to find out her parents just got divorced, or something just as drastic, that's important information because she may not feel too good about guys right now, and you will have to be even more careful about how you treat her.

5. Future

a. What if you are a senior and you start to date a girl in June? What would you want to know? Yeah, what's she gonna do next year? Is she gonna go to college? What's she gonna major in? Is she moving? If she is, you will have to decide if you want to spend a lot of time (and money) on her, knowing the relationship can't go very far.

b. What's she gonna do during the summer? Get a job? That will give you some idea of how busy she will be and if she'll be available to go out.

6. Faith

a. I never dated a girl for very long if I didn't know whether she believed in God or not. That was, and is, a very important part of my life. If it's not for you . . . OK.

b. Does she go to church anywhere? What's it like? Would she ever like to go to church with you?

So there's the six F's. That's just a starting place. You can take it from here. There are lots of other topics you could choose, so go to it. Just be prepared ahead of time. Make the girl feel special by being able to carry on a great conversation. If you use one of these topics and all of a sudden the conversation starts going off in some other direction, great. Just keep going in that direction. Then, if and when it starts to slow down, get ready with the next topic or question.

By the way, it's not bad to have quiet times while you're out together, even on the first date. It may seem uncomfortable at first, but sometimes the quiet is what she will remember and enjoy the most. Just be natural and relax.

Some guys put music on, which is OK, but a lot of guys tend to get so into the music that they never learn how to carry on a conversation. You don't want to seem so fascinated with your three-bazillion-decibel sound system that you forget the girl. Music in

the background is great, but don't let it be the center of your time together. It's really important to be able to talk, even though it can be scary. You might just as well learn it now, 'cause someday you're gonna get married, and ready or not, you'll have to face it.

To Kiss or Not to Kiss . . .

Kissing . . . ah, yes, kissing! See, kissing is one of those things everybody kinda expects . . . ya know what I mean? It's like it's no big deal any more. But hey, it IS a big deal! And why wouldn't you want it to be a big deal? You want a kiss to mean something, not just, "Hey, can I slobber a big one on ya? Cuz, hey man, I spent ten bucks takin' you out, ya know." So for what it's worth, my advice is: Never kiss a girl on the first date. Ever! And maybe not even the second or third. Most guys go for it as soon as they can, but it's never really special that way. And if the *first* kiss isn't special, why would a girl want to give you a second one? So don't cheapen it by kissing too soon, or too often. I lost a girlfriend in high school 'cause all I wanted to do was kiss. She got bored (and her mouth started bleeding), so she moved on. I never forgot that lesson.

This brings up the problem of what to do at the front door at the end of the date. If you haven't thought out what's gonna happen there beforehand, you'll be nervous and so will she. So plan out ahead of time what you'll do and say at her doorstep. Let her know you enjoyed being with her and that you'll give her a call again soon. (Then make sure you CALL HER!) You may even want to ask her out right then for next weekend (which, of course, means you'd better know in advance what you are going to do). Then thank her again, say goodnight, and leave. KEEP IT SHORT.

When you finally do kiss her for the first time, you might want to say something like, "Can I kiss you goodnight?" If she says yes, give her a simple little kiss. Don't do it like they do in the movies. "Would you mind if I bit your mouth off? Aaarrrgghhhhhh!!" Nope, just make it simple, short, and sweet.

Oh, yeah! Since you're now at the door at the end of the date, always make sure the girl actually gets IN the door, not just TO the door. One time I left a girl standing at her door, and after I was

long gone she discovered she'd forgotten her key and no one was home. She stayed out for hours by herself.

Kissing and Telling

What happens in a guy-girl relationship should remain private. It's between the two of you. When a girl confides in you, or kisses you, she is allowing you to see and experience a part of her that she doesn't want anyone else to see or know. This isn't a "group hug" thing, it's a "You and Me" thing, if you get what I mean. She is trusting you to hold that part of her in confidence. It's almost like you're being allowed to hold her heart in your hand. It's not information or a kiss you are holding, it's HER you are holding. If you go around blabbing about it to all the guys (even if it's just a simple kiss), you have cheapened IT and HER.

Dating Checklist

Here is a summary list of things you should think through before you leave your house to go on any date with a girl. You need to have a clear answer for each question before you leave, or it could spell disaster.

- Where will you be going, and what will you be doing there?
- Have you told her who you are double-dating with?
- Have you told her what you are wearing?
- What time does she need to be home? If you don't know, ask her parents before you leave. They'll be impressed.
- Have you called to remind her when you'll pick her up?
- Things you can talk about while on the date:
  1._____
  2._____
  3._____
- What is your contingency plan if the date flops?
- Know where and when your next date will take place so you can ask her tonight.

- At the end of the date, where will you go to get something to eat? Are you sure it's open at that time? Is she on a diet? (Don't ask if you don't know. Be sensitive.)
- Do you have $10 extra cash and a cell phone for an emergency?
- What will you say and do when you leave her at her door at the end of the date?
- Did you clean your car and put gas in it?
- How do you look and smell?
- How will you communicate to her that you really enjoyed being with her? (Phone call, note, flowers?)

Chapter 19. One Last Thing

Well, you made it! You finished this book. Congratulations! I hope it's helped you understand a little bit more about the opposite sex and what makes them tick, but most of all I hope it's helped you understand a better way to live. The advice I've given you in these pages isn't just *my* opinion about things, it includes the opinions of thousands of kids just like you—kids who did it the right way, and those who didn't. I've had hundreds of kids tell me, by letter or in personal conversations, "Please tell them what happened to me. Tell them not to make the same mistakes I did—that it's not worth going the way I went." Those kids know they'll have to live with the pain of their mistakes for the rest of their lives, but it sure would make it easier for them if they knew their stories were helping someone else. Let that someone be you!

So with that, let me tell you one last story. Unfortunately it's a sad one. A girl came up to me after an assembly one day and argued that she had the right to do whatever she wanted to do sexually. I agreed that she had the right to make her own choices, but I said I would personally sleep better at night knowing I had done everything I could to help her understand the consequences of the direction she was choosing. She wouldn't budge. Finally, in desperation, I pulled out a piece of paper I carry with me wherever

I go, for occasions just like this. I handed it to her and said, "Before you go, would you please read this? Then if you still feel the same way, sign it." Here's what the form said:

> I_____(your name) being of sound mind and free will, do now choose to live contrary to the standard of disciplined sexual behavior within the bounds of lawful marriage. With full knowledge of potential risks and liabilities (pregnancy, disease, and emotional distress) both to myself and to others, I choose to live for my own sexual pleasure.
>
> I hereby take full responsibility for my own actions and their resulting consequences by relinquishing all rights to support: resources, privileges, goods and services of any kind, from federal, state, or local governments, from social agencies, family members, and Almighty God.
>
> I choose my course freely and, therefore, hold no one other than myself responsible for my sexual decisions and their consequences.
>
> Signature_____ Date_____

She read it, and without any hesitation signed it and walked away.

The following year I came back to that school to do an assembly, and a girl came up afterwards and asked if I remembered her from the year before. I said no, but that she looked really familiar. Then she told me that her best friend was the girl who had signed the paper. I asked what had happened to her and, with deep emotion, she told me that several months after I had talked to her, the girl had gotten pregnant and now her boyfriend was nowhere to be found. Her life was in shambles. She didn't know what she was gonna do and was thinking about suicide. But the *real* reason this girl was now talking to me was because *she* had signed that paper too, and now she was scared to death.

It's Your Life

No one can decide for you what to do with your life. That's your decision! Live it the way you choose, but don't expect anyone else to pay for your mistakes. If you really read this book, you can no longer say no one ever told you what could happen, 'cause *I did*. People are likely to forgive you when you are *ignorant* of the truth, but they have a hard time forgiving you when you *ignore* the truth; and ignoring the truth can produce the most lonely, fearful life imaginable.

If you are still determined to go ahead and have a sexual relationship outside of marriage, that's your decision. But before you take that step, ask yourself, "Are the choices I'm making *today* worth dedicating *the rest of my life* to?" Because down the road a ways you will have NO choice but to dedicate your entire life to either running from, being responsible for, or enjoying the outcomes of those decisions. Every choice you make today will determine your future level of happiness. Decisions about sex, love, dating, and marriage are loaded with consequences. You make each choice just once—then comes the consequence, for better or for worse. My question is . . . can you live with that?

I wish you the *very best* in your future relationships and your marriage. I can only pray you have as much fun and enjoyment (and sex) as I have had in the first 32 years.

With deep and sincere love,

BRAD HENNING

P.P.S. This book's done and I'm goin' fishing!

Appendix
(OR KIDNEY . . . WHATEVER!)

A List of Differences

I thought it might be fun to give you a short list of some of the differences between men and women. This list is by no means ALL of the differences. These come from articles, magazines, personal experience and observation, and many of the books I've already listed in footnotes.

RELATIONAL DIFFERENCES BETWEEN MEN AND WOMEN

MEN	WOMEN
1. External—outward oriented	1. Internal—inward oriented
2. Interested in things (objects)	2. Interested in people (relationships)
3. Motivated by reward (hero)	3. Motivated by feeling valued
4. Competes for a prize (impersonal)	4. Competes with other women (personal)

5. Goal-oriented

5. Detail-oriented

6. Not concerned with other's opinions

6. Very concerned with others' opinions

7. Forgets fights

7. Remembers details of fights

8. Solves problems quickly on his own

8. Solves problems slowly with the help of others

9. Apologizes only when necessary

9. Apologizes to preserve relationship

10. Speaks his mind spontaneously

10. Talks about what she has been thinking about; processes her thoughts by talking

11. Takes word at face value

11. Looks for hidden meaning

12. Communicates directly

12. Talks "around" issue

13. Communicates facts

13. Communicates feelings

14. Talks (a lot) in public to gain attention

14. Quiet in public to build "connections"

15. Talks little in private— wants information

15. Verbal in private—wants intimacy; wants to be understood and listened to

16. Wants to be respected for what he does

16. Wants to be cherished for who she is

17. Satisfied with self

18. Very visual—hooked by what he sees (woman's physical appearance)

19. Values freedom

20. Romance = sex

21. Rarely asks for help (self-sufficient)

22. Arguments: becomes less communicative

23. Needs "space"

24. Fears being smothered

25. Identifies with performance

26. Independent of relationships

27. Logical

28. 12,000 words per day

29. Performance

17. Dissatisfied with self

18. Very observant—hooked by qualities (man's character traits)

19. Values security

20. Romance = communication (intimacy)

21. Gives advice as an act of love

22. Arguments: becomes more communicative

23. Needs "closeness"

24. Fears being abandoned

25. Identifies with people

26. Needs relationships (Having anyone is better than no one)

27. Emotional

28. 24,000 words a day

29. Beauty

30. Says what he wants (Doesn't read minds or get hints)

30. Wants him to "just know" what she wants (Hints at what she wants)

31. Offers advice when asked

31. Offers unsolicited advice

32. Feels blamed (why is it my fault?)

32. Feels guilty (It's my fault)

33. Needs to be needed

33. Needs to be validated

34. Self-confident

34. Confident in relationships

35. Responds to limits

35. Responds to listening

36. Holds pain inside

36. Verbalizes pain

37. Wants her to never change

37. Wants to change him

Physical and Mental Differences

Men and women are different in every cell of their bodies (DNA)
In the United States, women outlive men by four to seven years
Female metabolism is normally lower than that of men
She has shorter head, broader face, less protruding chin
She has shorter legs and longer trunk
Woman's index finger is usually longer than the third finger
His teeth last longer than hers
She has larger stomach, kidneys, liver, and appendix, but smaller lungs
She has menstruation, pregnancy, and lactation functions
Her thyroid is larger and more active
She has smoother skin and a relatively hairless body
She possesses 11 percent more brain cells in the area responsible for language comprehension

She can notice and remember positions of objects in complex arrangements (he can't find his socks)

Her blood contains 20 percent fewer red cells; therefore, she tires more easily

She is more prone to faint

He has 50 percent more brute strength

Her heart beats more rapidly (80 beats per minute versus 72)

Her blood pressure is 10 points lower than his

She has less tendency to have high blood pressure

She can stand high temperatures better (Her metabolism slows down less)

Men stutter more (four to one)

More men are color blind (16 to one)

He has more ulcers, hernias, and back problems

His death rates from heart disease, lung cancer, and emphysema are two to four times higher than hers

He outnumbers her in every one of the top 15 causes of death

He is taller, has heavier bones, and bigger muscles

He has quicker reaction times

Her left half of the cortex, which controls verbal ability, develops faster

He has a higher threshold of pain

He has 10 percent less body fat

His metabolism rate is 6 percent faster

He uses more oxygen

He throws off more heat

She has more acute hearing and keeps it longer

She has colder hands and feet but complains and suffers less

She is as healthy at home as at the office

Beyond age 80, females outnumber men two to one

She distinguishes colors better

She has sharper senses of taste and smell

She visits the doctor more often

She suffers more from illness on a day-to-day basis

She takes more prescriptions

She spends more days in bed

Wives outlive their husbands 11 times out of 12

He reacts more to visual stimuli (even as a baby)
His skull is thicker
He snores more
His daylight vision is superior
He has thicker veins
He has longer vocal cords
More guys are left-handed
He ages earlier
He wrinkles later
His immunity against disease is weaker
His death rate from cardiovascular disease is 77 percent higher than hers
He loses weight quicker
He has superior eye-hand coordination
She has an average of .8 gallons of blood
He has an average of one and a half gallons of blood
She has 1 million fewer red blood cells in each drop of blood than he does
She sweats 23 percent to 70 percent less
She, on average, can bench press 37 percent of what he can
Her average weight is about 143 pounds
His average weight is 173 pounds

SOCIAL DIFFERENCES

Men commit murder more than women (three to one)
He smokes and drinks more
Men commit suicide more often (two to three times more)
He has twice as many fatal automobile accidents per mile
He is more likely to drive through yellow or red lights
He is less likely to signal for turns
He is more likely to drink and drive

She laughs and cries more easily

About 60 percent of what comes out of a little boy's mouth is noise

Almost 100 percent of what comes out of a little girl's mouth is communication

He depends on road maps; she depends on landmarks

She is more sensitive to loud and repetitive noises (from infancy)

He fights more

She spends 6.6 hours per week eating, and 7.5 hours grooming

He spends 7.2 hours per week eating, and 5.3 hours grooming

95 percent of sufferers of anorexia are female

He is six to nine times more likely to be hyperactive as a child

To order additional copies of

Contact

Brad Henning Productions

www.bradhenning.com

Or Call

253.848.2239